Writing for Games

Writing for Games

Theory and Practice

Hannah Nicklin

CRC Press
Taylor & Francis Group
Boca Raton London New York

CRC Press is an imprint of the
Taylor & Francis Group, an **informa** business

First edition published 2022
by CRC Press
6000 Broken Sound Parkway NW, Suite 300, Boca Raton, FL 33487-2742

and by CRC Press
4 Park Square, Milton Park, Abingdon, Oxon, OX14 4RN
CRC Press is an imprint of Taylor & Francis Group, LLC

Library of Congress Cataloging-in-Publication Data

Names: Nicklin, Hannah, author.
Title: Writing for games : theory and practice / Hannah Nicklin.
Description: First edition. | Boca Raton : CRC Press, 2022. | Includes
bibliographical references and index. | Summary: "This book provides
readers with a vocabulary to articulate and build their games writing
practice, whether studying games or coming to games from another
storytelling discipline. It considers the material affordances of
videogames, and the practical realities of working in game development
processes"-- Provided by publisher.
Identifiers: LCCN 2021055527 | ISBN 9781032023069 (hardback) | ISBN
9781032023052 (paperback) | ISBN 9781003182832 (ebook)
Subjects: LCSH: Video games--Authorship. | Video
games--Authorship--Vocational guidance. | Video games--Design. | Video
games--Design--Vocational guidance.
Classification: LCC GV1469.34.A97 N53 2022 | DDC 794.8/3--dc23/eng/20220125
LC record available at https://lccn.loc.gov/2021055527

ISBN: 9781032023069 (hbk)
ISBN: 9781032023052 (pbk)
ISBN: 9781003182832 (ebk)

DOI: 10.1201/9781003182832

Typeset in Myriad Pro
by Deanta Global Publishing Services, Chennai, India

To Alex Kelly

I'd like to dedicate this book to my friend, mentor, and sometime collaborator Alexander Kelly, whose careful support gave me the tools to identify my practice, the skills to develop it, and an understanding of storytelling which is equal parts love, science, and forgiveness.

Contents

Introduction

When do you become a writer? When do you become a game designer? I would argue (without deep academic delving into child development studies) roughly around the same age. That is, as a very young child. We all start out as storytellers.[1] And we all play games; setting rules and trying out mechanics and thrilling in the 'magical circle'[2] of play as a means of imagining ourselves and the world in different, impossible, wonderful, terrible ways. Both inherit the same space of make-believe.

Writing is one of the tools we use to tell stories. Storytelling and play are both innate and ancient practices, and they are also crafts in which we learn how to develop skills and

---

[1] I use the term here to mean any kind of storytelling – from make-believe with friends or stuffed animals and lines drawn in the dirt; to singing, drawing, building, all the means of learning to imagine, retell, and process experiences for the pleasure of exploring or sharing with others. *This is not an exhaustive list, but I hope the spirit of my point is clear.*

[2] A term drawn from Johan Huizinga's play theory text *Homo Ludens* (1949).

DOI: 10.1201/9781003182832-1

tools for their practice. Or at least that's certainly my perspective as someone who trained in theatre (a game so old people forgot it's a game and called it a medium) and who now runs a videogame studio. I have worked in narrative design and game writing for just over half a decade, and have been paid to write – for interaction, installation, and more 'passive' audience reception – for nearly 15 years at this point.

Did I write this book just to make myself feel old? No, that's just an unfortunate side effect. Instead, as someone who has the privilege of an inter- and transdisciplinary practice, I want to share what I have learned about storytelling, from the combination of being grounded in the weight of centuries of literary and storytelling theory to finding wings in the relatively fledgling and often miraculous (in their actually working) practices of the games industry. This book is about the craft of writing, and more specifically, writing for games.

I want to emphasise that this is a book about writing because the industry often lacks coherent and common vocabularies. I will later on get much more into the difference between narrative design, worldbuilding, and writing. But just for now, let us say that while most videogames with story components need all of these things, writing is a specific subdiscipline of storytelling in videogames. Many books about stories in videogames conflate writing and narrative design,[3] but tackle writing specifically very little.

So, this is a book about writing. This book focuses primarily on how to write in the context of videogames. Some sections will be of use for people trained/working in videogames who want to know more about writing, and other sections might be more suited for people moving to videogames writing from other story disciplines. The book will trace a path from context for what the industry even is; to story theory; and then to the medium-specific details of character, story structure, and writing for videogames, including practical and material concerns. It will tackle three detailed case studies, and then offer a number of tools and exercises for practically developing your writing practice. I will tackle narrative design only where it intersects with writing (which isn't infrequent). This doesn't mean that narrative design and worldbuilding aren't important – but they play different roles and are different crafts.

I have read a lot of videogame-focused story books in preparation for the writing of this book, in the hope of being able to reference them as useful further reading, but in truth I found many of them to be lacking in craft and clarity around writing, especially in the context of indie videogames (more on the industry structures later).

If you are looking for an excellent source of further reading on story in videogames with more of a focus on narrative design, then I would recommend starting with Emily Short's invaluable blog. Take a look at the books category,[4] and you'll find an extraordinary and ongoing literature review where she explores texts from her expert perspective. Short's

---

[3] *For my definition of the difference of these two game storytelling disciplines,* look for the section titled 'Narrative Design Is Not Writing and Vice Versa' in Chapter 1, but nothing between here and there relies on you understanding this difference yet.
[4] emshort.blog/category/books.

blog is an accessible and robust starting point for further learning in the realm of games storytelling beyond writing. I will also recommend a wealth of other further readings as we go, and you can also check out the Bibliography for works I reference.

This book, then, stakes a slightly unusual and therefore hopefully useful niche in books about storytelling in videogames. If you're still unsure as to how to use this book, this next section will guide you on how to read it and how to know if it's for you.

Who Am I, Anyway?

Who am I and why am I talking to you? It's a fair question. And you should read my advice through the prism of my experience. I am someone who trained as a playwright; developed a practice as a devising-performance maker,[5] installation artist, sound artist, and pervasive game designer;[6] and a person working in the space between performance and games before making the conscious decision to transition full time into narrative design and writing for games. I've spent time as a producer, and have written and narrative designed on many projects that will never be released, or that I left when they ran out of money because I have never had savings, family wealth, or rev shares that enable me to work for free.

My biggest 'shipped' title was as writer and narrative designer for the multi-award-winning *Mutazione*, which I also took over production of in the final year, including running localisation, and sim shipping[7] the game on several platforms. It was around this point at which the owners offered me a chance to run the studio, and I'm now CEO and studio lead at Die Gute Fabrik. In terms of scale, I've worked from the DIY to the mid-scale indie. *Mutazione* cost somewhere around $4 million to make; and was launched on mobile, console, and PC in 14 languages; and is considered a mid-scale indie.

Somewhere amongst that I also wrote a bunch of zines and book articles and essays about games, and did a PhD on games-influenced theatre and theatre-influenced games as a 'political' practice. My writing has won awards, and I've spoken internationally at games festivals and events like Game Developers Conference (San Francisco), Freeplay (Melbourne),

---

[5] A prominent form of theatre and performance which is distinguished by using a different methodology to conventional playwriting. The traditional idea of 'theatre' is authorial – the idea that a single playwright sits down and authors a play which they then collaborate on with dramaturgs, directors, designers, and performers. Devising performance is much more like the way we think of a band putting music together – anyone bringing an idea and then developing together. I'll touch more on this later, but it's a wonderful practice not far off from good collaborative game design processes.

[6] Pervasive games are games which pervade the boundaries of time, space, and technology for games in unusual ways; games played across months, across cities (in 'non play' spaces), or which, for example, allow you to leave messages for strangers via a buoy at sea (Flock, 2012). For a great introduction to pervasive games, I recommend *Pervasive Games: Theory and Design* (Montola et al., 2009). And for examples of practitioners, look up the works of Hide and Seek, Invisible Flock, and Duncan Speakman.

[7] Sim shipping means simultaneously releasing a game on several platforms. It's much more complicated to line up more than one platform's certification (cert) and launch processes than it is a single one. 'Platforms' can be consoles like PlayStation or Xbox or, e.g., PC, Mac, mobile.

A MAZE (Berlin), Feral Vector (Yorkshire, UK), Now Play This (London), and at more universities than I can count, many of which probably still haven't paid me. I've also taken games practices to the cultural world with institutions like the Royal Shakespeare Company, the Wellcome Collection, the Victoria & Albert Museum, the Science Museum, and more (all UK-based).

In short, I can speak to crossing disciplines, getting into the games industry, the foundations of writing and writing practices, the full production cycle, and critical and artistic perspectives on videogames with a cumulative career of 15 years milling around in the centre of this strange Venn diagram.

Who Is This Book Aimed At?

This book is aimed at anyone who might pick up a book labelled 'writing for videogames'. That is, students on game courses eager to develop their skills, early career to experienced storytellers in other media interested in transitioning to videogames, and people with experience interested in another perspective on the practice of writing in a videogames context. I also hope that this book will provide different ways of thinking about *learning*. One of the key things you can do as a person learning a craft is to first understand *how you learn*.

When I learned to kayak at age 18 in a warm river in the Ardèche, my teacher (also 18, with soft curls in his hair, a severe buoyancy-aid shaped tan, and a grin full of wide teeth and freckles, and who was himself learning how to teach) told me he tended to find that he had three kinds of students: students who learned by seeing him demonstrate, students who learned by hearing the instructions and processing them intellectually, and students who only learned when he took the paddle in his hands and moved it so that their hands – also holding it – felt the movement. Hearing, thinking, doing.

There are probably many more kinds of learning. It's worth an afternoon's digression on Wikipedia for sure. But for here, let's keep things simple.

I am part thinker, part doer. I am definitely not a listener. I only learned a roll[8] when my teacher took my paddle and I felt the shape that my arms needed to move to right my kayak. That was probably one of the most formative movements for me. Knowing this about myself helps me in many ways – from learning a board game, to perfecting an area of a sport, to my practice as a writer. I also think that knowing that I learn by doing and reflecting is probably a good part of my shield against imposter syndrome – I have to do it to understand it, so I've got to start out somewhere. No use sitting around feeling bad that I don't know anything, because that's the beginning of knowing!

---

[8] In the 2000s when I was taught this, it was called an 'Eskimo roll', which I include as a detail in case it is useful technical knowledge to anyone. But we're all older and connected enough now to know that 'Eskimo' is at best a word of colonisers and at worst a slur. For those who want more detail on the move, it is effectively a technique of moving the kayak paddle underwater in a way that rights a kayak when you're capsized. It's kind of important to learn it quickly because if you don't, you remain upside down in the water and unable to breathe.

Theory, Practice, and Implementation

There are parts of the book which will be more relevant to some than others – both in subject matter and in *kinds of learning*. That's why I've laid out both a clear subject structure and a pedagogical (teaching/learning) structure. I have split the book into three parts: Part I: Theory, Part II: Case Studies, and Part III: A Practical Workbook.

Theory will discuss the ideas at the heart of this book; terminology we can use to discuss the craft of writing, and to do so across disciplines (as working in videogames will always necessitate). It will invite us to consider what we can learn about writing from other areas of the craft, and offers the basics of thinking about form, style, and the raw materials of telling a story through writing in videogames.

Case Studies will take explicit game case studies to develop some of these ideas further and in the specific context of videogames. Part I will prepare you for Part II, but if you feel like you haven't totally grasped Part I, Part II might help you see these principles at work.

Finally, the Practical Workbook part is for those who learn by doing. A section full of exercises, provocations, and means of setting your own curriculum in order to learn, reflect, and grow your practice as a writer and storyteller in the medium of videogames.

One part might suit you better or perhaps all three read in a different order. But mostly I hope that I have clearly marked each chapter and section so that you can navigate easily and in a manner that makes sense to you and your needs. For example, as we set out into theory you might find a chapter or section that is obvious to you because you're studying games or because you're an established writer. I encourage you to skip sections like that. Make this book work for you.

To paraphrase a sports science philosopher whose rambling podcasts I enjoy (Colby Pearce), 'nature is a novelty generator'. Just as no one nutrition plan or training regime will work for everyone (or even most people), so too do our wonderful and unique brains, histories, and contexts demand that we build specific toolboxes full of specific tools made just for us. I am showing you what has worked for me, not as a means of saying 'this will work for you too', but in showing you the underlying forces and materials so that you can name them and shape new tools which work in the way you need.

Focusing on Indie Productions

This book is particularly focused on *independent* (indie) to *triple I* levels of production in the videogames industry.[9]

---

[9] Not the 'gaming' industry, which means gambling. They sound super similar and it's easy to understand why people mix them up, and in parts of the industry there certainly is a gambling overlap, but if you want people in indie games to know you're talking about them, say 'games' industry, not 'gaming'.

From now on I'm going to use the terms 'videogames' and 'games' interchangeably (as it is in the industry), but remember that other texts might use 'games' more broadly; games are a much older medium than videogames, and board games, playground games, sports, etc. all have a connected heritage.

This is also a useful basis for noting that videogames aren't special (ineffable, magical, or like nothing else) but they are *specific* – that is, just like any other creative practice they are a medium and an industry with specific vocabularies and a scale of production which goes from tiny (one-person DIY projects) to enormous (multi-billion-dollar budget, 10-year development cycles).

In the next section I'm going to touch on what all this means, and why I feel my pitching this book at writing in an indie context is more useful to students and newcomers than only touching on the AAA. If you feel like you already know what indie and AAA games are, then skip to the section titled 'Why Not Write About Writing for AAA?'

How Is the Videogames Industry Structured?

If you are entirely new to games, it's likely you will have a working knowledge of another creative industry/practice, perhaps one of the ones which have penetrated the public consciousness a little more by virtue of being around a bit longer (or being a bit cooler so people make movies about it).

Let's take the music industry as an analogue: not every musician dreams of becoming a star through their music. Making a living and making good music, making something that brings people together, making a vehicle for a message you care about, or making cool stuff with friends might all be primary motivators. Certainly the dream of stardom is what builds (some might say pollutes) the business model of music and also what makes it possible to be so exploitative.

In the following table I have summarised a few analogous 'levels'[10] of the music industry set next to the game industry, and the economic and personnel scales which might roughly make them up.

Please note that some people like to spend a lot of time debating what 'indie' means (just as they did in music before indie became a genre and not just a mode of production). Can you truly be indie if you have publisher backing, for example? I'm going to be very broad in my definitions here for simple scene setting, and I will use 'indie' to discuss a scale of production and not a mode. My numbers are very general and of course the deeper you dig, the more nuanced it gets. My intention is to provide a very rough sense of things so that someone entirely new to the scale/structure of the games industry can build a foundation for understanding it.

---

[10] Scare quotes are used here because part of the problem is that I can't find a clearer term which is also non-hierarchical. I don't buy into the idea that bigger is better, but our vocabularies do, and I'd prefer to communicate clearly rather than redefining everything, especially in a book where we're trying to learn.

One final note: my use of 'professional' and 'amateur' should be strongly differentiated from *quality judgements*. The distinction for me is the difference between depending on the work for part or all of your income as a worker (professional), and developing the work outside of the needs of money-making, deadlines, and other like restrictions (amateur). Embroiled in capitalism as we are, industry structure and crafts designed to work within its structures are typically better defined in material terms from its labour/wage correlates. A professional needs different tools and practices from an amateur (though the skills overlap). For example, professionals need to worry about working to brief[11] and deadlines to earn their living; amateurs might have fewer resources and structures but more freedom. If you see me use either term, be reassured that at no point am I interested in quality judgements – they are simply different modes of engaging with a practice.

It's a bit icky to use economic terms to discuss a creative form, but also sometimes talking in the language of economies is necessary.[12]

Music	Games	'Level'
The band you're in at school with your mates that does covers.	Modders,[1] builders[2] (*Minecraft, Dreams*, etc.), people writing/making fan art.	**Amateur – cover artist.** Done for pleasure/ leisure, using tools/rules made by others.
The DIY music you make in your spare time, play gigs, maybe tour a bit. DIY labels might put out your records.	**DIY.** One- or two-person indie teams, perhaps making hugely ambitious avant-garde games, or small-scale/ experimental works. With no meaningful funding, and not as a 'job'. Might get some arts funding or local grant money for their costs. Or might run a Patreon (crowdfunding subscription site) to support their work alongside their day job.	**Amateur – DIY/ garage.** Can be by circumstance, or by choice – resisting the premise of 'professionalism'.

(*Continued*)

---

[11] I will use the term 'brief' throughout the book to describe the useful creative restrictions you may be given or develop yourself in order for you to fulfil the work you have been asked or set out to do. Briefs could contain genre; house style; existing worldbuilding and character details; previous iterations of the IP; and material details like tools, line length, word counts, etc. In Part III: A Practical Workbook, I offer a number of tools in order to support self-brief-setting throughout different stages of game-writing processes, and to think through the usefulness of working to or from briefs in your practice as a writer.

[12] Basically, don't @ me.

Music	Games	'Level'
The music that makes enough money that you can play it for a living. International mid-scale touring. Not pulling in loads, but it's your job. You might be aiming to be picked up by a minor label or you might just enjoy it.	**Indie.** Games made by a team of about 2–20 probably including a fair number of contractors and a smaller core team. Funders might include local grants; arts and academic money; or smaller publishing funds, minor investment, and often previous successes made at the DIY scale, which enabled a studio to establish itself. Budgets of approximately $100,000 to $2 million–$3 million.	**Precarious to sustainable living derived from the work.** I might call this as moving into 'professional' as compared to 'amateur'.
The music backed by the industry (from small-scale label to large). Made for a substantial audience, supported by lots of PR, touring internationally. Major label. And/or session musicians who make a comfortable living providing work for others.	**Triple I to AA.** Triple I is the several-million-dollar-plus budget end of indie (i.e. the indie version of triple A), perhaps a team of 20–100, with budgets in the multimillions. Funders could be previous successes, investors, publishers, or platforms (like a console). This scale also supports contractors who make a comfortable living working on several projects (writers are commonly contractors).	**Professional – resourced and substantial.**
Global mega super stars. You can probably just go by one name. You put out a bad record, people will complain, but they'll also buy it and your next one.	**AAA (or triple A).** The blockbuster end of the games industry. Multibillion-dollar budgets, teams of hundreds to over a thousand. Funders could be previous successes, investors, publishers, or platforms (like a console).	**Too big to fail.**

[1] Someone who 'mods' is someone who 'modifies' an existing game to change it somehow. That might be adding new quests, it might be removing all the dragons because they annoy you, or improving the character generator's ability to model Black hair.

[2] This is the term I'm using for people who use games-built-as-tools to build cool things in their leisure time. They might have professional-level design sensibilities, spend hours and hours on their works, and produce professional-quality output, and/or they might be your five-year-old making a space to play with their friends.

The comparison works with other art forms too: AAA games is Hollywood, is Broadway, is a headline exhibit at the Met. Indie is independent film, small-scale touring performance practices, and artists who have work commissioned and exhibited in smaller-scale galleries.

Why Not Write About Writing for AAA?

Why is it that I am aiming this book at people writing for indie games, not the AAA studio experience on which a lot of previous publications centre their narrative design and writing advice? Honestly, because I think this is a much more useful foundation for both early career practitioners, university students, and those considering moving to games from a parallel discipline.

Firstly, when writing in an indie studio, or for a small team of like-minded indies, you will need a much wider games-storytelling foundation, have much more creative input (or at least be part of the design discussions), need to be able to communicate a lot more across disciplines, and have fewer resources at your disposal. Even if you want to move to AAA games, the experience and development you'll get in indie will mean you can build a portfolio and practice to make that step. Anyone can be an indie.

Secondly, for those of you moving between disciplines – if you're currently a professional poet, playwright, novelist, etc. – indie games are probably closest to the level of creative input and practice that you're actually used to. Writing for AAA can certainly involve creative input, especially if you work your way up to lead creative and design roles, but you will very often be slotting into a monolithic process, where huge departments work in parallel, and department leads take the responsibility for decision-making and communications. Likewise, a lot of studios at an AAA level will be working with 'existing IP'[13] and house styles, which means that there's little room for authorial instincts to be exercised.

In AAA you will often be given extremely specific tasks, to do in extremely specific tools, as part of a whole writing team. Narrative designers may work separately to you, designing quests and content with level designers. Your job might be a month of writing the three-second lines archer-class characters shout as they run into battle. There is more variety of expression and experimentation at an indie level (not to denigrate the hard-won innovation that does go in at AAA, but there's less of it, because it's playing with much larger monetary gambits). If you're excited about games as an experimental form, you probably want to be seeking out the avant-garde indie circles.

Thirdly, it is extremely rare to find entry-level positions in AAA, especially for non-programmer roles. They will usually expect three to five-plus years' experience, published games, or notoriety.

Finally, there is a preponderance of film practice and theory that has made its way into AAA games, which has made it a little homogenous in its aim for realism, the imitation of reality, the drive for immersion, etc., which honestly, is deeply uninteresting to me and denies all of the rich affordances of such an interdisciplinary form as videogames.

In this book, I am going to be drawing on what people interested in writing for games can learn from theatre, poetry, art, comics, literary theory, and much more. There is a rich

---

[13] Here I mean 'sequels' or 'a series of games which a studio is known for' or 'drawn from a popular movie', but in general 'IP' means 'intellectual property'.

heritage of storytelling that goes back to the very genesis of our ... well, genus.[14] I think the preponderance of film as a gold standard of storytelling impoverishes games' possibilities, and I think produces writers missing a whole host of vocabularies and tools which might otherwise prove invaluable.

Focusing on Writing

As I've said, one thing which I hope sets this book apart from other guides on storytelling for games is that while touching on narrative design principles this is a book first and foremost designed at improving or understanding the context for games *writing*. If you want to skip ahead for the full definitional difference between narrative design and writing, look for the section titled 'Narrative Design Is Not Writing and Vice Versa' in Chapter 1 (though nothing before then will rely on your knowing the difference in detail).

A lot of game design/development degrees (already overstretched in having to cram in so many disciplines and practices) will have to pack their 'story' teaching into a single class/module that will naturally focus on the most broadly applicable skills of worldbuilding and storytelling through environment and quest/level design, maybe a little narrative design. This kind of storytelling foundation will benefit designers, generalists, creative directors, and mechanics/gameplay-first interested folks.[15] But it's no substitute for learning the specialist craft of writing and storytelling (though it's a good foundation!) if you want to be a dedicated games storyteller.

Likewise, those coming from non-university backgrounds or other writing disciplines can use other narrative design texts to understand story-through-game-design practices. Here, I hope to provide tools and vocabularies for people who write for games, or want to better understand writing for games, to develop a fuller storytelling practice.

Two of the biggest requests after I teach or speak are the very general 'Where can I learn to make my writing better?' and the very specific 'How do you make a good character/world/story structure?'. My answer, I hope, is in the pages of this book.

---

[14] Okay, I said 'genus' rather than 'species' because it sounded better. If you're interested, however, there are plenty of philosophers/scientists/anthropologists who posit that the reason Homo sapiens became the dominant species is precisely because we were the 'storytelling ape'. Yuval Noah Harari's *Sapiens* and Terry Pratchett's *Science of the Discworld* are two widely different but very readable pop-sci approaches to this question. Though these are worth pairing with Graeber and Wengrow's *The Dawn of Everything: A New History of Humanity* which is an excellent challenge to a lot of the premises about early human civilisations that the aforementioned trade in, and especially the one which lead us towards capitalism and inequality as a natural conclusion.

[15] I hate drawing such broad conclusions, honestly. Obviously, there are some courses and professors doing an excellent job of cramming everything in, including writing practices. But what I mean to say here most of all is that I understand that videogames include so many disciplines. Of course on generalist courses nothing gets a deep dive, and of course these areas are where you might focus to begin with. It's tough to teach 'videogames'.

Games Are Not Special

Did you ever hear someone explain that games are the medium of the future? Or that games can do something that no other art form can do?

Here are some headlines and ideas that I picked up on using a quick search online:

- Games are uniquely immersive.[16]
- Videogames are the only 'total' art form.[17]
- Games are uniquely capable of empathy.[18]
- Games are uniquely interactive.[19]
- Videogames are a uniquely young medium.[20]
- Videogames are the medium for our era.[21]
- Games are unique in how they deal in agency.[22]
- Games are unique in duration.[23]

Games exceptionalism – as I'm going to term it – is a totally understandable position, but not a healthy one. The ideas that games are special, games alone are the medium for the future (or for now), or that games express things no other form can express are ones which will only impoverish the medium.

A lot of this comes from the understandable need to stake out a space for games as part of the spectrum of culture. Games haven't always been taken seriously, and in many areas of the arts and academia still aren't well understood. That's partly because of the heritage of videogames drawing from technological disciplines as well as artistic ones – the art world doesn't know how to treat games, we don't all train alongside or practise in the same sphere – and it's also partly because of the snobbery of some of the art and academic world.

Because of this and other reasons, the world has been resistant to seeing games as part of 'culture', and the games industry has often responded by justifying its belonging by explaining that *games alone can do X, Y, and Z.*

I am here to reassure you that videogames are not special, are not unique, and that's okay. If you believe that if you tell a story in a game, that it is automatically immersive, then you

---

[16] No one tell LARPers.

[17] No one tell Wagner.

[18] No one tell Boal.

[19] No one tell Ontroerend Goed or Yoko Ono.

[20] Is 60–70 years young? And isn't there a much, much older heritage of all the component parts (other than the screen) that can be built on?

[21] No one tell Netflix.

[22] You get a damn sight more agency in most interactive and promenade theatre than you do videogames because no one has had to spend three years inventing how 'up', 'down', and 'stairs' work.

[23] Oh, you spent 100 hours playing a videogame, did you? Mate, I know some artworks which are designed to last for hundreds of years. And opera which is designed to go on for days. And durational performances which last for months.

are failing to understand videogames as a material. You have to *make* it immersive; it is not naturally so. And it's also worth pausing for a minute to think about why immersion is desirable. Is it? For the story you want to tell, or the effect you want to have? Either way, if you believe the very medium is built of immersion, you may make accidental design choices which break it.

Technologist Tom Armitage is the person who first articulated for me the incredibly useful conception of *technology as a material* (Armitage, 2011). He's a creative programmer who has made many interactive and pervasive experiences over the years, and in speaking on his practice he talks about the *affordances* of technology, of code, of making things out of internet-enabled devices or wireless technologies.

Affordances[24] are things like the grain of a piece of wood or the texture of a particular kind of clay; you can work with them or against them. *But assuming that those qualities are general and inherent will make you think you can work the wood in any direction or treat the clay in any way, and get the same result.* You won't; you'll risk ending up with a weak and splintered thing, or a pot that explodes in the kiln because of your glaze choice.

What I'm proposing here when I talk about understanding the quality of games as a medium is quite similar to how Armitage talks about technology: I'm asking that we look at videogames like they are a porcelain clay or a piece of mahogany wood. Immersion, interaction, empathy, totality, agency; these things are not inherent qualities of games alone, but possibilities. Games' affordances are made specific and complicated by where and with whom they happen, the genres and conventions they build their foundations in, and what systems of interaction and reaction they employ.

It's also useful to separate *affordances* from *effects* – interactivity is an affordance of forms based on human–computer interaction; immersion is an effect of those forms used in a certain way (and neither of these things are necessarily done 'best' by videogames). Role play is an affordance (not unique to games); empathy is an effect (again, something I think many games assume is inherent in first-person play, wrongly so).

Games aren't *special*, but they are *specific*. Many other art forms exhibit agency, interactivity, human–computer interaction, screens, etc., but together they are some of the medium-specific affordances of games. They aren't *unique* (special) to games, but games tend to bring these things together. When we set it out like that, we're freed to reflect on how other media explore these affordances and use them to different effects. As practitioners, this equips us to better understand the material we work with in games – their affordances. We might even develop or synthesise a form better suited to the effect we want or discover alternative collaborators who can better help us get there.

---

[24] This is a kind of design thinking which owes much to Don Norman's classic product design book *The Design of Everyday Things* (2002).

In walking away from the idea of inherent qualities, and in separating the affordances of a material from the effect we want to have, we can ask ourselves what story or experience is best expressed through these mechanics, tools, or constraints; or what mechanics, tools, or constraints are best suited to exploring this story or feeling we're interested in. As writers we can ask: What does line length do to my writing? How can I build my characters in a way that enhances the themes the creative director is interested in? What of this plot is better implied rather than explicitly shown?

In fighting the impulse to make bold claims about videogames being *the* medium of a particular affordance or effect, we can gather fresh influences, new thoughts, and build on the centuries of work that has already been done around these questions. We are then better equipped to assess the specific context of games' affordances and the effects they might have.

Games aren't important, aren't exceptional, aren't revolutionary, and they aren't the medium best able to express the modern age. Understanding what games aren't inherently and exclusively will help us make a better, more important, more exceptional, and more revolutionary game better able to express the modern age (or whatever it is you want it to express).

Therefore, the Intention of the Book

That leaves me to summarise the intention of this book, which is simply

- To provide you with the vocabulary to articulate and build a writing practice in the context of videogames.
- To provide you with examples and tools to develop your understanding of how to practise and improve as a writer in videogames.
- To provide you with resources to start out on a journey that will better equip you to express yourself to collaborators, reflect on your practice, advocate for better storytelling, and to consider your journey as a writer as one of lifelong learning in whatever medium you choose to operate.

How to Read My Perspective

Throughout the book I will draw on example works when trying to illustrate smaller points, but the problem with referencing games is that quite quickly a new generation of consoles or the fall of an online game platform might render them inaccessible. The practice of writing in other mediums, however, is a bit more robust in terms of its own preservation, and writing about writing has been going on for a few centuries or so. For that reason, a lot of my resources are not games-specific, but drawn from TV, film, theatre, and literature.

In Chapter 8, 'Further Reading', I've broadened my references to feature texts founded on different philosophies around craft and practice. If you find some of my approaches don't work for you there will be others to discover there. You can also look up the full details of every reference in the Bibliography at the end; I haven't included anything I wouldn't directly recommend.

Every work I recommend herein has been instrumental for me in how I think about my own writing and games practice. In lack of other writing-specific guides for games, I hope that this book will complete the circuit between a general writing text and games-specific writing.

That isn't to say that there are no good books on storytelling in games; just that they serve other purposes than this book is interested in. They look at how film storytelling techniques can be applied to AAA studio practices, focus almost completely on narrative design and not at all on the craft and practice of writing, or are extremely specialist. I very much enjoyed *Procedural Storytelling in Game Design* (2019, edited by T. Adams and T. Short), for example, and it's a fascinating and well-edited collection of essays from practitioners playing with story and randomness in game design practices. But it's certainly not entry-level.

While I'm trying to fill this gap on our shelves, it's worth saying that I think the 'uniqueness' of games (as I have touched on) can be vastly overstated. What you will learn from the non-games writing texts – if you can learn to consider other practitioners not as 'magic talents' but as craftspeople with specific toolboxes – can be easily reshaped to develop your own practice in games writing.

A final caveat: I was taught as part of an anglophone Western literary paradigm of canon/writing which is largely formed of White, Western, cis, het men. How I think about writing and storytelling has been irrevocably shaped by that. I have done some work as I became a mentor and teacher to diversify my recommended texts and the lessons I draw, but it's something you should be aware of nevertheless.

When recommending works and methodologies to you, my context is of White supremacy, cis-het patriarchy, the preponderance of the Western world, written storytelling (as opposed to oral traditions), and especially American and British anglophone culture. If you are someone marginalised by these hegemonies, you *do not have to make do with tools ill-fitted to your work*. But it can be hard to find expertise outside of these realms because people outside of those hegemonies are rarely asked to record their craft for posterity in a book. Most people marginalised by these hegemonies are at best corralled into writing and teaching on their marginalisation. Forever stuck in the box marked 'Other'.

For that reason, you may find your further reading in places less gatekept than books: in talks recorded online; articles on blogs; by following women, writers of colour or indigenous backgrounds, LGBTQ+ folks, and people from non-Western non-anglophone cultures online and seeing the influences they share. By absorbing other disciplines (dance, poetry, craft, experimental and folk art, etc.) and reaching out to mentors.

Read my book with my background in mind. Excavate it for what is useful and relevant to you. Open my toolbox, look inside, and try out what's in there. Feel the heft of each piece of advice and practical exercise in your mind like you're holding something that you will use every day of your life. Work out if you need to reshape it, discard it entirely, or build something yourself influenced by its intended use.

The further reading suggestions listed throughout the book also exist because after I do lectures about a lot of the things that I'm going to set up in this book I'm always asked 'Where can I find out more?'. It's a valuable impulse to want to broaden your influences and deepen your expertise, and I want to honour it.

Before we get there, though, let's fill ourselves in on some lovely foundational theory.

PART I
Theory

CHAPTER 1

Craft

This first chapter in the Theory part of the book is going to set the context and foundations for everything else, so it's worth sticking with this one, even if you only want to dive into one or two of the others. The central thesis of this chapter is something I touched upon in the Introduction: essentially, the idea that storytelling is a *craft*.

What Do You Mean, 'Storytelling Is a Craft'?

Storytelling is a craft, and writing is a means of practising that craft. When asserting the idea that storytelling is a craft I am attempting to shift us away from the ideal that *storytelling is magical*. Like much art and design, when storytelling works well, you rarely see the artifice (unless intended, like Brecht or brutalism) – that is, all of the hard work and considered decisions that make it sing. Storytelling is a craft, but it's easy to forget that because it's an ancient one, practised for generations, and one that we all have a grounding in. It's a craft

DOI: 10.1201/9781003182832-3

and practice which surrounds us; we all learn and communicate and develop our relationship to the world in part through storytelling.

For that reason, there are often two perceptions damaging our ability to communicate about (and develop our ability to practise) writing, which I see particularly in games. If you're coming from a different storytelling discipline, then the principles here may seem obvious, but you'd do well to equip yourself with the knowledge of what people often *don't* know.

First, there's the idea that the building of story stops at the world building and plot (the world the player/characters are in and what happens to them). This is the level of storytelling we're all equipped with as children and as adults experience daily as the audience for storytelling. For that reason, many people dismiss storytelling as easy or unimportant, or naively assume it doesn't take training, expertise, and material design decisions to make a game story and its writing effective.

The second common misconception (which has developed more because of the gatekeeping of literacy and the literary canon) is that writing and storytelling are solely instinctive or innate in only some people. That people have aptitudes for certain practices isn't something I would wish to dispute. But I strongly believe that *wherever you start from*, if you work at it, you will become a better writer and storyteller. And that if you rest on the laurels of your initial aptitude, you will equally have a practice which will never develop for the better.

I'll use the words 'craft' and 'practice' often because these are both words which speak to lifelong learning, the continual building of a toolset, and a thing you learn by *doing*, a living thing. The main takeaways here are

- Storytelling is not magical.
- Storytelling is an expert discipline of which writing is a part.
- Storytelling is something everyone can learn to be better at.
- Storytelling is a lifelong practice.
- Storytelling in games is made up of much else besides plot and world building.

In games it's fairly common that a creative lead or design lead in a small indie studio may get excited about cobbling together a world, characters, creatures, and broad-brushstrokes plot and motivations for the player, and either never hire a storytelling professional or wait a long time before they hire one. They will do so because they believe that writing and storytelling is not a craft and that writing is something that fills in the gaps to make a story legible. Or they hire too late, meaning it will be very difficult for the professional to do their job well. If a writer is good, they might need to advocate for design changes, new tools, workflow adjustments (i.e. 'you can't rearrange the levels without telling me because it also rearranges the set-ups and pay-offs of the character interactions I have written'), the reduction of clichés, the pruning of the plot, the nurturing of more distinct characters, and more. If they are lucky, they might be listened to.

But they will do much less good work than if the lead had understood storytelling as a practice. The idea here is that a lead who understands storytelling as a practice both understands the need for placeholder content and that a less practised storyteller may often imbue their plot and worldbuilding with unknown clichés, broken design, and plot and narrative decisions that break the effectiveness of their game design. A lead who understands storytelling as a practice will know that they need initial expert consultation (if they can't afford a full-time expert yet) to avoid any undoable poor design, tool, and workflow decisions. They will know that storytelling in games is made up of backend tools, material gameplay and design decisions, narrative, UI, character design and development, text styles and effects, and writing, as well as plot, world building, and filling in the gaps between them with dialogue.

Finally, in understanding storytelling and writing as a practice and a craft, we can also appreciate it as something done joyfully and well by both professionals and amateurs, like music, ceramics, garment-making, and more. The point of this definition is not to gatekeep but to welcome all in the understanding that you place yourself somewhere on the developmental spectrum of lifelong learning.

Educated Fan, Amateur, or Professional

Is writing something you don't want to specialise in? Welcome! That's totally fine; familiarise yourself enough with the vocabularies and core contexts so you can usefully collaborate with specialists and know where you want to draw your limitations. A good metaphor here is of a sports fan who watches the sport play, knows the rules and the players, and understands the contexts in which the players and coaches can excel, but doesn't want to play the sport.

Is writing something you want to do as an amateur? That is, not to deadline, to the briefs of others, or as your primary means of income? Welcome! You won't need any of the tools which enable you to be creative every day, to deadline, and the shortcuts for collaborating and communicating in professional settings. Define your lifelong learning as something which brings you joy and satisfaction. In the sports metaphor, you are a weekend warrior – you focus on your life, health, and well-being, and you practise the sport of your choice as part of that. You play in five-a-side tournaments, but don't have to train every day. You may get serious about equipment, competition, and workouts, but no one will mind if you take a week off. And you can just as easily find joy in the process; you can suddenly decide that instead of the interval workout you had planned, you're going to go for a long run through the countryside and just smell the roses.

Is writing something you want to do as a professional? That is to deadline, often to the briefs of others, and as part of the means by which you sustain yourself and those you have caring responsibilities for? Welcome! You will need to be much more strategic about the tools you build, the vocabulary, and the communication and collaboration skills, but most of all, you will need to be able to develop a practice of problem solving, solution building, and creative practice which *does not rely on inspiration*. You will want to seek out dedicated coaches (peer mentors); you will want to keep records of your training and knowledge as it grows, so you can reflect on it as you progress to the next season; and you will want expert knowledge of every part of the sport (practice) and will need to be ready to perform even on the days you don't feel like it.

In the Introduction I invited you to think about yourself and how you learn best; here I invite you to think about how you relate to the different levels of investment that exist: Do you want context for your adjacent work? Do you want to find joy and well-being through creative work? And/or do you want to do this, frankly, for money?

As you progress through this text, and learn from the wider world, use this to measure where you want to invest your time. If you need adjacent professional context, you might want to focus on vocabulary (for comms) and how writing can be best produced in order to improve your related processes. If you wish to develop your skills in an amateur context, focus on concepts, case studies, and practical exercises for exploring your ideas at leisure. If you're a professional, or want to be, then you want all of the above, plus the exercises and practices which concentrate on process, communication, collaboration, and working to deadline.

Unsure? Try it out and see how you feel! None of these approaches are better or worse than the others; the aim is to know yourself and your needs.

The Material Context of Games

The next few chapters will cover a variety of essential vocabulary in specific areas: from games studio structures, to story structure, and story components. But before we run the gamut, I wish to lay down one more set of foundations about storytelling in games.

Here's the most important thing:

Games are really hard to make.[1]

Theatre is also hard to make; dance, ceramics, quilt making, all of it. I know. All media and art forms have their own challenges, but when you make a film, sure, you have to write a script and hire actors, and direct and film and edit. But you don't also have to invent gravity, and build the actors as puppets made out of flesh and bone and weird perspectives. That you have to define 'up' and 'down' and 'sky' and 'ground' is also part of the joy and inventive potential of games, but please believe me when I say the defining thing about game development is that it is a goddamn miracle if any game functions at all, and still if it functions on most computers, most of the time.

It can take half a year for a team to resource, design, implement, and fix the display of italics in onscreen text (this happened to me). It can take several months to build the tools for defining the logic of, implementing, and displaying a character's dialogue in the right

---

[1] 'Nobody told me when you make a video game you have to make the whole thing' (Esposito, 2018).

format. A large part of game development is project planning, MVP,[2] and communicating with others about what's needed, what's a priority, and when a change is being made – so that other departments can understand how it will have a knock-on effect.

The material context of writing and storytelling in games is that you rarely work alone – especially as a writer – and the practice of writing will as much be about communication, priorities, project planning, spreadsheets, and resources, as often as it's about being able to actually do it.

Then you face the huge lack of common vocabulary for what we mean when we talk about story in games.

Narrative Design Is Not Writing and Vice Versa

Writing is not narrative design, and narrative design is not writing. One of the common misconceptions in videogames around storytelling is that narrative designers can write and vice versa. Sometimes you get people who do both (often you will be expected to be a dual narrative designer/writer in a small indie development team), but this problem is endemic and often means that the actual brief or recruitment copy for a piece of work isn't clear about what's wanted. And it's even possible the people writing the job description don't know what they need.

So, let's set this out as clearly as possible:

> *Narrative design* is the practice of game design with story at its heart. You are the advocate for the story in the design of the game. Narrative is (and we will dig down more into this in the next chapter) the design of the telling of a story. Not just a *plot in a world with characters*, but also the decisions around in what order the plot is communicated, how characters and the environment build together, structure, pacing, choice design, voice, perspective, role-play relationships, UI, the key decisions around tools, player agency, and much else. *It is storytelling through design.*

> *Writing* is the building of characters, worlds, plot, structure pacing, cadence, dialogue, UI text, choice text, exposition, characterisation, character journeys, format, genre, and medial expressivity (i.e. What is this sentence to be read as? Is it a line of dialogue like in a script, a book, for speaking, a comic?). *It is storytelling through words.*

Even if you are practising – or wish to practise – in both of these areas, separating them is extremely useful, as you will develop both strands through different processes, and both will provide different solutions to a challenge or problem. It's also useful to be able to articulate the difference to others. If you're hired as a narrative designer, but the team that hires you isn't willing to include you in design discussions or consider design proposals from you,

---

[2] Minimum viable product: part of the Agile practice of design. The idea is to make the design idea, tool, or piece of gameplay in its most minimally functional way, and then to test or play it in order to know in which direction to improve and build on it.

then you are not actually being given the means to do your job. If you're hired as a writer, but someone is suddenly asking you to co-design a dialogue system, it can be empowering to assess that as a narrative design task and ask for more resources (money, time, or hiring a collaborator) to do so.

The Different Layers of Writing in a Game

Not all writing is storytelling. Some writing will be a part of communicating how the player should and can interact with the interfaces and mechanics of a game. One affordance of writing for games is focusing on the *utility* of your writing. A game may need several levels of 'voice' or 'register', from the 'creative' register of the story and its characters, to the informational register of tutorial instructions, UI, inventory descriptions, and quest reminders. Sometimes they combine in conventions such as inner monologue – in many games, characters will converse naturalistically in all manners except that the player character will also talk out loud to themselves in an extremely unnaturalistic manner in order to give the player hints and reminders. And the writing of a UI text is not a simple thing – it is a sub-discipline which also works with genre and formal conventions.

When writing for a game you will need to think about how these registers intersect. Perhaps you're writing for a game where the characters individually don't have distinguishable voices because the *game* voice is the important thing (this is most common in jokey or internet-humour-driven games, where the voice of the game is referential, and characters frequently break the fourth wall). And don't forget – your choices (if offered) will have a register too! Does the game UI describe the choices, or does a narrator in the world offer them or does the character? Following is one choice expressed in three different kinds of 'voices':

- Move on.
- Priya wants to leave.
- Priya: Come on, let's go.

(More on choice voice, later.)

You also need to think about how the writing in the game sits in the layer of importance for the player. Are they front and centre (in a story-driven game), are they holding two parts together (cutscene writing), or are they part of the supporting framework (a small dialogue encounter in a puzzle-driven game, or 'barks'[3] in a battle)?

For example, games with puzzles can be simplistically split into story-driven and puzzle-driven. In the former, all the puzzles should move the character or the story forwards; in the latter, the joy should centre on a puzzle well-solved, and the writing is more focused on a

---

[3] Barks: One-off lines which reinforce character and the drama of a moment, delivered not as part of conversation, but to liven up travel, battle, or the exploration of an open world area.

supportive background for the puzzle-solving. Neither of these approaches are inherently better – instead consider the effect you want to have and how the working with the affordances of your game can help you achieve it.

Now that we've laid these final foundations, I think we have everything we need to relate to how you want to learn from the book and for setting that learning in context.

Without further ado, let's move to vocabulary.

Why Is Vocabulary Important?

The key thing about working in games is that it's an extremely broad interdisciplinary practice, so it will be common for you to need to communicate with people with widely different training and media/artform backgrounds from you. Understanding the vocabulary of game development will help you understand what kind of background or foundation from which a person might be speaking to you. This will be the subject of Chapter 2.

The act of learning the basic building blocks of storytelling vocabulary benefits everyone; if you are already a game developer without story expertise, it will allow you to understand the storytellers you communicate with. If you are someone who wants to tell stories with games, understanding the specificities of storytelling deeply enough to communicate them clearly will help you fight for the story in the design meeting, development process, and the game's production. This will be the subject for Chapters 3 and 4 – the first is a grounding in story structure ideas, and the second a run through key story components.

As a writer it's vital to be able to articulate your practice to yourself and your peers – not only does it help you practise your craft more effectively, but it also allows you to better critique (crit)[4] other works, and therefore understand how they have their effects, and in turn help you better understand how you can learn from them.

If you're someone confident in your game development background, then you might like to read Chapter 2 lightly or skip to Chapter 3. If you're already someone with a good foundation in literary theory, concentrate on Chapter 2, and read Chapter 3/4 by looking for how the concepts might particularly apply or differ in a videogames context.

---

[4] I set out a detailed proposal for a critical methodology in Part III of the book, but for now we can loosely define 'crit' as *the practice of analysing and understanding how a work uses its affordances to achieve its intended effects.*

Vocabulary: Games

A Beginner Vocabulary for Game Development

I will develop more detail around things like game genre and the specific formal constraints of working creatively in games in later sections. This section is about laying a foundational vocabulary for roles, tools, and material processes which will help you make sense of entering the world of indie game dev as a writer or as a game design degree graduate.

There is, of course, much greater detail and nuance I could go into, but this isn't a book on project management so am staying fairly top-level here.[1] A basic understanding of the following roles will offer a good idea of who you're collaborating with, what their background and responsibilities might be, and what you might expect from them as a writer working on their team.

---

[1] The excellent *A Playful Production Process* is a good reference for that approach (Lemarchand, 2021).

DOI: 10.1201/9781003182832-4

Remember, if you already have a working understanding of game development, feel free to skim or skip to story vocabulary in Chapters 3 and 4.

Creative Director

The creative director is also sometimes called the creative lead. Oftentimes in indie dev, this person will have founded the studio or team, be an owner or co-owner of the studio, and/or share the title with a legal role such as CEO or combine it with the role they had before the company grew (such as lead programmer). In indie studios this person more often than not comes from the programmer/designer side of the spectrum. The creative director's job is to lead the game from a creative and design perspective. They will often have been instrumental in ideating the IP[2]/game idea and will lead design discussions. It will be their job to make final decisions on the creative direction of the game: the world it depicts, the headline story, plot and characters, the gameplay, core values, player journey, that kind of thing.

For a writer coming to an established team, the creative director will define the parameters of your brief, and often the basics of the world, gameplay, character possibilities, and have ideas for plot. If you don't have a direct narrative report, they may be the person to whom you'll make proposals, request changes, or suggest revisions and redevelopments, and who will sign off on your work.

Tech Lead

A studio with a fairly robust legal structure might have a CTO (chief technology officer), who would in essence be a tech lead, but in smaller indie teams it's rare someone will go around calling themselves a CTO unless they're seeking outside investment. In most studios, a large proportion of the team will be made up of programmers of some kind, and if they have a structure (many teams won't and that can come with problems of its own), there will be a lead or senior programmer who collaborates with the CEO/creative lead to define the technological aspects of the development of the game. They will discuss scope, and the building of tools, systems, features, and implementation of all departments' designs, usually in a game engine.

---

[2] While we've defined IP in the context of AAA's working with 'existing IP', it's worth explaining that 'intellectual property' is often used more generally as a term for 'idea for a game/game world'. It's the stuff that you can trademark/copyright, protect via a non-disclosure agreement, and licence. Often when people say they're working on 'a new IP' it's a way of saying they're not working on a sequel or an 'existing IP' which has been licensed to them, like *Game of Thrones* or Lego.

Note that it's unhelpful to regard programmers as 'not creatives', as they almost always will be involved in design – whether UX, gameplay/gamefeel,[3] UI, level design, etc. Programmers on games are often creative coders.

As a writer coming to an established team, the tech lead is the person from whom you might request tools and tool improvements, text styles and effects, and systemic needs (i.e. you might need a variable and variable checker to prevent players from accessing a specific conversation until the player has a specific item in their inventory – this is a system that needs designing and implementing, if it doesn't already exist).[4]

Art Roles

Sometimes one and the same in a small team, sometimes divided up into the following roles (and more besides), art has a very wide remit in game development.
- Artist/lead artist
  - 3D artist
  - 2D artist
  - Concept artist
  - Technical (tech) artist
  - Rigger
  - Animator

An art director or lead artist will define the overall art style for the game. They might also define perspectives (isometric, top-down, first person), camera behaviours, tech workflows, asset pipelines, animations, effects, art style, and more. Specifically, 2D and 3D artists will specialise in either 2D or 3D art (although many 2D effects are made using 2.5 or 3D assets, and many 2D worlds are built like theatre sets, with layers of scenery which can be expressed in 3D space, shot 'front on' by a 'camera' in the game engine). Their job will be to produce and often implement assets, and they may also be a part of concepting.

---

[3] *Gameplay* is how the player *plays* the game. It describes things like the 'core loop' of the game (the patterns of play the game teaches and expresses itself through), mechanics, and include gamefeel, the resistances, frictions, satisfactions, and tactility of the gameplay systems. A simple jump can be made infinitely more satisfying by adding *juice* to improve the gamefeel. If you're looking for an image to remember this, think of the act of squeezing an orange. Imagine you simply command your hand to squeeze, and then you have a hand full of mush, not so interesting. Then imagine you add resistance that is high at the beginning of the squeeze and then easier before a sudden stop; imagine that liquid squirts out, there is a squishing sound, and a drip afterwards. Congratulations, you added 'juice' to the experience and improved the game feel of the orange-squeezing gameplay experience. The mechanic is the fact you can squeeze. The gameplay includes orange squeezing. The gamefeel can be improved by adding juice.

[4] 'Gating' is a piece of common terminology for discussing how you pace access to story and other experiences throughout the player's exploration of space and time. In the metaphor you need the 'key' to the gate in order to open it and progress. The key you might need could be one or more of inventory checks for a certain item or number of items, having experienced a specific line or conversation, 'has met' variables (that you've met a character before), a certain time, or proximity to a place, a threshold of something is met · (clues, areas explored, level of character, tokens of another kind), etc.

Concept artists can be a continual part of the team – bringing the leads' vision to life before it's built and implemented – or might be hired as part of a pitch and prototype process. All artists will be comfortable working digitally, but not all will work directly in-engine. Tech artists specialise in bridging art and tech, they may focus on implementation and smoothing art workflows/pipelines, and might build their own tools or shaders[5] to help bring the art and animation to life. Or they might simply ('simply!') be an artist who can comfortably complete the pipeline from concept to asset to implementation.

Animators and riggers focus on setting up physical objects in the game and defining how they look when they move or are moved by the player. A 3D artist might produce a concept and the materials for a model, but before it can be played or animated, it will need to be 'rigged' (articulated so it can move – like applying the outside of a puppet to a skeleton that allows it to move) by a rigger. Animators will define how characters and game objects look when they move or are moved by the player.

A writer coming to an established team will want to collaborate closely with the art team to describe or adapt character concepts, add to, co-develop, or understand the art style of the game world, characters, and genre, and you will want to respond to the art style in the kind of writing you provide. A noir detective style when applied to a puzzle game might demand either 'straight' noir or self-aware noir writing. A cartoonish aesthetic will mean a writer needs to decide to either humanise the cartoonishness through a naturalistic style of writing or lean into the effect by producing cartoonish characterisation and dialogue.

Narrative Lead

We've touched on the role of narrative designer before now, and it's rare that a smaller studio will have several story roles, but if there is a story or narrative lead they will be who a writer reports to. They will define systems and workflows and tools with other team members; they will fight for the plot, story design, and gameplay decisions around the story. If you are a writer on a team with a narrative designer or narrative lead, your job is likely to be producing writing; contributing to story meetings; developing characters; and writing conversations, encounters, and dialogue.

---

[5] The dark art of shaders in my experience bewilders both programmers and artists alike. Shader specialists focus on conjuring visual effects and producing tools for their implementation and editing. A shader manipulates pixels in the game to render dynamic effects like shadows, water, smoke, wind through trees, and much more. A shader specialist will produce tools for their implementation and editing. For the effect of smoke they might create a particle system, define how it curves, moves, dissipates, and is coloured, and make an interface so these variables can be placed and set.

Programming Roles

Programmers can specialise in a wide array of areas and disciplines. We've touched on shader specialists and tech artists who cross over from the art side of things, and a fair amount of narrative design can be visual programming. But otherwise, here are some types of programming areas of specialism you might encounter:

- Gameplay specialist
- Tools specialist
- UX/UI specialist (programming focus)
- Unity/Unreal generalist
- Generalist
- Audio programmer

A gameplay specialist will focus on the feel of the game in the hands of the player. A tools specialist will build the tools other team members need to complete their job and document them for ease of use. A UX/UI person focuses on user experience and interface design – think menus, layouts, buttons, etc. (I am very much simplifying here; UI/UX people could be designers without a programming focus.) Then you might get 'generalists' who can work in anything with a wide array of experience, or someone who can work generally but excels in a particular game engine like Unity or Unreal,[6] or making a game that works on PC work on a specific console or platform ('porting').

As a writer you might intersect with the programming team for: tools requests, implementation, documentation, and support; as part of voice over (VO), localisation (loc) processes, and systems design; as a playtester in quality assurance (QA) processes; and in defining the display, style, line length, and restrictions on your writing. For example, menu text might have character limits to adhere to because of the size of screen area it needs to be displayed in.

Design Roles

In very general terms (and especially on a small team), pretty much everyone designs the game – any decision about how the game works and feels to the player is design. You may have some programmers who work entirely to a design brief set by other designers, but if they make independent decisions or inferences about how the game works or feels for the player, they're designing.

---

[6] Unity and Unreal are two popular game engines in the indie game dev world, but there are others, and studios can also build (or roll) their own. The game engine is an environment specifically geared towards the programming and making of games. It will have a bunch of basic systems, interfaces, and built-in tools, and allow you to build new tools, behaviours, and systems on top of these. Game engines are a little like Word or Pages is a text editor which provides an environment for writing, and encodes things like italics, footnotes, and heading styles for you ahead of time.

In small teams you might find design roles combined with another, and on larger teams find design roles which are very specialist. The type of game will also influence what design roles are invested in. For example, for games which rely on hundreds of levels (i.e. where traversing the level is the challenge, like in a platformer such as *Celeste*) a studio might hire specific level or game designers. Whereas in a game where the place is a backdrop for other kinds of action rather than a function of the game's challenge (*Night in the Woods*, for example), the creative director and art director might design the 'levels' more like scene setting and instead focus their design resources on a narrative designer.

Design roles don't need to have programming skills at all (though often they're familiar with engines and programming conventions – even if they're not writing code directly) and their work might include concepting and proposing mechanics and encounters; systems for storytelling, exchange, and encounter; level layouts; the structure, pacing, and order of place, space, and progression; the distribution of items or encounters, and much more.

As a writer working with a game, systems, or level designer, you might expect to work with them to understand where dialogue encounters will be necessary and the affordances of these encounters, such as conditions for their occurring, frequency, repetition, and line length. If you also have narrative design responsibilities, you will work closely with a game or level designer to fight for the story being reinforced and supported by game or level design decisions. This might be designing puzzles which drive the character or story forwards, it might be pacing the exploration of an environment and how the setting tells a story, or the placing of clues and comments.

Audio Programmer, SFX Artist, Composer

Audio programmer, sound effects (SFX) artist, composer – someone might be all of these or one of these audio roles. An audio programmer builds and implements audio systems; music is often implemented using bespoke tools or middleware.[7] Audio will need to be composed, recorded, implemented, and mixed, and can take the form of music, VO, and sound effects (ranging from foley editing footsteps to the sound of the sea).

As a writer, you might collaborate with audio teams over VO, the desired sound or feeling for a particular place or moment, or even agree on some notation along with the audio programmer so you can implement sounds within your writing.

Producer, Project Manager

I've asked many peers about the difference between a producer and project manager and it appears to be another area which is a little confused. So bear in mind these roles (like

---

[7] Middleware is software which connects two things. FMOD and WWISE are two pieces of popular audio middleware which connect musicians with Unity through an audio-specific interface.

narrative designer and writer) might need to be checked against internal definitions. But for our purposes, let's describe the producer as someone who focuses on the game as arising from the team, and the project manager as focused on the game as arising from the planning, resources, and timeline.

A producer will develop tools and procedures for good comms, collaboration, and grease the wheels of the making of the game. A project manager (PM) will make sure the production runs on time, on spec, and on budget (or more typically, two of those three) – especially relevant if your team has external funding milestones it needs to meet. A PM will hold the procedural overview, and the producer the people one. Both might work to scope, cut, and resource features, and revise planning and process when things inevitably do not go according to plan. They both might also make sure departments are communicating effectively, led well, and have the personnel and resources they need to do the job they are being asked to do.

As a writer, the producer and/or project manager will work with you or your lead to produce work estimates, scope features, improve comms, set standards, and support your team with resources or new hires, and follow your work to assess when you might need additional support or cuts to deliver.

QA, Localisation, Community Manager, PR, Etc.

QA, localisation, community manager, and public relations (PR) are roles most commonly outsourced in small studios, and so I've grouped them together here despite not having a huge degree of similarity.

QA, or quality assurance, are the people who will test the game to destruction. Their job is to seek out bugs and tell you their conditions (how to reproduce, or 'repro' them), so that they can be fixed by a member of the team. They might, for example, see what happens if a hypothetical cat walks across the keyboard and mashes all the keys at once. Or test leaving the game running on pause for 24 hours before resuming. Or try skipping fast through some lovingly crafted writing to see what effect it has on the printing of the text. Or unplug and re-plug the controller. There will be a QA process of bug identification, fixing, retesting, and resolving towards the end of a production process. The process of submitting a game to a particular platform or console is often generally called 'cert' or 'certification', and will require a certain level of performance and presentation, and working within the cert requirements of the platform specifies. QA will also support that.

As a writer, QA will support you in fixing bugs in your writing. They might spot typos and grammar issues (although you might want to lobby for a proofreader, as QA will not typically be geared towards grammar and spelling); and any logic which might be broken, delivering the wrong lines, or where lines are inappropriate for context.

Localisation (loc) is the team that will translate the text of the game into other languages (depending on who is funding the game and what they might require, as well as key audiences the studio itself might wish to reach).

Often writers will either annotate their writing for loc teams via a comment system, or if comment systems aren't built, provide support to loc teams in defining the intent and meaning of lines in the game. Sometimes explaining a previous line, another context, subtext, intonation, and the meaning of idiomatic or unusual expressions. There's much more detail on loc processes throughout the book, so don't worry about details right now.

Community managers and PR folks tend to also be part of the end of production and post-launch. *They will often work with story writers* on copy for the game, for press releases, and in generating content for the community that you will hope to build around the game after launch. While written content is likely to be locked long before the launch of the game so it can be, for example, tested, voiced, localised, you might move on to working on post-launch content during the final phases of the main release.

Process Vocabulary

Phew! I hope you found some or all of that useful. Finally, I'm going to very lightly touch on a few process and project management terms that are useful to know about and think through with regard to the role of writing for videogames.

Funding and Milestones

When you join a project, work out where in the process you are fitting in. A four- to eight-hour indie videogame worked on in a 'full-time' manner could take anywhere between one and five years to produce (team size, polish level, and budget size and consistency being funding-dependent). How the process is designed will also depend on how the project or studio is funded: Does it have equity investment? Publisher funding for a specific project? Arts grants? Is the studio owned by part of a console company like PlayStation or Microsoft and funded to develop directly for them? Or is the studio run on the profits of a previous success? This and many other funding scenarios will change how the studio is accountable for its spending, how long delays will be tolerated, and how and if further funds can be negotiated. The most relevant thing to understand for writers is whether there are internal or external 'milestone' deliverables between ideation and launch which will structure their work.

If you are joining a project funded by a publisher (where to receive advance payments the studio needs to deliver predetermined milestones on time and on budget), you will need to work in a more structured and defined way than if you're joining a studio early on in a project (when it is coming up with ideas and trying to produce a prototype). In the latter case the work may be freer, more 'up for grabs' and with room to explore and pivot at your own pace.

Vertical Slice, Horizontal Slice, Demo, Playable Prototype, Early Access

Vertical slice, horizontal slice, demo, playable prototype, and early access are all different terms for the kind of proof-of-concept builds[8] which might be used to pitch to a funder, exhibit to press and expo/conference/festival attendees, or be produced internally or externally in order to test the game with players. Demos tend to be released as teasers to the public. A vertical or horizontal slice is perhaps the opaquest term here, meaning a literal 'slice' of the game, demonstrating core gameplay, a core loop. A 'vertical' slice is a 'finished' level of polish on a very small slice of the game; and for 'horizontal', less polish but a longer excerpt that shows, for example, how several puzzles interact or how characters develop. This is all a bit like producing a pilot episode or a sample chapter.

Early access games are released before they're fully ready (perhaps they aren't 'balanced' yet, or don't have full level design, art polish, or complement of items, levels, character variants, etc.) in order that they reach a much wider community of free playtesters and/or to build hype, expectations, and increase the swell of attention in marketing terms. It might also be used to seed a loyal player base for word-of-mouth marketing and for when a healthy online community is needed for online co-op features to be effective. Often you will also run a community space where players can discuss, debate, and feed back on the feel of the game, so you can polish and fix it before an official release.

NDAs, Rights Assignment, and Revenue Shares

It is extremely common to have to sign non-disclosure agreements (NDAs) when joining a studio. They are often required by platform and funding partners in order to protect information about proprietary technology, or IP, before it is publicly announced. An NDA will prevent you from sharing any information about the tech or IP with people outside of the company and its partners until it becomes part of the public domain (there might be years where you can't talk about your work, therefore).

Many studios will also require a full rights assignment of your work to the studio – that is, any words you write, characters you develop, and worlds you build, as well as systems and tools contributions, will belong to the studio and will be theirs to assign to others (e.g. publishers) and exploit as they wish (through 'ancillaries' like stuffed toys, or t-shirts, or sequels and TV adaptations).

---

[8] A 'build' is a version of the game-in-progress which has been compiled for playing or testing.

.

Some contracts even take ownership of *anything you make while you are employed by them* – whether on company machines/grounds/time or off. While the former is necessary in order to collaborate with publishers/platforms, the latter is something I personally think is a poor practice and don't include in our studio's contracts. Look out for the details of the rights transfers you sign up to, and do try to negotiate if you're not happy with the terms. If they say they're non-negotiable, ask why.

Rev shares (revenue, but sometimes people call 'profit shares' rev shares too) can also be part of the agreements that you discuss on entering a studio to work on a project, sometimes for a reduced fee, sometimes as part of the compensation package. This is less common in larger indies where the revenue share will be between the studio and the funder. And is more common in smaller teams. You might work for nothing upfront, but then receive a 10% rev share from day 0, in perpetuity. Or you might take a fee as an 'advance' against a rev share. There are a lot of different models here and I can't describe them all, but it's worth knowing that they exist.

Design Processes

Programming – as part of iterative game design processes – is time consuming and expensive. For this reason, an idea, mechanic, or design will be more efficient if it can go through a number of design processes which don't involve programming (or much of it) before it is figured out in code. This is something that, as a writer, it's useful to know because you will often be a part of producing mock-up content, working with storyboards, and producing placeholder content for prototypes, before seeing features and content implemented.

The simplest and quickest version of a design idea is a design proposal – a one-pager which comes out of a design discussion that summarises a tool or feature, what it sets out to do, and how it achieves it. Art might provide still or animated mock-ups. Story might work with art to storyboard an encounter or sketch a level design. A writer might mock up something in a standalone story tool/text document or a programmer might mock up something using simple shapes or other placeholder content.

All of these stages help those working on a feature or content iterate on it in order that it might be better scoped and understood before it's implemented. It will almost always need iterating on after first implementation, but the point is to get it to the strongest possible foundation before spending programming resources on it. The more you know, the better you will scope how long it will take everyone involved to build it, and what minimum viable product (MVP) might be.

Not all studios will use these terms or work in this order. Some might let programming lead, others might define a different workflow or set of progressions. So bear in mind that when you join a team, part of the job might be fitting into an existing workflow, or – if the team isn't very structured – working out what structures you can develop yourself to communicate your needs and priorities, and to make your writing the best it can be.

It has been necessary to cut a lot of nuance and detail in attempting to summarise game design processes and roles in so short a space, so if you would like a whole book dedicated to it, I recommend Richard Lemarchand's *A Playful Production Process: For Game Designers (and Everyone)*.

Story Tools

It's worth briefly discussing tools (although I do want – where possible – for this book to outlive the fast-changing world of software, and also acknowledge that you may often be required to work in bespoke tools made by the studio).

Tools like Twine, Ink, Yarn, Fungus, Ren'Py, etc. can have two uses: either for prototyping, or for integration and implementation.

A studio might use one of these tools to implement writing in the engine it's working with. In this case you will have the advantage of knowledgeable communities and thorough documentation. On the other hand, your storytelling will need to be governed by the restrictions the tool offers.

Alternatively, you may work with a tool made by the studio itself (and which is likely still in progress). Then your role may be to test the tool, request features (like markup for italics or bold text), and for testing the writing 'in game' in a quick and simple manner. You lose out on documentation and probably a bunch of features you might expect,[9] but you get to define precisely the features and implementation that your project requires.

And finally, you might be working in a bespoke tool which isn't built at all or which is onerous, and you might want to use a tool like Twine, Ink, or Yarn to prototype a structure, encounter, or progression of a plot line.

Remember that tools will affect the constraints of your design and writing. Just as the size of notebook you write into can alter the feel of sentences on the page and change your writing's expansiveness, so too can the kinds of agency, choice making, default mechanics, and visualisation that different tools define change the writing you do in them. For example, Twine encourages visually supported branching, whereas Ink encourages more linear passages and word swapping/option burning.

It's good to be literate in tools, but better than that is to be articulate about them too – their affordances and uses. When you investigate a writing tool, bear that in mind.

---

[9] I use 'italics' as an example a lot, but it took me about nine months of advocating and just going ahead and defining my own markup for the programming team to be able to resource the display of italic text in one game I worked on. Longer for copy and paste. And I never got an 'undo'. Never assume the features of a word processor like Word or Pages will automatically be part of a story tool or its integration.

Project Management and Collaboration

A studio will use a number of tools for different kinds of communication and collaboration. One tool for immediate conversation and communications (Slack is currently most in vogue). Another tool for documentation and wiki-keeping (Google docs, or Notion), others for task management and bug tracking (Trello, Jira, a billion others), and on top of that *version control* – a tool that will enable you to 'pull' a version of the project from a repository with everyone's most recent changes in it, and then 'push' your changes when they are ready.

Version control produces something a bit like an edit history, meaning you will then be able to track down and roll back a change if someone's pushed content breaks something. Pushed content is often called a 'commit', because when you push your changes they are 'committed' to the project repository.

This requires making sure that you're never working on the same file or part of a project as someone else. If you both change it on your computer locally, and then push it to the repository, your edits might clash (be in conflict), and you will need to choose whose changes the repo should accept and lose the other's changes. This is something you should expect your team to support you on learning, and there may be different vocabulary and processes depending on what kind of version control and version control software the team is using – some tools automatically lock things if someone is working on them, others don't.

Finally, as a writer, do not underestimate how often you will need to build, use, and maintain *spreadsheets*. You might use one sheet to define or understand the conditions or variables attached to an encounter, another to mark things as in-progress or drafted/redrafted. And a third to write dialogue directly, from which a programmer can export it into the game.

Everyone will have different approaches, and you may need to set up workflows yourself, too.

When you build a portfolio as a game writer, you may want to show you can write good dialogue and use common tools, but just as important will be demonstrating you can fit into the process and collaborate – that might be by drawing up character sheets, one-page plot proposals, a sheet for all the encounters in a level, and a one-page request for a new writing tool feature. All of this will demonstrate a much fuller toolkit for a writer working in games than several pieces of writing all in the same tool.

Defining Your Process

Finally, while part of being a game writer is fitting into a studio's process and workflows, part of it will also be to define your processes and personal workflows.

- Where do you start?
- How do you separate and manage tasks? Do you set up the tech steps in bulk, so you can just write dialogue in bulk afterwards?

- How do you separate or bring together the tech workflow and your creative process?
- How do you manage who's doing what?
- Where do you draft, test, review, comment, mark up, and implement?
- How do you request and advocate for features?
- How soon until you can test it in game?
- How many steps to do everything?

It's okay to start with a pen and paper, or with a thousand Post-its and a Sharpie, or in a text edit document. I certainly went through the early days of getting to grips with *Mutazione*'s world, characters, plot, and narrative design using whiteboards, Post-its, and diagrams. Then when it came to writing dialogue, I preferred to spend several days setting up all of the technical implementation, variables, and conversation 'shells' in between Unity and the story editor (bespoke tool) before beginning writing.

When I began writing, I would also have already defined the narrative design of a whole day, the specific time of day, and know who was in the conversation, where they were, and have a one-line headline for what happens – agreed through design and overall plotting proposals by the creative director. I would have accounted for everything (and made it filterable and searchable) by adding it to the Truth Sheet[10] so I could, for example, look for all the conversations featuring a certain character, or affected by a certain variable, or in a certain place and time of day.

I also knew the characters well, and had developed distinct descriptions and voices for them over many months in collaboration with the creative lead's foundations and vision. All of this meant that when I sat down to write, I had only to sit down and transcribe the conversation as it played out in my head.

Part of the job of writing in games might be making existing processes and workflows work for you, and part of it might be defining them for yourself. Knowing which situation you're in, and pushing back or redefining when you see inefficiencies or miscommunications is also part of the role; the other half is knowing how your mind works best and making room for that. I hope that's what I've been able to prepare you for through this section of the book.

Let's move into storytelling vocabulary.

---

[10] The Truth Sheet is a spreadsheet I made when I realised there was no way of tracking and searching content in the game (which, by the end of the game, contained thousands of 'conversations' – units of dialogue exchanged between characters in a discrete time and place). It had a number of columns which tracked different information about each conversation in the game, from where and with whom it happened, time of day, unique ID, attached animations and assets, priority levels, variables and conditions, etc. It was the sheet which contained the 'true' content of the game writing, and I had to set the internal rule that only I edited it and maintained it, so changes would flow through me and I could spot issues, conflicts, and make sure things were implemented in the game accordingly. This was not an ideal process, but it was the one which fixed a lot of the problems I encountered.

39

CHAPTER 3

Vocabulary: Story Structure

The first thing to know is that the discussion and debate around how to tell a story well (and how to name its components usefully) is a centuries-long practice, with plenty of disagreement and different schools of thought. I'm going to keep things fairly simple and approachable here, but know that if you want to dig into this stuff, it will get more complicated and discursive – in a good way. And if you do investigate further reading, and a literary theory book you dig into disagrees with me, that's both to be expected and okay.

The most important thing for our purposes is *to have a vocabulary at all*. Being able to name and describe the components of your practice make you much more able to reflect, crit, and grow your practice, and in the context of games, will be crucial to being able to advocate for the story with non-expert storytellers.

If a puzzle designer doesn't know what a set-up and a pay-off are (a simple two-part comedic micro structure, where one encounter might set up the joke and a separate second

DOI: 10.1201/9781003182832-5

41

encounter completes it[1]), then they might assume they can move your encounters around in a puzzle redesign without disrupting anything or undoing any work. Being able to mark, describe, and keep a record of your crucial set-ups and pay-offs enables a puzzle designer to alert you when they've made impactful changes or be mindful of writing while working (which of these two approaches you take will be a production question).

My storytelling vocabulary is more theatre-driven than literature-driven, and also borrows from TV and film terminologies. Again, be aware of my context and make decisions – further reading choices, decisions on what tools you want to pick up, reshape, or pass over – based on yours.

The Tyranny of Film

Film storytelling is by far the vocabulary that AAA games attempt to replicate, and because film is (in theory) a writing business in which you can actually make money, the preponderance of snake-oil merchants selling books on film structure and storytelling theory is high, and the quality tends to be low and underdeveloped. This has also trickled down into indie games, and means that to get to grips with good game writing theory, we need to slay some film-writing dragons.

Two of the most over-referenced books in screenwriting are Robert McKee's *Story* and Blake Snyder's *Save the Cat*. They present a set of principles for screenwriting as a recipe for storytelling success, which at this point is extremely outdated, and has formed the basis for so many works that they have become overwhelming cliches. The problem is not being influenced by them, but *only* being influenced by them. I also (as I'll explore in more depth in the next section) think that screenwriting structure is often not a great model for many game storytelling intentions.

As a writer it is highly likely that you will face audiences and colleagues who quote McKee and Snyder as though they know all there is to know about storytelling and structure. *Do not trust someone whose only source is McKee and Snyder with game story decisions.* I'm not saying don't work with them – and I'm not saying McKee and Snyder don't occasionally have something useful to offer. I'm saying equip yourself with a wider vocabulary so you can take your collaborators by the hand and lead them to a whole number of other structures, forms, and formats which might better suit interactivity, choice, explorable worlds, and all of the design affordances that games offer to better intended effect.

Videogames are an artform intimately connected with the screen (though of course not necessarily using it). And film, for a large part of the twentieth century – before 'prestige'

---

[1] Not even just comedy really. Set-ups and pay-offs can in general be a nice way to provide depth to a collage-style story structure in a more open world. And sometimes you might write them so it has a different texture if reversed and you don't mind that the player experience could vary. For example, encounter 1: character X has lost a beautiful cow. Encounter 2: character Y has found a beautiful cow. If you want comedy, Y follows X. If you want tragedy, X follows Y.

television – was considered the greatest thing you could do with a story and a screen. I can understand why videogames have aspired uncritically to ideas like 'immersion', of lifting 'filmlike' sequences directly into games to glue together gameplay, and get stuck in the rhetoric of realism being the most expressive and 'true' form for story to take.

But there is *such* a rich and deeper foundation we can build by broadening the source for our vocabularies. And by thinking critically about them. The next section is by no means exhaustive but a select history of approaches to story structure beyond that of just film, which opens up some of the questions of where story vocabulary can come from, and hopefully make room for rejecting some orthodoxies to encourage conscious decision-making.

Structure

Let's start with beginning, middle, end.

This is something we're taught at school, and something which is in our bones; defined by the arrow of time and biological life. That is, our lives have a beginning and they have an end. What happens in between is (by process of elimination) a 'middle'. Maybe you might throw 'childhood', 'adolescence', 'young adult', 'middle age' and 'old age' in there. Congratulations, you invented the five-act structure. Now add in some events or rites of passage: a coming-of-age moment, early-20s mistakes, a midlife crisis, and retirement. These key moments are our plot points around which the story can be shaped: build up to, culminate in, and provide the energy for the story's resolution. We have some innate understanding of structure. But how can we express it for use in our craft?

My education is deeply biased towards the Western paradigm, which, like most Western things, begins with the Greeks and Romans, and in English is refined by the progression of literature, art, and theatre from Beowulf to the contemporary era. That progression also defines a lot of English-language storytelling, so it's reasonable, I think, to draw some basic definitions from that journey which can in turn be useful vocabulary for a game writer.

Acts

Acts are part of the hierarchy of storytelling as defined originally by theatre. You might draw that hierarchy simply as

1. Line (a single piece of action or dialogue/monologue)
2. Scene (a collection of action and dialogue/monologue usually centred on a single location/time)
3. Act (a collection of scenes, or a single scene, which forms a key unit of the overall storytelling structure)
4. Play (the whole storied event)

Plays have tended to fall into one-act, three-act, and five-act structures. Bear in mind that the kinds of stories that plays tell are (because of human context) governed by the attention span of the average bladder. That is, where do you put the interval (or the ad break). One-act plays don't have a break; in film you might also call these a 'short'. In games something like *Wide Ocean Big Jacket*, playable in 60–90 minutes, could be called a one-act story; it captures a moment. A shorter structure doesn't make it less good storytelling; it simply defines the structure of the storytelling and its scope. Three-act and five-act stories told in theatre often choose to put the interval between acts 2 and 3, or 3 and 4. Ad breaks in TV storytelling can go between each act.

But games are most often *not* an event or broadcast format. Sometimes they can be one hour long, or two–three hours, but sometimes can span a hundred hours of gameplay. What does it mean to write for characters who develop over that timespan? How do you build a story structure which can sustain that level of meandering attention? More on this soon, but for now we've defined 'acts', and let us return to 'beginning, middle, end'.

Aristotle and Horace

One of the earliest records we have of someone saying there should be a beginning, middle, and an end was Aristotle. We tend to over-represent the authority of people like Aristotle because of a mix of distance and coincidence. Sure, he wrote down a bunch of ideas, but there were loads of writers ignoring him and working before him using the same ideas. It was just a cosmic coincidence that his records survive and not someone else's. Nevertheless, we must admit that his theory survived and became authority and so let us acknowledge him.

Basically, everything I've said earlier is essentially what Aristotle concluded: beginnings, middles, endings, along with some thoughts about protagonists and antagonists (the character who wants something whom we're on the side of, and the conflicting desires of the antagonist standing in their way). He also, because he was a philosopher, was required to come up with bigger reasons for these theories, and wrote about the political efficacy in showing protagonists learning from (or failing because of) their flaws ('fatal flaw').

Obviously a 'flaw' was defined by those with the authority to commission, author, and produce such stories. I will touch on Augusto Boal later, but for a brilliant and excoriating take down of the political orthodoxies at work in Aristotle, check out *The Theatre of the Oppressed* (Boal, 1993).

The Romans brought us Horace's 'Ars Poetica' ('The Art of Poetry'), which went further than two/three acts (depending on how you interpret Aristotle's structure) in demanding everything fit into a five-act structure. Most of Shakespeare does this. The five-act structure basically goes:

- Beginning/establishing – Romeo and Juliet are two young people from significant families.
- Set-up – Romeo and Juliet are in love! But their families are at war!

- Complication – Romeo and Juliet have a cunning plan.
- Unravelling – Romeo and Juliet's cunning plan goes very wrong.
- Resolution – Oh no, everyone died but that should teach us a lesson.

This description is hampered by the fact that I am trying very hard not to plagiarise Gustav Freytag's development on Horace's five-act structure, and one which is very prevalent in film storytelling and vocabulary, so let's just explain Freytag.

Freytag's Pyramid

Faithfully redrawn in many a writing handbook, Gustav Freytag's defining work *Die Technik des Dramas* was to define the rising and falling action of a story (the bit that happens between the beginning and the end), usually shaped around a five-act structure.

Here's a pyramid .

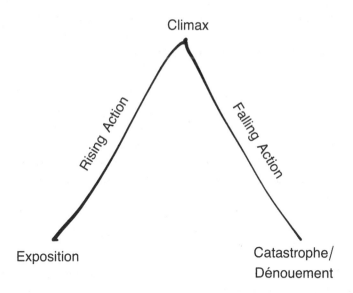

Starting with exposition, through the rising action to the climax, then the falling action, ending in the catastrophe or dénoument. The diagram is often enriched with key points on this dramatic arc; the inciting incident, the turning point, the dénouement (French roughly for 'the untangling of the mess') has replaced 'catastrophe' as the common word for the last part of the story structure. The triangle is nice and neat and fairly self-explanatory.

The Monomyth and the Hero's Journey

Finally, in our adventures in overused story vocabularies, let us turn to Joseph Campbell's Monomyth from his book *The Hero with a Thousand Faces* (written in 1949, with 17 stages for the hero to pass through) and later adapted by Christopher Vogler's *Hero's Journey* (who refined it to 12).

Was a triangle not good enough for you? Three to five acts insufficient? Well, fear not, we have the whole 17 to 12 trials and tribulations through which you can press your long-suffering protagonist. Let's summarise Vogler (the shorter of the two) here, through the lens of a fairly well-known story: *Lord of the Rings.*

1. Ordinary world – Frodo Baggins lives a nice life in the Shire.
2. Call to adventure – But then Gandalf shows up, and offers him an adventure.
3. Refusal of the call – He's just a little hobbit! Not for him, adventure. But … maybe … he should?
4. Meeting the mentor – That's Gandalf. The one who gives you what you need to reach the next step.
5. Crossing the threshold – Leaving the Shire.
6. Tests, allies, and enemies – Can Frodo really be trusted with the ring? He meets the Fellowship! They face lots of enemies; one by one most of his allies are stripped away. It's just him and Sam!
7. Approach to the inmost cave – The meeting with Gollum, who promises to lead them to the place they must go, but also threatens to reveal to them something deeper about themselves.
8. Ordeal – Really, at the point giant spiders are involved, most people would give up. But this isn't about a spider, it's about whether Frodo can trust anyone. The ordeal is betrayal. Not just tests and enemies now; this is that which strikes at the heart of the protagonist and of the story's premise. Without trust in others, a hobbit isn't really a hobbit, and if he isn't a hobbit, he can't do what he needs to do: which is not be a man, elf, wizard, dwarf, or otherwise racist cypher and therefore be capable of destroying the ring.
9. Reward – Frodo has what he needs! Namely the fortitude and friendship of Sam, and a whole host of other people making their last stand to distract from and help him.
10. The road back – They find where they set out to go in the first place, which is also the beginning of their return (either home or to their graves).
11. Resurrection – They are saved, and so is everyone else.
12. Return with the elixir – In this case, returning with not the ring, that is, the defeat of evil and the balm of inter-species kinship.

My irreverent tone shouldn't be read here as dismissal. I'm not saying don't read up on these storytelling principles. I'm saying *treat them as choices and not orthodoxies.* That's why I'm trying to counter the too-often reverence with which they're treated. I hope that's okay.

Christopher Booker's Seven Basic Plots

Let's very lightly touch on structural theory when applied to plot. Many works have attempted this, but none with such ferocity as Christopher Booker, whose life's work is the doorstop known as *Seven Basic Plots.*

You may have a structure and terms like 'the reversal', but how does that differ between, say, a comedy and a tragedy? I really don't want my light tone to diminish the achievement of this work; it really is impressive in its clarity and ruthless depth. In it, Booker defines seven 'basic plots' to which he claims the psychological profile of all stories can be pinned. He deconstructs each of the stories, discusses why we tell them, and how their inner workings are effective. Here's each summarised by a well-known example.

- Overcoming the monster (*Jaws*)
- Rags to riches (*Aladdin*)
- The quest (*Lord of the Rings*)
- Voyage and return (*The Emperor's Lost Groove*)
- Comedy (*Singin' in the Rain*)
- Tragedy (*Romeo & Juliet*)
- Rebirth (*A Christmas Carol*)

I think summarising the details of the book is beyond our scope, but I really do recommend reading more about any of these theories and analyses of story if they intrigue you. They can be immensely useful diagnostic tools for looking at a piece of writing and considering why a character's journey doesn't make sense, or why the middle of a work feels soggy and lacking pacing.

The Problem with All of This

The problem is not that these structures don't work. The problem is it that they aren't the only way to make things work. Because the actual practice of writing is in cobbling together a whole toolbox of different approaches, diagnostic tools, and possible solutions, not a single truth. What's more, all of these orthodoxies have in common that they centre on

- A single pathway
- A discrete time for the story to be paced and told
- A single hero
- A single author/authority

Many of these aren't relevant to or at the very least are significantly disrupted by the space of game design. The more agency you offer, the less authorial control you have. The longer your storytelling time, the flabbier a solo hero's tale will feel as you have to pad more and more between each incident. And if you want the player's agency to affect the story, we need new structures and to think through how we can maintain the effectiveness of the storytelling through multiple middles, multiple endings, multiple characters, and more.

There are also ethical and moral implications wrapped up in the hero's tale. The hero's tale focuses on

- One central character (usually framed around a cis, het, White, male gaze, and even if it isn't, it is limited to a singular psychology and experience)
- Other characters serve their forward arc (NPCs are there solely to be mined for story)
- Man vs. everything (including environment – context and interrelation is stripped away)
- Psychological rather than sociological storytelling

There is an excellent article on precisely this last point by Zeynep Tufekci for *The Scientific American* called 'The Real Reason Fans Hate the Last Season of Game of Thrones'. If you are too young to have experienced people being annoyed at the last season of *Game of Thrones*, I suggest you search your preferred web browser for the discourse (try 'last season game of thrones bad').

In the article, Tufekci (2019) explains that 'whether we tell our stories primarily from a sociological or psychological point of view has great consequences for how we deal with our world and the problems we encounter'. People like to discuss the perceived plot problems with *Game of Thrones*, but Tufekci instead describes the influence of Hollywood-style *psychological* storytelling replacing the *sociological* storytelling of previous seasons:

> In sociological storytelling, the characters have personal stories and agency, of course, but those are also greatly shaped by institutions and events around them. The incentives for characters' behavior come noticeably from these external forces, too, and even strongly influence their inner life.
>
> **(Tufekci, 2019)**

Whereas in the hero-centred view of storytelling, it is the psychology of the hero from which we derive everything. The hero contains the potential for greatness, the flaws, and the potential solutions. It is a storytelling structure shaped around revealing the inner landscape of a single character or characters who are solely shaped by their morals and experiences 'often' *out of context*.

In an era of global economies, climate crisis, and the failure of nation-state politics, perhaps we need other story structures, ones where we follow characters *in the context* of others. Where we acknowledge that the collective is often as important as a leader. Where in nudging characters' journeys down different paths, individuals act within and are changed in turn by communities, and where communities reshape and flow around them, opening up and closing down different possible paths through the world based on the collective not individual perspective.

There's an excellent Rebecca Solnit article 'When the Hero is the Problem' (2019) which explores the precise socio-political problem with the 'hero' of contemporary storytelling, if you wish to dig further into this sentiment.

On top of this political point, there are the practical affordances of game storytelling. As I have already touched on, I believe that the hero format prominent in games is largely not suited to the majority of game stories that intend to run longer than two to four hours. Two to four hours is roughly the length of a film or a piece of theatre – a perfect unit in which to hold the attention of the audience/player (and their bladder) and to explore the inner workings of a single character as they are put under pressure and changed in the heat of whatever kind of story that you're trying to tell.

When we're talking longer than that single unit of human attention, everything changes: you need new structures and foundations to make your story stand up. As players are able to explore a world, rather than follow a directorial eye; and as they choose their own camera angles, and pacing and characterisation are shifted by choice, focus becomes dissipated. It becomes hard to compose the concentrated interiority you need to explore a single, authored psyche when the psyche of the player has freer rein – the hero's tale begins to feel thin, interrupted.

Games (driven by commercial pressures for longer experiences) also often pad out the single unit of storytelling with filler to make it longer, for example, convoluted plotting or tasks which don't move the story or characters forward. Which can in turn begin to make the story feel like it's decoupling from the gameplay and that the world is there to occupy you rather than enthral.

And that's well before we even get to the question of agency, choice, and making multiple pathways rewarding. That's not to say the structures I've described never work, but if you think they are the only or the 'winning' ones, then you are losing out on a whole host of possibilities for making your writing and your storytelling better.

Where Else Might We Turn?

In that case, what else is there? With the caveat that a lot of my influences are drawn from the world of live art, performance, and theatre, following are some other examples from a history of storytelling we could turn to.

Promenade, Panorama, Pass It On

Agency in storytelling did not wait around for videogames to show up. In every culture around the world, you will find oral and folk storytelling traditions which eschew the idea of a single author and/or a single story to tell – storytelling which rejects the idea of a static story or a static audience. We have promenade performances, where the audience would walk through and past tableaux from the Bible (medieval mystery plays). Or a huge panorama and rotunda, designed to immerse (and propagandise) the populace in the scenes of successful battles that the powers-that-be-rich-enough-to-commission sought to portray. In fact, creative movements have – since the production of the idea of the author – gone to great lengths to challenge the idea of the relationship between author, audience, and story to produce new structures and forms.

In the movements in art and storytelling in the 20th century, you see artists and authors disrupting all of the following:

- The text (The idea that there is one true version of the story)
- The form and structure (Expectations of what storytelling *is* – that, for example, a story will have a beginning, middle, and an end, or that it will be told sequentially)

- The environment (Where it happens and all of the contexts that will therefore intersect with it)
- The performer and the audience (Where do they start and where do they end? Are they one and the same, like in instruction pieces?)
- The frame that tells you story is happening (Is it a screen? Or a stage? Or is it happening on the street in front of you?)
- The body of the audience/spectator/participant (Do they move through the piece; do they press buttons to engage with it? Who is with or around them when they do these things? How does that change it?)

Here are some concrete examples of ways in which people throughout the 20th century have broken the rules we've just set out to structure the stories they needed to tell.

Ibsen Crumbles the Walls of *A Doll's House*

Story is inextricably tied up with the idea of the author(s). And through that, with 'authority'. Throughout the history of story, it has been wielded alongside or against authority. When we author something, we take power over the lives of the characters we describe, and how our players, readers, and audiences reflect on the world in which we live through the lens of how we have (re)presented it.

I tell you this not to be fancy and highfalutin. I tell you this because power is an orthodoxy you deal with when dealing with story, and your writing reinforces or deconstructs perceptions of the world with every line.

Why is this all under an 'Ibsen' section? Well, Ibsen tore up the five-act structure not just because he wanted to do something different – but because his storytelling about the structures of power demanded it. Ibsen was writing as the foundations of the ruling classes of late 1800s Europe crumbled beneath them and at the beginning of the faltering of the patriarchy and a bunch of other cruel ways of organising the world. He crumbled his structure with it – to make his audience feel it in form as well as content.

In *A Doll's House* (1879) we find Ibsen focusing on a woman's story: Nora. Nora is a married Norwegian woman struggling with the strictures and expectations of a woman of the time (and capitalism in its never-ending dance with the patriarchy).

As the play progresses you discover that she faked a man's signature on a loan application so she could afford to take her husband somewhere sunny to recover from an illness. She told her husband she inherited the money from her father.[2] The person who gave her the loan tries to blackmail her when her husband tries to fire him. And in general, she does all she can

---

[2] Unfun fact: Did you know in the UK it was illegal for a woman to open a bank account without a man's permission until 1975 (Moore, 2014)? Women of colour were refused a lot longer for spurious reasons, and members of the Gypsy, Roma, and Traveller (GRT) community and homeless people without access to a fixed address weren't able to secure a bank account until September 2016 (gypsy-traveller.org, 2021).

with the little power she has to stop the truth coming out (tries to seduce people, considers suicide) and embarrassing them out of all their relative power and situation.

But the important part is how it ends. Her husband discovers what happened, and 'fixes' it for her. But instead of offering his solidarity and understanding, he offers her forgiveness. He explains that her foolishness makes him feel like more of a man, as it makes her as defenceless as a child he can take responsibility for. She realises she is just a pretty doll to him, an object, not a subject. She snaps: abandons her wedding ring, her husband (and child), and leaves. The final note of the play is the door slamming behind her.

What makes this wreak havoc in story terms is not just that she leaves and that the play ends. *It is that it happens in act 3.* Plays are meant to have five acts! This is like sitting down to a Marvel blockbuster and having the hero die and the film end 45 minutes in! It works on more levels still: the second Nora leaves her doll's house; her story is no longer the property of the audience. Perhaps those further acts are not for us.

I tell you all of this because it's an example of how in taking structural orthodoxies and subverting them, you can underline your content. Want a relevant game example? Consider the exploding of formal expectations in the big perspective shift in *Fez* where you think you're playing a 2D platformer, but suddenly discover you can rotate perspectives as though they're in a 3D world.

It's a very meaningful way to underline the *power* of the player character's central mechanic – so strong it can warp genres.

Dada and Meaning-Making in a World of Meaningless Horror

For many across the world, the World Wars were a watershed, a wound; a huge shift in our way of thinking about what it is to be human in the context of other humans. Such horror. Such meaningless loss of life. What is the beginning, middle, and end of someone born into a ghetto, snuffed out in a concentration camp? What the hell can a hero's tale or a three-act structure tell us about living in a world of such horror? What do you do with that horror if you try to neaten and refine it into legibility or meaning?

This was the context that gave rise to surrealism: Dada in Europe, the Happenings and Fluxus in the US. Let us briefly consider one of them: Dada.

Dada is a nonsense word. That's the point. Dada was reacting to a post-war Europe, to the terrible destructive capability of man armed with machine. But Dada's use of nonsense was not for nonsensical ends – it was to search for how to represent it in form, not content. Dada performers did things like turn their backs from the audience and speak to the back wall, cover their speech with noise, speak over one another incomprehensibly, dress up as geometric shapes.

Dada was either anti-fascist (practitioners such as Hugo Ball) or embodied a nihilistic rejection of politics and meaning altogether (practitioners like Tzara). Much of the work happened in the interregnum between the two World Wars, and in a Europe inextricably bound up in or in-between two monumental conflicts. Dadaism often rejected reality, rejected the possibilities of sense-making, and rejected the notion of communication through art and story altogether.

The beauty and permanence that art and story was supposed to embody for previous generations was impossible in their Europe. The work participants made recycled media images and propaganda posters, it took place as demonstrations on the streets, it recycled and mangled thought and language. The Dadas turned to noise and nonsense – not through joy (as some nihilism does), but through despair at there being no other option.

I tell you all of this because it's an example of one of the early wholesale rejections of structure and meaning-making in 20th century Western storytelling. It is possible to try to let go of meaning for effect. For further reading on games that follow a similar trajectory in challenging the language and meaning-making of games, take a look at *Avant-Garde Videogames: Playing with Technoculture* (Schrank, 2014).

Brecht

More theatre![3]

Brecht rejected immersion. He wanted to frame experience for 'scientific consideration'. He described an 'experience error' that (through immersion) stops the individual from seeing the systems in which they are implicated. If you are immersed in a story, how can you learn from it in an objective fashion? Surely anything else is manipulation! Brecht suggests that a new 'scientific' way of looking at the world should be encouraged. He was interested in producing an audience that was put into an encounter with the 'everyday' where nothing was 'universally accepted'; a mode of processing stories that observed, measured, and theorised multiple possibilities for action and reaction to the content they portrayed.

In Brecht's theatre the audience are not told how to feel, but presented with the facts of the matter. They are invited to assemble the facts, to see how the situation in front of them can be constructed, and, in taking a more active perceptual part in piecing it together, recognise how it might in turn be alterable. In the 'Indirect Impact of Epic Theatre', Brecht explains that by 'means of a certain interchangeability of circumstances and occurrences the spectator must be given the possibility (and duty) of assembling, experimenting and abstracting' (1964a, p. 60), and in that way discover a 'practical attitude, directed towards changing the world' (p. 57).

Brecht liked musicals and the use of song, because they don't draw you in and pretend that they're real; they offered archetypes and themes from which you might draw lessons, rather

---

[3] If you want to dig into more theatre influences I strongly recommend the thrilling, experimental, and wildly creative world of contemporary performance (Brecht was over a century ago, after all). Steve Dixon's *Digital Theatre* will provide you with a neat and game-relevant 20th-century primer, and from there I'd recommend Robert Daniels' two collections *DIY (Do. It. Yourself)* and *DIY Too*, which surveys a good portion of the 2000s UK performance scene, which operates on a scale at which you might draw an equivalence to indie games.

than characters you believe stood only for themselves. He experimented with breaking the fourth wall, with labelling a scene with a title which might be considered a 'spoiler' so you weren't caught up in the action. For a useful example, take a look at Brecht's *Mother Courage and Her Children*, an anti-fascist, anti-war play (though I'm oversimplifying, of course) first produced in Germany in 1941 (Brecht et al., 1995).[4]

There's an excellent documentary about the 2009 National Theatre production (Tony Kushner's adaptation) available on YouTube – obviously I can't promise it will still be up when you read this, but search for 'Mother Courage Documentary (Featuring Duke Special)'.[5] It's an excellent opportunity to listen to many of the cast and crew describe how they tried to stage the work in a 'Brechtian' fashion, including footage from a performance/the staging itself.[6] They discuss design decisions like leaving the theatre background workings exposed; having stage crew wear their 'regular' clothes (not all black), stand onstage, react and laugh along with the audience; making sound effects with voices; etc.

I tell you this, because Brecht, amongst others, is an example of the rejection of the assumptions of what art is supposed to *do* to its audience. Of how it might change its format as it strives to produce action and intellectual change instead of immersion and emotional escapism and resolution. In games, Molleindustria's *Phone Story* exhibits similar instincts for using the mobile game to re-present (make present instead of invisible) the platform you use to play the game as a point on a supply chain (and the suffering that supply chain represents). The form reinforces the content of the story about global exploitation in technology that the designer wants you to consider (Molleindustria, 2011).

Boal

Boal was a radical anti-colonial Brazilian theatre practitioner (1931–2009) who sought to design a method of performance which let the audience take agency over the performance in order that they see how they might take agency in their wider lives. He uses a number of techniques – many of which he describes as 'games' – to provide his playing audience with the tools to de-colonise their minds and empower them to challenge their class status. He sought what Randy Martin describes in 'Staging the Political' as 'a theory of the audience, of what a public in attendance can do to "decolonize the mind"' (2006, pp. 26–27).

Boal's work is incredibly relevant to videogames because so much of his practice was in performance games and interaction. In my PhD I described Boal's practice as a kind of 'first person theatre'.[7] The Boalian technique continues a line of thought from Brecht about trying

---

[4] My version is David Hare, but Tony Kushner's adaptation is the more recent/pertinent. Also, remember that theatre is a living art, and a visual one. It's worth taking time to look up the various stagings of the play and, in particular, look through the videos I've referenced here, if they're still available.

[5] https://youtu.be/x6obtAUsju8.

[6] It's also collected as part of YouTube user Sarah Passfield's incredible Brecht National Theatre Files playlist collecting related films and features (Passfield, 2018).

[7] Y'know, like first-person shooters … academia is a lonely practice.

to find ways to produce impetus for change – but Boal identifies a much more practical thesis for what change is, and a collective and class analysis for how change might be accomplished.

Boal concentrates on the embodied investigation of social structures of oppression through a performing audience, and also attempts to embed these discussions in everyday life. For example, Invisible Theatre is the practice of constructing a situation of the everyday political in the street that is performed 'as if real' by actors in a manner that aims to engage and bring in passers-by. He had workers perform scenarios like disputes with their bosses and try means of exploring and disrupting the bosses' exploitation of them. Boal used performance games as a microscope to offer people with which they could examine their lives, and then empower themselves to make change.

If you're interested in finding more about Boal's extraordinary practice, check out his *Theatre of the Oppressed* (Boal, 1993) where he extrapolates from the theory and foundation of his ideas to the philosophy of their practice. Then there's *Games for Actors and Non-Actors* (2002), which describes many of the 'games' which he designed and used. These games are designed to unpick ourselves from the world we have become used to and empower us to imagine ourselves otherwise. They offer the opportunity for the performing audience to resituate themselves in their own body, in time, in place, in the context of others, and in the context of the state, before asking them to consider power, relationships, the politics of space, and the possibility of solidarity and community through embodied agency.

This is getting a bit chewy, so let me bring it back: I'm telling you this because (in our context) Boal is a mid-20th century example of the turning away from the idea that the audience were *inert observers*. He devised structures to bring them in and give them agency. To try out solutions, not just observe a problem.

We shouldn't remove Boal from his radical working class and anti-colonial context by blithely suggesting he should in general inspire videogames. I offer his work here as an example that actually agency – and the offering of it – is a radical gesture in storytelling that we should by no means take for granted. It can (and should) change our thinking. There is no such thing as 'film plus interaction'; there is only interactive storytelling. And also, we should think of storytelling as a potentially radical (and therefore potentially status-quo maintaining) means of presenting or re-presenting the world, and think carefully about the ethics of portrayal, interaction, and agency as we work with videogames' affordances.

For further reading on videogames as a radical practice, Mary Flanagan's *Critical Play* (2009) is a useful starting point.

Television

A step away from theatre towards long-running TV shows can offer us another different storytelling structure to that of film. And, in the context of games, I'd suggest long-running ensemble television casts can offer us a much better model for TV's oftentimes longer storytelling timescales.

Do you remember 'sociological rather than psychological storytelling' (Tufekci, 2019)? The ensemble (group) cast TV show (when written well) focuses on a group of characters rather than one central hero-style character in precisely this way. In an episodic approach to structuring story you can more effectively offer the interplay of community, rather than the victory of the hero, as the focus of the story. We can now add an additional unit in the hierarchy of story structure: the episode.

Think of something like *Star Trek: Deep Space Nine* – leaving aside the science fiction genre setting. In this long-running show, the ensemble cast's multiple perspectives on living on the border of a recent brutal occupation allow the showrunners to explore the complex and interconnected nature of the relationship between occupier and occupied communities over time. It also uses the episodic format to keep the pacing snappy and interesting – comedy episodes, romance episodes, cliffhangers; it weaves the wounds of post-colonial trauma through the lived lives of the ensemble, and with a pace that keeps the audience compelled.

Let's try to define the qualities of an episodic, ensemble cast structure:

1. A group of characters of the same dramatic importance (community).
2. Drama arises from community in context (their environment and each other).
3. Variety (more characters/locations) – can tell longer, more complex stories.
4. The 'new start' of each episode allows you to play with format and tone, and for time to pass without having to account for it.
5. Conflicting points of view leave you guessing/making up your own mind.
6. No false jeopardy as in stretched-out hero's tales, as the episodic format allows you to pace through sub-genre and character focus switches.
7. Can examine cause and effect over longer periods (generations), and thus progress over a longer timespan naturally and without padding.

This is not a better structure to the monomyth, it's a different one, and it might be the one you need.

So … I Have to Do a PhD in Literary Theory throughout History?

No. You don't. But you should consider anything that you care to learn from is a single approach for a specific storytelling context. You should know that you can change and resist orthodoxies. That you can challenge anything which doesn't allow you to write your story in the best way possible. That film isn't the only or best source of theory. And that when approaching a game writing context, you will often be told how to do something by a non-expert, and your job is not to do what they tell you to but to ask them what effect they want to have, and to check whether their proposal achieves it, and if it doesn't, support them in building a structure and form that will get you there.[8] With that in mind, here are some

---

[8] They may not listen to you, of course. And solutions might be in narrative design rather than writing.

useful questions for thinking about what structures might support the writing and intent for the storytelling when working in a games context.

- Multiple middles? Multiple endings? Or something else?

This may be a narrative design decision, but as a writer you will be dealing with the consequence and may be part of the team leading the decision. What does player choice do to the story structure? How does agency affect outcomes, pathways, and possibilities? Can player choices provide them with multiple middles, multiple endings, neither, or both? None of these are better – but they are different and demand different pacing, laying of exposition, character development, and more. And different approaches will also have practical implications (such as do you manage the variability programmatically or through just a lot of writing). We'll touch on this in more detail later, but for further reading, see Emily Short's *Beyond Branching Narratives* (2016).

- Working with or against ideas of form and structure (expectations of what storytelling is or should be – that, for example, a story will have a beginning, middle, and an end).

Choice and agency aren't the only affordances that are a part of the form and structure of game storytelling – you can also make conscious decisions about how form and structure either support or interestingly contrast with interaction, content, and player expectation. Five-act, single-protagonist-led structures are one approach, but so too are vignette storytelling, collage-based storytelling, competing-narrator storytelling, ensemble-cast storytelling, episodic, and more.

Form can mean genre, format, perspective; the pieces from which the story is made and how it's offered for the player to put together (player-driven structuring). There are established ideas about how most kinds of storytelling should progress, but a good storyteller will think about how the different levels interplay and use the affordance of the expectations of the player.

What does that actually mean? Let's consider the premise that your small puzzle-driven adventure game is about police corruption. You could build a story around the structure of a typical fugitive format – solely told from the perspective of the person subject to the corruption trying to avoid capture working towards the goal of clearing their name.

But what if you take a multi-protagonist approach to the story? Use the form of one thing, then subverting it against expectations? In this version of the game, we set out in a noir setting, playing as the detective. We begin to explore a murder and try to discover who committed it through simple puzzle-solving. After some smaller puzzles which enable you to uncover the first major clue (say around act 1 in the story arc), you begin act 2 playing a different character in the story: the prime suspect. Now you're the person who's been framed, and in adding in details by playing this person's version of events, you create an extra 'piece' for the master plot. In act 3 you return to the cop and discover your puzzle could be put together differently, with the very piece of information you found in act 2. The cop is concealing that information. You'd want to tell it over five acts so you could play more with the back-and-forth, but hopefully that presents an interesting initial proposal for a structural expectation twist. We choose noir at the beginning because it's a very comfortable ready-made world for the player, and we don't have to lose time world building when we're going to ask the player to do a lot of work in dealing with the twist.

It's an interesting way to upend copaganda,[9] by setting up a reliable cop narrator, and then using the form and structure to undermine them as well as the content. This is certain a narrative design series of decisions, but it is a part of what the writer should understand in their writing – indeed, in hearing that the narrative designer wants to flip this expectation, a writer could advise noir as a means of setting expectations quickly, and in turn make relevant decisions about characterisation, plotting, tone, and pacing.

• Psychological or sociological?

To return to the excellent consideration of psychological vs. sociological storytelling set out by Tufekci (2019), we can ask ourselves whether the protagonist is the only one shaped and shaping the story, or are society, environment, and social relationships also part of the picture. When writing for games, drawing up characters, and participating in narrative design discussions around player agency, is it the psychological journey of one or several characters which you're telling (make sure those characters' journeys are really well mapped and shift meaningfully) or is this a story of interweaving and interdependence and more zoomed out than the individual? Perhaps in that case you might like to map the community like it's a character, and make sure that the story develops there, too.

• How do you treat the land, its resources, and NPCs?

Following on from the preceding point, is the land a character? Are NPCs and resources there for the mining/taking, or do you want to say something else with your storytelling? One of the biggest strengths of *Avatar: The Last Airbender* (a Nickelodeon TV show) is that as often as the core characters furthering their great quest, they are pausing to try and solve the problems of the communities they move through. They leave a mark in a way which powerfully reinforces the ethos of the central character and the value of the story. Many of the often-used game mechanic 'verbs' are exploitative ones and you may not be able to affect their being part of the design, but you can think about how to acknowledge that in your writing. It might be explaining why it's okay to mine indiscriminately for a resource, or it might be acknowledging an effect of it on the characters or world.

---

[9] Copaganda is the lionisation of the police in prevailing culture and storytelling which works to obscure the very real and substantial data that funding contemporary policing and prison systems causes more harm than it stops. See *The End of Policing* (Vitale, 2017) for an excellent resource.

- One big story or lots of little ones?

When you expand your game into 100-plus hours or you expect many repeat playthroughs, you really need to consider how the writing and storytelling sit as part of that picture. That might mean close work with narrative design and programming solutions to keeping dialogue feeling fresh. It might be co-designing a world in which an unlimited amount of 'missions' (story-lets) can sit. And don't forget to have in mind how post-launch downloadable content or sequels might work with the storytelling.

- First person, third person, other.

Consider: who is the player. Are they role playing a single character? Are they dealing with pieces on a board? Do you need the player character to be empty enough that the player can fill them up? If so, be prepared to struggle with meaningfully developing the player character. Is the player character very clear and full-formed in their identity? How do you then make that clear and make guiding the character rewarding? Also, how is the voice of the author/game present? Who is the author? Who is the game? And how do they all talk to one another?

- Immersion, interaction, or reflection.

Immersion is another orthodoxy we would do well to consider objectively, rather than as an automatically desirable outcome. Used uncritically the word 'immersion' often just means 'enjoyable', but as a storytelling outcome, it's an unreflective mode. It is the washing away of the player's context, life, and character, and pulling them wholly into a new world or character context.[10]

Perhaps that's ideal for the ethos of your game and studio, but perhaps you want to make work where players test out ethics, reflect on how the game speaks to real-world themes, or perhaps you want them to hold a more systems-level view? In the latter case, you don't want to whisk the player away, you want to pepper their experience with an enjoyable scene setting. And if you want space for people to think about the implications of their choices or story experience in the context of the 'real' world, you'd better leave enough of a gap that

---

[10] Also remember that some people are able to hold their identities more lightly than others. Someone who is White, cis, het, male, able-bodied has rarely been othered by the stories in the world. They are 'Everyman', and can flit about, their gaze and experience replicated by directors and lead actors everywhere. For someone who is not those things, their identity may be something they feel friction for every day, and also something which they therefore build necessary resiliencies around and a different relationship to. No less strong, but certainly more guarded. What do you do when you ask this person to immerse themselves in an Everyman? Or offer character creation which could never represent them? When we work with games and design for 'players' our idea of 'player' is a part of the material we work with. For more on this concept, check out my talk 'The Player Is a Material Made Up of People', currently hosted on YouTube by Freeplay Independent Games Festival (Nicklin, 2019).

the player can distinguish the frame that says 'this isn't real, but it could be, what do you think of that?'.

The ultimate form of interaction is not immersion. Things can be immersive and absolutely uninteractive (film!). And immersion can be negative in many ways – addictive, or just plain impossible and therefore straying into the uncanny valley. It's actually the latter point which makes me think that immersion is not a good aim for games storytelling. I also think immersion should be separated in storytelling terms from the 'flow' of mastering enjoyable mechanics.

Do you want to vanish the player into a new place, like in a film? Do you want them to experience the systems and mechanics more like a board game? Or do you want to provide them with a place to build their own meaning, character, and contexts? All of these things will demand radically different writing approaches.

Many of these themes have drawn out implications which may not involve a writer's input, but whether or not they do (whether or not someone has already made these decisions for you), you need to make decisions about character development, plotting, exposition, style, genre, pacing, line length, etc. that consciously respond to them. If you understand the desired effect, your job becomes about how you twist the affordances of the writing to better achieve it.

Now that we've set this foundation in structural questions, let's find a specific vocabulary for precisely that: the components of story and how a writer can use them.

CHAPTER 4

Vocabulary: Story Components

We've been on vocabulary for a while now, but all of that foundation we've lain means that now we can be quite punchy and quick, promise!

Part of representing the story in game design processes is being able to represent your practice and its components clearly and articulately, and part of that is knowing, for example, the difference between narrative, story, and plot. Your director might say 'the story isn't working', but it's down to you to be able to ask questions and define terms: Is the plot unsatisfying or too confusing? Is the exposition not clear or well paced? Is the narrative too formulaic? Are the characters not credible? Etc.

Likewise, if you know the difference between these terms you can also separate them in your own practice, and pick out where something might not be working, or where tweaking one of the components in a certain way will make things work better, or a change will break things that you now need to fix.

DOI: 10.1201/9781003182832-6

61

I'm drawing on my foundation in theatre but also from *The Cambridge Introduction to Narrative* (Abbott, 2008) when drawing up these definitions – so if you want to really dig in further, that's a good starting point. Remember that you will encounter other people – story specialists or otherwise – who might use these words differently either because of their different backgrounds or because they don't have a detailed background in story. The most important thing when collaborating is to build a shared and specialist vocabulary: knowing where *you* stand will help you collaborate and work more effectively no matter what.

Some of these terms will be explained quite straightforwardly, and some we'll touch on with a little more depth. Chances are that if you dig into in the annals of writing theory, you'll find slight shifts in definitions, maybe even larger variations on what I've set out here. That's okay. The most important thing is that you can separate the components and name them and describe them.

Story

Story is the *whole* thing that you are then using techniques and conventions to tell. If I were to consider the story of my life, it would be everything that happened to me and in the wider world from autumn 1984 until present day. Every choice you make about what to show and how to show it is using techniques and devices which have different names.

Story is the whole thing before you do anything to tell it, and I also think it is useful in its colloquial form – the term for the whole thing once we've finished using all those tools: the interplay of character, story-world, plot, narrative, genre, form, choice, agency, and writing.

I have a fairly large bugbear about story-driven games being frequently labelled 'narrative-driven' because *they are not equivalent terms*. Narrative is 'the representation of a story'; story is the sum of all the technical aspects and practices of storytelling including narrative (Abbott, 2008, p. 237). Narrative is the choices we make in representing the story (this is explored in more detail a few definitions on from here).

I think that the word 'narrative' is often used inaccurately in game circles solely because *it sounds more technical*. Beware: sounding technical and actually doing a good job of having a technical understanding of your practice which you communicate well to others are often in opposition to one another.

Anyway, story: the whole thing.

Story-World

The story-world is the setting for the story you are telling. Games may often be set in fantastical, sci-fi, historical, dystopian, speculative fiction, or otherwise fictional worlds. Or they may be set in our 'real' world – though in doing so you will still make decisions on where in the world it is set and how that is represented in the story. Worldbuilding is often something game studios will be quite comfortable with, and world bibles are wonderful resources which at some point you should be referencing or adding to very rarely. World bibles can be satisfying documents to create and especially useful if you're developing a world that is not ours, but they are not a story (which also comprises a plot and narrative decisions, and might include characters, dialogue, genre choices, etc.).

A good story-world can contain complex politics, wonderful locations, inventively drawn communities, creatures, environments, and more. A good story will use these details sparingly, sprinkling them only when they are necessary for understanding or delightful in discovery.

When working on story-worlds as a writer I also believe it's ethically imperative that you consider what orthodoxies or principles from 'our' world you might choose to reproduce. For example, our Western society might be based on monogamous and heteronormative family units, but what if we chose other examples of social organisation from our world now, from history, or our imaginations?

You don't have to change or challenge everything, but you do – in good conscience – have to consider what you put into the imaginations of others and what of our world you uphold. Do you need your Black character to have a criminal past? Do you need your female character to be the nurturing emotional labour-bearer of your story? Does a physical workplace need to be cis-male dominated? Does childcare shape around elders rather than parents in this world? How does that change society? There are a lot of unnecessarily boring decisions made in worldbuilding. You don't have to front and centre the world and experience of the cis, het, White, able-bodied, Western man, which is a minority in our world and already so well mined.

Games which are less story-driven or contain little writing often demand a lot of their story-world (an excellent example of inventive storytelling without words is the puzzle game *The Gardens Between*, which produces a really interesting story-world out of the psychogeography of the characters).

While this book is focused on writing (for which worldbuilding is a process it's good not to lose yourself in), if you'd like to delve more into the practice of worldbuilding in games, I recommend Emily Short's excellent blog post 'Worldbuilding from a Mechanic' (Short, 2018; Short and Adams, 2019), which includes a link to her literature review on the subject. There are also later sections in Part III of this book on building world, place, and communities to support storytelling with writing.

Plot

Many writers turn to Russian formalism when trying to define the difference between story and plot – specifically the two concepts of the *fabula* (commonly translated as the story) and the *syuzhet* (the plot).

The Russian formalist tradition defines 'story' as everything that happens in the time linear order (as I described earlier), and 'plot' being what you choose to show and in what order.

If you're trying to define the plot of my life, perhaps the first plot point might be the circumstances of my birth (I was born jaundiced and into a substantial blizzard, there seems to be enough drama there), but babies are pretty boring, so following that you might skip forward to a formative moment – perhaps my first swimming lesson. The second you make choices on what to show, you are designing a plot.

It's also worth noting that even *The Cambridge Introduction to Narrative* describes plot as a 'vexed term' (Abbott, 2008, p. 240). Remind yourself – if you meet a different definition – that the important thing is that you know what you mean when you say plot and that you can communicate that meaning easily to others.

So, this is what I teach and practise: plot is what happens in the story – *select events in a select order*. Imagine plotting waypoints in a route on a map. The waypoints you place which get you from A (beginning) to Z (end) – B, C, D, etc. – are plot points. Plot points describe the arc of the story structure through events. You can have several plots in some story formats, and that's our next definition.

Some people also call plot events 'beats' (a 'beat sheet' is a common screenwriting design proposal), while other people define 'beats' as a much smaller unit within scenes (scenes are used to connect the dots between plot points, and beats are the tiny components of the drama of a scene, like mini plot points within a scene only).

For clarity, when I use the term 'beat' to refer to plot, I'll make it clear by saying 'plot beat' and it will mean 'event that contributes to a plot arc'.

It's also very common to have more than one 'level' of plot arc or focus on several characters, and in that way weave different plot arcs together. This leads us neatly to subplots.

Subplots

A good central plot has a sense of what the crucial information is, but in bringing the world to life – especially in the context of longer games – you will also want to understand how to fill out the world and develop characters through subplots. Not all stories need all these layers, but anything long running, episodic, or mission based will benefit from considering this approach. I believe any five-plus hour, well-paced story is an interplay of A, B, and C plots. Light relief in the C plots, secondary character and world development over longer B plots, and the crucial plot in the A plot.

And if we're drawing from the kind of format-driven episodic storytelling you might find in long-running TV series, there's often also a season-long Ur plot. Not all ensemble cast episodic shows have Ur plots, especially not slice-of-life ones, but having a central theme or problem that the plot of the show returns and develops throughout a season can be a pleasing and useful underlying rhythm against which the characters and world can meaningfully develop.

Here's how I describe a general hierarchy of plot:

- The *Ur plot* is the whole story of the season or game told at a high level; the crucial events and theme.
- The *A plot* is the driving theme or problem of the episode or a part of the game.
- *B plots* are the secondary stories in an episode or a part of the game, often lighter, comedic, or contrasting thematically in a way that reflects on the A plot – all of which make the A plot more compelling when you return to it.
- *C plots* are the smallest unit and might resemble 'empty' side quests or single scenes with a recurring comedy character, for example. The difference between a well-written C plot and a poorly written one is usually just good writing for that C plot character/ event. Perhaps you encourage the player/viewer to invest in C plot characters/events in previous encounters/episodes, or you set them up in a previous event or episode to be a comedic pay-off, or the C plot meaningfully illuminates the world with a new detail on the environment or character. Good C plots are both totally unnecessary for understanding the story and totally necessary for adding to the feeling of worldbuilding fullness.

Star Trek: Deep Space Nine is (by now obviously) my go-to example of an ensemble cast TV show. It often uses season-long Ur plots for the big historical shifts in the world (plus worldbuilding and lead character development), but develops the ensemble and the community through the A, B, and C plots.

The A, B, and C plots happen within episodes. The shifting focus of an ensemble cast allows an episode to deal with one big theme or problem in the A plot, whilst also varying pace and levity with smaller subplots. By not placing this all on a single hero (where the shifts in tone could feel unbalancing) the season gives itself far more room to fill time with diversions, contrasts that highlight the central theme, and lots of nice moments for details on worlds and characters as they grow.

- Example: *Star Trek: Deep Space Nine*, season 1, episode 15 (1993)
  - Ur plot: Thematic. Sisko and his crew of misfits must navigate the tensions of being a neutral territory on the edge of the boundary between the recently occupied planet of Bajor and its retreating colonisers, the Cardassian Union.
  - A plot: Drama. Kira must secure the evacuation of a Bajoran moon which is being turned into an inhabitable power-generation resource moving on the residents unwilling to leave. She meets a recalcitrant but charismatic older Bajoran, who is the last to remain and refuses to budge.
  - B plot: Comedy. Jake and Nog discover there is a surplus of yamok sauce on the station. They take it to try to make a profit out of increasingly unprofitable and amusing trades amongst the members of and visitors to the station. They end up

with a surplus of self-sealing stem bolts, which even chief mechanic O'Brien doesn't know what to do with, and which becomes a long-running joke in the *Star Trek* universe.

- C plot: Cameos. Woven into the B plot are minor encounters with the various people the trades intersect with, offering cameos for characters who don't feature continually in the episode and filling out the world of the show, making it feel real and grounded in routine living.

I drew a lot of influence from this structure in *Mutazione*. The game was essentially set up episodically – told over several days, with each 'day' being constructed like an episode. I made a conscious decision to make each day's A plot beats (which contributed in turn to the full game Ur plot) mandatory. In each time of day, the player has two or three A plot conversations or actions that when completed will move time forward. We always mark the mandatory conversations with clear 'clues' in a journal, and in the world when the player finds the final mandatory plot beat of that time of day, a timer symbol tells them it will move time forward. This gives them the choice to explore all of the other conversations from that time of day, or move on and lose them. The plot structure became a narrative design and player agency decision. However, in my role as writer, the writing flowed from understanding that as the structure.

So, in *Mutazione*, each 'day' in the game has an A plot, which contributes to the Ur plot. Then there is a great deal of choice in terms of which B and C plots you dig deeper into, who you make deeper connections with, and how much of the complex and thoroughly plotted history you uncover. I wove a different character's B plot into the A plot each day, encouraging you to return to them when they weren't connected to the main plot. And peppered the world with C plots connected to character, habit, ritual, and amusing situations, all intended to thicken the presence of the community and their environment – the plots made sense alone but if you collected a few of them they'd be even better together.

In writing each conversation, I therefore knew whether a player would definitely play through it and could scope my writing accordingly. An A plot conversation could not be missed because you needed all of them to progress – meaning that the writing/story needed to make sense if these were the only conversations you experienced, and it's where I could really invest because I knew everyone would see them. Everything else was possible to miss, and either scoped as mid-size and for the purpose of a B plot (a subtheme that developed every character over several days but with no vital information, and which you could enter at any point) or a small C plot (usually standalone one-offs, or riffing on a very light theme).

Enough of plots, let's look at our next term.

Narrative

So, we know the word for all of the thing is 'story', and that a story is set in a story-world, and that the plot(s) are the events you show. Subplots can divide the 'plot' into different layers of length, affect, and meaning-making.

Narrative, then, is *how you tell it*. Or as Abbott summarises in *The Cambridge Introduction to Narrative*, the 'representation of a story' (2008, p. 237).

Sometimes 'narrative' is the right word, for example, narrative design as a practice is literally the *design of how you tell (represent) the story*. I find it very useful to have two different words for 'story' (the whole thing) and 'narrative' (how it's told).

Naturally, much of the narrative work in games is done by a narrative designer, and is also hugely defined by mechanics and probably a bunch of decisions the creative lead has already made without thinking of them as narrative design considerations.

Narrative considerations for a writer might be:

• Perspective. (Is it third person, first person, etc.? Is that perspective 'reliable'?)
• Is it told in order?
• What don't you tell?
• What is told through writing, and what is told through other means?
• How does time work?
• Do you focus on one character? Or many?
• Is there a (literal) narrator/author in the work?
• Does the game have a different voice to the story (UI, tutorials, instructions)?
• What formats do you use in the telling? (More later on formats.)
• How do the verbs the player has at their disposal enhance or detract from the themes of the story, and how can your writing tackle that?
• Do you need all those subplots?
• How do you expose the world, character, etc. in a way which is appropriate for your genre and form? (It may be naturalistic, but if it isn't, what is appropriate?[1])
• The emotional arcs of the characters and how they can be drawn.
• Pacing (very much down to mechanics).
• Line length. (More later.)
• Is the writing meant to be read like writing in a book (reported), or a script/comic book (readable but more like talking), or will it be voiced and subtitled?

There are many more, but that gives you a feel for a few ways in which *the way we tell a story* intersects with writing and produces different effects.

Writing

In this book, 'writing' is used to define literal words which will be read or spoken in a video game.

---

[1] Imagine a noir detective game where whenever you're introduced to a major non-player character (NPC) a 'file' is pulled on them, and it appears on screen, adding crucial clues when they come up. That's character exposition (if there are details the player didn't know but the file does). It's still diegetic (of the world of the fiction), but it's not naturalistic, where a character might talk and you're just expected to remember the clues.

Genre

Genre has two possibilities: genre of the story and genre of the game. This is where it could also get a bit muddy. Is a puzzle game a 'form' or a 'genre'? I've decided to categorise at that level as 'game genre'.

Storytelling genre might be things such as

- Murder mystery
- Detective
- Romance
- Science fiction
- Fantasy
- Period drama
- Historical fiction

How you play with or against the grain of a genre decision (faithful? pastiche?[2] satire?) will be a thing you need to know before you write. You may also want to do a mini literature review if you're coming to a genre you've not worked on before. How do different writers in different mediums in different eras treat this genre? As a writer you could try taking a plain paragraph and writing it in the style of several interpretations of the genre, test them on your team, then ask them which one they prefer.

Now let's offer some examples of game genres, which are generally a little more self-referential and opaquer than fiction genres:

- Rogue-like
- Rogue-light/lite
- Souls-like
- Metroidvania
- First-person shooter (FPS)
- Massive multiplayer online role-playing game (MMORPG)
- Sim
- Strategy
- 4X (explore, expand, exploit, exterminate)
- Block-pushing
- Adventure
- Action
- Walking simulator
- Deck-building
- Side-scrolling platformer

---

[2] Kind of like a self-aware but affectionate version of the genre.

- Battle royale
- Role-playing game (RPG)
- Sports
- Interactive fiction
- Story-driven

This isn't really the space, I think, to go into detail on the provenance of these genre labels, and the internet is fairly good at providing examples as definitions. If you're new to games and eager to work in the sector, I recommend you put the time in to watch some online playthroughs of different genres, and make some notes on what makes them different.

The important thing for a writer is that different genres of games will not only have formal expectations around mechanics and narrative design, they will also have attached expectations about how writing and story works in them. Then we're back to the same question of how you work with or against the grain of those genre expectations on the spectrum of faithful, pastiche, and satire.

Form

'Form' might feel a little woolly as a definitional term at this point. Sometimes I've used it to describe what I've also called 'structure' (the form a story takes), and also the formal expectations of the medium and of genre. That's okay though, because 'form' is a word that simply means the 'shape' of something – the shape we design or a set of expectations about how things are usually shaped.

The meaning of 'form' is modified by context – structural form, media form, genre form. I've touched on 'form-driven design/storytelling' as a kind of *approach* too – using the shape of structure, genre, or medium to underline or contrast with the content. Elements of form in games are ways the storytelling is shaped by the writer, the design, the gameplay, and by the player. These elements include:

- Register (poetic, prose-like, script-like, sitcom-like)
- Length (vignette, 3–5 acts, epic)
- Parcelling of story (episodic, sequel based, mission based, through environment, through encounters)
- Agency (play between cutscenes, open world, multiple middles, multiple endings)
- Platform and proximity (mobile, console, PC, local multiplayer, online multiplayer, non-screen focused)
- Unit of attention (how long a play session is meant to be – a commute, a bathroom break, an evening, a weekend day)

Again, you won't always (or even often) be in control of these things as a game writer, but they should definitely shape your decisions and approach.

For example, here's the shape of a game form: a poetic vignette game, which is largely explorational, open world, designed for mobiles, and for consumption in one to two short play sessions. Let's assume the studio hired a theoretical writer, so they want writing in it.

Here's some things which I would recommend as a writer thinking about these formal constraints:

- *Poetic register* should mean that the dialogue will link themes and imagery, but never explain anything too literally. I would do a lot of research into poetry around the same themes from contemporary practitioners to see how I can faithfully reproduce a relevant effect without being cliché. And I would also ask my director: pastiche, satire, or faithful approach?
- *Exploration and open world* means that writing needs to be sparse, not crowding the player in, and it needs to feel rewarding discovered in any order. If the environment is important, I would think about how the writing can be (in its actual presentation) connected to the world of the game. Does it appear from the mist? Is it hanging from tree branches? Or is it spoken by a narrator or character?
- *Mobiles* mean very short line length, in order to be comfortably read on the screen.
- *One to two short play sessions* means that it needs to operate like a short poem, not an epic one – be something that unfolds in the mind of the player long past its length on the page rather than a clear story with plot points. It needs to feel compelling and not wishy-washy though, because a lot of people tend to try a mobile game a bit after downloading before deciding whether to play further. I would want something good and chewy in the first three minutes that pulls the player back. It might not be writing, but I would want to try to figure if it should be with the designers.

Setting

This is a short one. Setting can mean world, universe, time period, place, or culture. Basically, anything which can follow the line 'it's set in …'. Examples:

- Past
- Future
- Contemporary
- Dystopian
- Utopian
- Anti-colonial
- Feminist
- Afro-futurist
- Pastoral
- Urban
- Suburban

- Occupied territories
- Space station

I think all of these can be usefully called 'settings', and link more to genre or worldbuilding in different ways. All of them describe a place and perspective which will influence your storytelling, and how the writing, dialogue, register, characterisation, and exposition could and should work.

Literary Devices

This is quite a fun one. Literary devices are commonly used story mechanics which have been deployed so often by storytellers around the world that they have developed names. Sometimes they're called 'tropes', and often they're used to short cut the story so you can usefully manipulate it or the audience to a desirable place more efficiently. They're not bad, but you shouldn't use them too often and lazily,[3] otherwise they might begin to lose their effect. You might find the TV Tropes website[4] useful if you really want to dig into specific genres or a lot of detail, but for now I'm going to list some of the most common literary devices as examples of what we're talking about and how they're useful.

Deus ex Machina

Literally 'god from the machine', deus ex machina is when something completely unlikely and unrelated appears at the last minute to whisk the hero(es) out of trouble, and solves whatever problem is driving the drama of the moment. They can sometimes be enjoyable. The central character in *Doctor Who* has made a whole career out of being a deus ex machina. But if you have a naturalistic world where a very tense drama is suddenly and conveniently relieved by an unlikely and unexpected solution, then you risk the trust the audience places in your ability to provide compelling clues.

Red Herrings

Speaking of clues, no set of clues is complete without some red herrings to lead you on a wild goose chase[5] and to keep the audience guessing until the solution is revealed. Red herrings that are easier for the audience to spot than for the characters can feel exciting and rewarding. Red herrings over longer storytelling periods which truly lead the audience on divergent paths can produce exciting fan communities. Red herrings are part of your clue arsenal – and should be deployed with consideration.

---

[3] Unless they're part of pastiche or satire, in which case they're not 'lazy' uses but effective.
[4] https://tvtropes.org/pmwiki/pmwiki.php/Main/Tropes.
[5] Honk.

Dramatic Irony

Leading on from the differential knowledge between character and audience clue knowledge that I described earlier, dramatic irony describes just that sort of thing – a difference in the knowledge between the audience and the characters on stage. Maybe there's one character confiding in the audience or whose full actions are clear to the audience, but hidden to the rest of the characters. Or perhaps you know something none of the characters do (the beginning of *Titanic*). Dramatic irony deployed well can make the audience feel pleasingly invested – watching how a thing plays out or is pulled off with panache is fun!

MacGuffins

To return to *Doctor Who*: The sonic screwdriver (at least in the reboot of the show) is a classic MacGuffin. It's not important in and of itself; it exists to be a multipurpose tool which can move the action along in a way that's useful to the writer. A MacGuffin of this variety can be deployed too often, however, so that drama no longer holds tension because the MacGuffin can always solve it. Sometimes you might end up needing to introduce reasons why the MacGuffin *can't* solve the problem this time. But the object-equivalent of a deus ex machina is sometimes what you need to move a story along. And is often pleasing and expected in certain genres.

Cliffhangers

A cliffhanger is the hanging dilemma at the end of an episode or chapter that makes you turn the page or tune in next time to see how it's resolved. Too many of these and you will exhaust the potential for dramatic tension, but just enough will keep an audience thrilled and invested.

Foreshadowing

Foreshadowing is a fluffier version of clue laying – placing hints to later plot events. Hints don't necessarily have to be physical or diegetic clues; sometimes foreshadowing works best in the slightly more immaterial space of imagery and motif. Maybe you introduce in the beginning the thing which will undo the character or resolve the story in a small and off-hand way, for example, a fondness for a hobby which later becomes vital, or a newspaper lying on the table slightly out of focus which contains an article about a yet-unknown villain who later attacks our lead character. Or maybe someone who turns out to be a werewolf is given a name which is only a letter or two away from the Latin for 'wolf-like'.

A famous example of foreshadowing can be found in *Macbeth*. Early on, he meets with the witches, and they set up an apparently unbreakable fate for his great success in the form of their visions, including the most famous 'none of woman born / Shall harm Macbeth'.

Macbeth therefore sets out bravely in the face of the idea he is unvanquishable. But he is defeated. In his final moments he realises that each prophecy was struck down by, well, frankly, as he says, 'double sense' (clever wordplay). Macduff, his vanquisher, tells him:

> Despair thy charm;[6]
> And let the angel whom thou still hast served
> Tell thee, Macduff was from his mother's womb
> Untimely ripp'd.[7]

(Shakespeare, 1606)

Macduff was born by caesarean section! And thus, not of 'natural' birth (this is a long time ago), he is able to work his way around the prophecy to defeat Macbeth. His fate was foreshadowed by the prophecy's loophole.

Chekhov's gun is another common means of talking about foreshadowing. The playwright Anton Chekhov repeatedly laid out in a number of letters a rule on the theme of 'if you place a loaded rifle on the wall in Act I, by the final Act it should be fired'. In actual fact, he's talking more about cutting what's superfluous – if the rifle isn't going to go off, why would you put it there? (Unless it's a red herring, of course.) But it's a useful thought in either direction. There, we've dealt with another literary device while we were at it.

Set-Ups and Pay-Offs

I learned this concept when studying comedy writing – via the farces of Alan Ayckbourn. In that context a set-up is usually for a comedic situation which pays off in the punchline. But it can be a dramatic or romantic or horrific combo if you want. In a set-up you lay a piece of information which later on will become important. Here's David Edgar, an eminent British playwright, interviewed as part of an Open University panel on the concept (which he calls 'figuring' but I think 'set-up and pay-off' is a little easier):

> I do a lot of what I call 'figuring', which in other words is things that you set-up, you reiterate, and then you pay off. A very good example of that is in Alan Bennett's *The Madness of King George*, where the king has an irritating verbal tick, which is to say 'what what!', and we get very irritated by that, as does his staff, and then when he goes mad, suddenly after a while one of the servants notices that he isn't saying it, and he says, 'I wish he'd say "what what!", it was really irritating but I miss it'. And of course

---

[6] 'Give up on your protection you have inferred from your prophecy'.
[7] Oh no. I put some Shakespeare in my book. Sorry. If you're looking for a more up-to-date reference, think of when Luke Skywalker sees his own face under Vader's mask in a dream. Dreams are an excellent place for foreshadowing. And when audiences spot foreshadowing, imagery, and subtext as it comes together in the story, it makes them feel satisfied and very clever, and then they can make YouTube videos about the 20 secret meanings in Childish Gambino's 'This Is America', etc. A lot of the basics of storytelling is about being satisfying in that way.

what Alan Bennett has then [...] set-up, and obviously, very brilliantly, the clue, that when he says 'what what!' again, he's better, and that's a very obvious example of a piece of figuring.

(Edgar, 2009)[8]

When you move away from single-track authored writing towards games where the player has the ability to move around, choose who to talk to in what order, or different pathways to follow, set-ups and pay-offs become a quick and dirty way to provide compelling structure for collage-based storytelling. If you know the rough possible pathways through a puzzle space or world, you can set up jokes or meaningful encounters in earlier dialogues, and then later on pay them off. It doesn't matter if you don't find all the set-ups or pay-offs. But some will land and it can feel rewarding.

Extremely simple example: in the starting village, someone is distracted because they have lost their favourite cow. How unlucky they are, to have done such a thing! Then, in the first area outside the village, perhaps another person has found a free cow! How lucky they are! To have found such a thing! They will name her Daisy. Alone, both are a nice bit of colour for the world; together, they are a nice reward for exploring and taking an interest in the world and its characters.

Reversals

Reversals are sharp turns in the story which enliven the pace, surprise the audience, and keep them guessing. Think someone's on your side? Oh no, now they're not!

Allegory

Really more of a mode than a device, but you can put allegory in your story, as well as operate in an allegorical mode. Essentially an allegory is the idea that there's a wider (and often specific moral or political) lesson to be learned from the story. It sets up that the creator/writer/designer has an eye on the audience/reader/player taking a lesson from as well as being affected by the world they're creating. Allegories set out to prove a lesson by broad example.

Allegories often use simplified, cartoonish, or otherwise anti-immersive frameworks to have their effect. 'The Tale of the Three Brothers' in *Harry Potter and the Deathly Hallows* is an allegory within a story – the ancient fairy tale speaks of power and its use and abuse in a way

---

[8] This is actually from an Open University free OpenLearn online course called 'Start Writing Plays' and is a collated series of interviews with some very eminent British playwrights on dialogue, structure, character, and more (audio and with transcript). There are hundreds of these mini lectures and practical courses on critical reading, writing dialogue, and lots more. The Open University is beautiful part of an egalitarian vision for education in recent British history, and if you're looking for wonderful free resources on writing which would be delivered at a bachelor's degree level, I strongly recommend looking up OpenLearn.

which foreshadows Harry Potter's future.[9] *Animal Farm* is an allegorical work (putting politics in a children's book mode of a farmyard).

Allegories are often more useful than immersion in providing political points of view to a player, because while they themselves might be crude, a well-presented allegory understands you're trying to tell a story as an example rather than as 'full' reality. This is a particularly pertinent thing to consider set against the rise of games designed to produce political change, and places us back in the realm of Brecht and Boal.

Skip past this section if you want to just continue with definitions, but *let's have a quick formal think about games that do try to advocate for change* – and the political 'potential' of games as a form, which is something you may need to contend with as writer with a particular set of ethics.

I am someone who profoundly believes games should not be used as 'machines for change' – there are too many lazy 'games for good' or 'games for change' or 'empathy games' which misunderstand 'empathy' as an *affordance* of games, rather than an effect you need to work for. I also don't think using games to try to change people is ethical. If we get good at it, we end up with coercion machines, which are a terrible tool to hand to the world. It's much better (as Boal and Brecht practised) to offer perspectives for consideration, and leave the change up to the player.

But isn't it special and good to be able to play as someone else? To empathise with them? People are not holidays you can take. And truly understanding a person and their experience as you do your own is fundamentally impossible. Empathy, in fact, is the act of trying to cross that gulf, a profound act because to do it is impossible – empathy is an act of beautiful failure. That is why (I believe) difficult decisions with difficult outcomes are much more human and compelling than the obvious answer the game wants you to pick. Empathy is not an affordance (innate quality) of games. It is a very difficult effect you need to design for.

What's more, this concept of empathy games continues to centre the *person who needs to change*. If the change you want to make is to give people the tools to challenge structural racism, perhaps centring White people isn't the only or best way to do so. If you assume your audience is White, aren't you perpetuating the idea they're the most important people in the room? What might a game for anti-racist change look like which centres audiences of colour and their needs?

The assumption that telling a story in first person is equivalent to empathy, misunderstands that empathy is not about understanding the personal experience of oppression, but *in trusting the accounts and worth of people who aren't you*. Empathy is a

---

[9] I'm uncomfortable using the work of an author whose public presence has been so cruel and damaging to the trans community as a supporting example, but I can't think of a clearer and (crucially) accessible contemporary comparison. If you wish to reference this moment in print, I recommend you look it up in a book from a charity shop or another means which doesn't produce profit for the author and her estate.

first-person act about a third-person experience. So-called empathy games also often charge the player with making decisions which change an outcome for the better or worse. And while individual actions can be important, this attitude to change obscures the fact that most systemic oppressions can't be overturned by one person's actions within those systems.

Don't get me wrong, there's a lot of other art forms that make art aimed at changing people's minds, and the problem is also often the same: a lack of understanding of what empathy is and how it is a *practice* and not an *outcome*. And that politics arises from collective action and consent, not individuals.

Take most civilisation sims for example: there's no sim which could truly allow you to explore P/politics[10] as it's practised without modelling genuinely human-level AI and imbuing every NPC in the system with it. And even then, the P/politics of the game could not avoid the deeply encoded biases, assumptions, and perspectives of its designers. It may be useful to consider the systems that govern our societies at a high level, but only if you acknowledge they are *not real* and their presentation and encoding *not neutral*.

For Boal, P/political and personal change is a kind of muscle that needs to be discovered and exercised by the oppressed themselves. Boal (2002) didn't want to change the colonisers; he wanted to empower the colonised to decolonise their minds and bodies, and then consider what action they wanted to take together – what new relations they wanted to build.

P/political agency is what happens after the game or art or story has ended and the player incorporates their reflection on it into their worldview and political praxis. It can never and should never be the output. Otherwise, what you're describing is brainwashing.

What does this mean in the context of allegory? Allegory takes care to frame that what is being presented is not coercive. It is a story told to present a moral lesson or question, and in doing so leaves the player the decision on how to reflect on and incorporate that lesson. It's not the only way to engage with P/politics within games, but it's a good example of how to use the form interestingly to do so.

To offer an example, consider *Democratic Socialism Simulator* (Molleindustria, 2020) by Paolo Pedercini, a game which engages with Politics in an open and empowering admission of its limits. *Democratic Socialism Simulator* is an excellent allegorical use of the *Reigns*/Tinder swipe mechanic with a bit of *Animal Farm* zoomorphism thrown in for good measure. It doesn't pretend to be a neutral sim of Politics, instead it's very open about its systems (to the point that Pedercini has released the precise calculations behind how the voters react[11]), and – in the title itself – it's clear about its Political values. Then,

---

[10] This is a commonly used way to distinguish between 'big P' political systems (voting, writing to your representative in government, attending a rally) and 'small p' politics (the interplay of power and actions between people and communities).

[11] Paolo Pedercini, Democratic Socialism Simulator Release Notes, *Molleindustria* (blog), 22 February 2020, molleindustria.org/blog/democratic-socialism-simulator-release-notes.

in the spirit of Orwell, the use of animals rather than people in the artwork, it further alienates you from the idea you're playing with 'reality', instead it's clear that you're being asked to play with the interplay of socialist policy proposals modelled on an explicitly USA-like Political system.

There'll be more about the ethics of making games later on; for now, let's return to our definition rundown.

Imagery, Motifs, Symbolism

Sometimes the way to really have a player pay attention – imagine something, or read something and really feel it – is to describe something in a way it hasn't been described before. I would also define this as infusing a kind of 'poetry' in your work. Poetry, on the page, is the act of folding meaning into a new shape, and then letting the reader unfold and refold it in turn. Expressed simply that might be the difference between a character saying 'it's cold today' and 'air like iced cream'. Imagery, motifs, and symbolism can all be used to draw pictures in your writing which bring it to life in a way which makes a reader/player pay attention.

From the pragmatic – all your characters in a community that rear cattle use cow imagery in their idioms ('why you look flat as a cowpat') – to the thematic, a recurring motif is an idea or image which arises as thematically important. A recurring motif in *Mutazione* is that of grief and intergenerational trauma. Objects can be imbued with symbolism (a wedding ring is a symbol in our world), and actions can be symbolic (like a widowed character's unwillingness to remove a wedding ring) – a way of speaking to meaning without having to write out 'they are very sad'.

Narrator(s)

If narrative is the telling of a story, a narrator is a person or voice which tells the story.

The use of a narrator allows you to build a presence in the storytelling for commentary, perspective, and orientation. Whether they be a diegetic narrator (a character from the story) or a non-diegetic one (set outside of the story-world, a means of the author speaking to the player/reader). Certain forms and genre will often have expectations around how a narrator's voice works. A narrator might impartially guide the reader/audience/player, or fill in scene transitions, catch the audience up on what happened previously, or add a layer of jokes and observations.

A non-diegetic narrator offers another layer to the storytelling which is outside of the story-world, the diegetic narrator offers a deeper and potentially interestingly flawed perspective on events from within the story.

Thinking about the different kinds of narrator you can use can also give you room to play with the audience's expectations: perhaps your reliable narrator is – in a twist – proven to be unreliable, or perhaps you think they're a non-diegetic narrator, but they turn out to have been a diegetic character the whole time.[12]

Here are a few useful things to think about when writing a narrator:

- Perspective: First person, third person, other. Does the narrator tell the story from their perspective? From outside of the story? Are you inside the mind of a single character, or can you flit to many? Does it inhabit a 'studio voice' that your game studio is cultivating or known for – or an imagined author's?
- Focalisation: How much and how far can the narrator see? Is it a tight focus, in line with the characters they're narrating the action of? Or a wide focus – can they describe something in the distance the characters haven't seen yet? Do they know what the characters know? Or do they know more? Are they omnipotent or omniscient (can they comment on the future, past, and any place)?
- Reliability: Is the narrator telling the absolute truth? Are they able to lie to the player? Are they able to lie to themselves? Can they miss things?
- Relativity: Where is the narrator 'sat'? With the player, watching the story play out? In the world but after the fact, remembering what happened to a later person?
- Purpose: What is your intent as a writer? To add show-don't-tell nuances like in settings or stage directions? Is it to provide a commentary for comedic purposes? Is it to situate you with the thoughts of recollections, the inner voice of a character?

To dig into this more, I strongly recommend reading Chapter 6 'Narration' in *The Cambridge Introduction to Narrative* (Abbott, 2008); though be prepared, it's a usefully complicating, rather than clarifying, read.

Wow, we're really knocking this vocabulary-building out of the park! If you're reading sequentially, just take a moment to flick back through the bits of the book you just read and all the things you just internalised. Maybe you knew most of it already, but I hope at least some of it was usefully articulated or re-articulated for you. Take stock of that. Appreciate it. Write down the things you found most useful. Try to explain it to a friend, loved one, pet, or nearby houseplant to see if you can express it in your own words. Or write a summary.

Writing notes or explaining to others is a really useful way of making sure things stick in your head. Remember what kind of a learner you are – maybe go back and read a bit you didn't quite get out loud (auditory); or draw a diagram to represent the building blocks of a story (visual); or take a favourite TV series, film, or book, then try to describe each of these concepts through the lens of that story (practical, doing learner).

Good work.

---

[12] Spoiler for *Jane the Virgin*: For most of *Jane the Virgin* you believe you have a non-diegetic narrator, which is fairly common and understood in the telenovela format. But in the finale, the narrator's voice is revealed to be a character from the world of the story. The revelation provides a nice extra bow tied on the top of the resolution of the series.

We're now going to touch on one final piece of story terminology for us to understand, and then we'll move on to vocabulary specific to writing in and for games.

Format

This is a fun one. One of my favourite things to play with is format. Remember how 'form' means 'shape'? 'Format' in this context means 'a well-known shape' – a well-known story structure or set of conventions. Think the courtroom scene, the interview/audition scene, the investigation, the heist, meet-the-parents. Storytelling format is a useful shorthand that everyone recognises and which can do a bunch of the heavy lifting of context and subtext, opening room for the writer to subvert or exploit the format to dig quickly and efficiently into character, plot, and more.

Some formats:

- A court scene
- A sports match
- An audition/interview
- An investigation
- A heist
- A wedding
- A funeral
- Historical pastiche
- Holodeck episode
- Spooky/Halloween episode
- Religious festival (Eid, Christmas, Passover)
- Family dinner
- A resort/holiday
- A fish-out-of-water

Some of these could be combined or be 'subformats' but hopefully they paint a picture – each of these is a situation which has a *way of working* and a *context* which is instantly familiar. When in a court scene the truth is at stake, two arguments are laid out, someone presides, and a jury decides. When at a family dinner, you deal with the context you grew out of and its expectations for you versus who you actually are. Weddings, funerals, heists, and investigations all have a predetermined structure and often symbolic aspects which you can either allow to flow and provide the backdrop, or you can subvert or break them and see what that does to the characters.

To see the use of format in all its glory consider these examples:

1. *Star Trek: The Next Generation*
   Given the (alleged) showrunner's maxim of 'no conflict between the characters', the writers turn to format to develop tension, stakes, and character. They use the

holodeck and time travel, especially to play with historical and literary pastiche (Data as a detective, inevitably used to develop the Data motif of using an articulate naïf to reflect on what it is to be human). They have the sexy holiday planet Risa on which to place the uptight Captain Picard to force him to be a fish-out-of-water, refusing to relax, and nicely developing his character. They pull heists, investigate mysteries (plenty of sci-fi red herrings), and use the occasional wedding and funeral to allow characters room to reminisce and reflect. Because it's all in space, the formats have room to feel fresh, and all the strange characters and worlds get a chance to feature and develop in a form that always helps the audience feel oriented.

2. *When Harry Met Sally*

There are several formats used in this film to provide a structure for Norah Ephron's characters to sit easily in order that she can quickly dispose of the plot and get to the business of amusing situations. Whether it be funny misunderstandings, set-ups for amusing quips, or getting you to fall in love with her characters so that by the time they realise they're in love, you're rooting for them. The men in the (admittedly dated) story only discuss their feelings when looking straight ahead at a sports match or activity. The road trip is the format which kicks it all off. The blind date set-up is subverted into a wedding to provide a useful backdrop for the characters' discordance (paid off wonderfully in the toast the happy couple pay-off). And the New Year's kiss format is refused beautifully, twice. Watch this film! Bask in it!

3. *Firewatch*

Campo Santo's 2016 videogame *Firewatch* uses a series of formats. The person running away sets it up in place and basic character, then there's the doing a job to someone else's instructions, which provides a structure for the player's engaging with the environment and other main character. Then, as soon as you're on top of that, there's a mystery introduced, through which the full story and characters can emerge. The set-up format, the reason-to-explore format, and the reason-to-continue format all give room for the relationship between the walkie-talkie woman and the central character to emerge, develop, and expose. Format gives the story a reason to have the characters talk, develop their character, expose their history, and reflect on their experiences.

Never underestimate the power of using and subverting plot to do the heavy lifting, and provide structure, context, and contrast for your characters to be placed in and against.

Enough Vocabulary

There are plenty more terms, vocabularies, and craft methodologies to dig into within the craft of writing and storytelling as a whole, but I hope that this summary will be a useful handle to begin your own glossary and to begin to consider more widely how storytelling is a craft, full of the experience of centuries of craftspeople. Vocabulary allows us to articulate, understand, and build shortcuts into both our practice as storytellers (i.e. you understand story structure, and can more easily diagnose character development issues rather than having to tweak by feel) and into our ability to advocate for necessary change.

CHAPTER 5

Games Writing As a Discipline

So, we have a start on story vocabulary, but wasn't that all quite … general? It could work for film, theatre, and fiction as easily as games? Well, yes. And while there are plenty universalities to be found in storytelling across media, there are also some considerations specific to the discipline of writing for games.

I've asked us to separate the craft of narrative design from writing for games and have proposed that this book is much more about writing than the craft of game design through story that is narrative design. I want to remind us of this again, because there are very specific disciplinary differences in writing for games which often get lost behind the differences that the practice of narrative design demands (which might be new tools, logic and variable thinking, interaction design, gameplay-driven story or story-driven gameplay, UI design). So, what is different about writing for games?

This chapter is about some of the specifics around writing and storytelling in videogames, when it's not narrative design. It explores some of the affordances and qualities of writing for

DOI: 10.1201/9781003182832-7

videogames – gives us vocabulary to think them through, communicate with others about, and if you're an experienced writer new to games, gives you some new creative restrictions to contend with. This is still fairly general and punchy theory we'll go on to look at more detailed case studies of some of this theory in application in Part II.

A final note: remember that I'm talking about an indie to III context here. I'm providing tools for someone writing for a game in which they are making almost all of the decisions about the writing and telling of the story through writing to when they're collaborating directly with programmers, designers, artist/animators, possibly with a sound artist/musician, and a creative director to develop and refine a game's story-world, storytelling, and writing. And also when they are either the entire story department (with game designers doing the narrative design), or working under a narrative design or story lead.

Let's get into it.

Writing for Games

When you write for a film or play or a performance poem, you know you're writing words which will never be seen by the audience on the page (as you and the performers see them). When you write for a book, or a page poem, you know precisely the opposite. There is a big difference between writing for being spoken and writing for reading – even if what you're writing for reading is dialogue. Before we can talk specifically about writing for games, let's first consider a few affordances of these two modes of writing when considered in any medium.

- *Writing for speaking isn't within the control of the audience when it comes to pacing.* They can miss things, characters can argue over one another, things cannot make sense. Writing for speaking needs more anchors for the audience. If it's a mystery, you might seed more clues than for a text being read or make them more obvious in how they're played.
- *Writing for speaking also needs to understand the closeness of the audience to the performance.* Can they see anything at all (radio)? Can they see the close-up of the body language and micro-expressions of a character (film or TV)? Or are they 50 m away in the cheap seats (performance)? Without visuals, you will need to think more about how to communicate what characters are doing without being unnaturalistic. (Are they baking in a radio drama? Have a character refer to the recipe or ingredients somehow. 'It says here "butter: room temperature"'. 'Ah, it's fine, just beat it a bit longer and it'll cream up all the same'.). In writing for the screen, you can leave a lot more unsaid. Performers can draw more with their faces and body language. And in writing for theatre, you can use the expressiveness of the performers' bodies in the space, and can use more of the less naturalistic meaning-making of theatre.
- *Writing for speaking needs to be understandable but convincing in terms of voice and characterisation.* People don't speak in sentences. However, real people speak in ways which would be very hard to follow in a storytelling setting where we're used to some basic distillation and intentionality. You also want the voices of characters to come

out in how they speak – their own personal rhythms, pauses, idioms, and more. Many things you'd write on paper for reading would end up feeling stilted in the mouths of performers; it has to be constructed differently.

So, what about writing for reading?

- *Pacing is in the control of the reader.* Poetry on the page can be much more complex and elliptical because a reader can unfold the meaning again and again, as long as they want. They can return to a line and reconsider it in the context of a previous one. In a heavily plotted mystery story, a reader returning after a gap in reading can flick through and remind themselves of what has gone before.
- *The mind's eye is an extremely powerful multisensory camera.* Want to transform someone into a giant obelisk? Just describe it. Want to discuss the scent of someone just after they've saved you from an oncoming car? Done! More work has to be done to build characters and settings interestingly and without cliché, but the writer can flit into the minds of characters, they can play with the textures of lies and misgivings; the experience of being in bodies, not just the bodies' performances.
- *Writing for reading needs to feel good on the page.* When speech isn't informed by the context of performance, it needs to read differently. It needs to be something the eye can skip along on, as well as sounding like something someone would say.

(These, it should be noted, are general rules, plenty of people break with purpose, but it's most useful to set out the baseline here.)

Writing for Speaking vs. Writing for Reading: Examples

Take a naturalistic play (writing for speaking) with regional specificity, something like *Road* by Jim Cartwright (a favourite of many a drama-school auditionee because of Cartwright's fondness for monologue). Here's a small excerpt from a speech to the audience by a character called Valerie:

> I'm fed up of sitting here waiting for him, he'll be another hundred years at his rate. What a life, get up, feed every baby in the house. Do everything else I can, without cash. While he drinks, drinks it, drinks it, and shoves nothing my way except his fat hard hands in bed at night. Rough dog he is. Big rough heavy dog. Dog with sick in its fur. He has me pulling my hair out. Look at my hair, it's so dry. So sadly dried. I'd cry but I don't think tears would come. And there's nothing worse than an empty cry. It's like choking.

(Cartwright, 1996)

And here's a monologue (comparable in length, interrupted by one line), as an example of writing made for reading, from N. K. Jemisin's *The Fifth Season* (book one in the Broken Earth Trilogy):

'I'm not interested in mentoring a sycophant. I want you to be yourself with me. And when you are, you can barely speak a civil word to me, no matter how civil I am to you'. Hearing it put that way, she feels a little guilty.

'What do you mean, then, that I hate the world?'

'You hate the way we live. The way the world makes us live. Either the Fulcrum owns us, or we have to hide and be hunted down like dogs if we're ever discovered. Or we become monsters and try to kill everything. Even within the Fulcrum we always have to think about how they want us to act. We can never just … be'. He sighs, closing his eyes.

(Jemisin, 2015)

Compare these two examples. One made for performance and the other for reading on the page. Compare the naturalism of Valerie's repetitions. The shortness of her sentences. The rhythm of her imagery. The way she expands on an image (dog) cyclically: 'Rough dog he is'; a second thought, 'Rough heavy dog'; a third thought, 'Dog with sick in its fur'. Notice how her sentences miss articles like *a* and *the* where they wouldn't be natural to say. Look how her thoughts skip from image to image. And foreground the physicality of the performer. Can you see Valerie holding up her flat, thin hair?

Then consider N. K. Jemisin's thrilling fantasy novel. It still feels like a person speaking, but here it's more about the ideas than the naturalism. The sentences are longer. They make better grammatical sense on the page, but still express thinking-as-someone-speaks. 'You hate the way we live. The way the world makes us live'. It's still a character honing in on their meaning, but longer, fuller, and more easily read. There's one pause, and it's written out by the author, underlined by the description that follows. Do you see the difference? If you're interested in this distinction, seek out more contemporary scripts[1] and compare them to some of your favourite novels.

But, why am I talking about all of this? Well, it leads us to a pressing question: Which one of these is games? I've been holding back on you. There's one medium I haven't mentioned: comics. Games dialogue is, I think, closest to comics in that it is writing for reading like speaking. They have the ability to provide action sequences, but no live human performances (as close as some AAA games might come to it, we're in the indie sphere here, remember). And while some games will have voice performances (VO), they will almost always need to also exist as writing for reading like speaking. Many people have VO turned off, they still lack full-embodied visual human performances, and player-driven pacing (pausing or entirely skipping the performance once you've read the subtitle) and rereadability will interrupt and challenge the fluidity of the performances.

---

[1] If you're unsure where to start with scripts, here are three scripts I have recently enjoyed: *Barber Shop Chronicles* by Inua Ellams; *Mr Burns: A Post-Electric Play* by Anne Washburn; and *Fleabag: The Original Play* by Phoebe Waller-Bridge.

Some Affordances of Writing for Games

In games, what are some of the affordances of writing for reading like speaking?

- *Pacing is often in the control of the player.* They will often press a button to progress the writing, although there are plenty of choices for the writer and game designers on how that text appears (in one block? line by line? at different speeds depending on the emotion you've tagged it as?). One difference from comics is that sometimes the ability to recap previous exchanges is missing and many text systems in games will vanish previous lines. Players can also misread a line's pacing and rhythm unless they are well communicated. This pacing/missing information point also means you need to have systems which collect and preserve tasks and knowledge (journals, lists, etc.) if the player is expected to play the story in more than one sitting. Player-driven pacing can also ruin comedy, which is based on timing and delivery.
- *You will need to strike a character voice and speech quality which works on the screen, and builds character, and which oftentimes would work in the mouth of a VO performer.* This is a very difficult task. You want to find somewhere in between written (legible as read) and spoken dialogue (feels like it's being said). You want more characterisation in the character's speech so they feel alive on the page, because you do not have the mind's eye and all the room in the world for narration to fill in all the details for you. (Adhere to the playwriting adage that you should be able to remove all visual character markers and just see lines on the page, but still be able to tell who is speaking.) It may also need to feel natural enough to work for a VO performer to say out loud if that's part of your brief.
- *The distance from the screen is much greater than the distance to the page.* Almost all text for videogames is too small. This is a hangover from people writing for reading or working close to their own screens, and not considering the affordances of TVs, consoles, and accessibility. There are also just lots of other visual things going on in a videogame compared to a page; you need writing to feel simpler to work within the whole. If you write thick, overwrought paragraphs, you will encourage players to treat your writing as superfluous. The words you write have got to do a lot: fit comfortably on the screen, read easily, communicate within the pacing of gameplay, convey crucial information (characterisation, exposition, etc.), and come together with active visuals and player interaction.

This is where I think the comics comparison comes strongly into play. Imagine the space in a speech bubble or the width of a panel. Even if a long monologue is necessary (see *Watchmen* for example) it needs to be spread out over several panels – contrasted, complimented, or counterpointed by the art. Here's the character Rorschach's opening monologue in the very first issue of *Watchmen*, where each new line is a new panel's contents and where a double forward slash (//) denotes a new bubble inside a panel:

Rorschach's Journal. October 12th, 1985: // Dog carcass in alley this morning, tire tread on burst stomach. This city is afraid of me. I have seen it's true face.

The streets are extended gutters and the gutters are full of blood and when the drains finally scab over, all the vermin will drown.

The accumulated filth of all their sex and murder will foam up about their waists and all the whores and politicians will look up and shout 'Save us!'... //... and I'll look down, and whisper 'no'.

(Moore and Gibbons, 2012)

The lines have clear staccato character, the imagery is uniformly dark and horrific – in that way the voice is strong and clear. The lines are also shorter than in the novel example we considered earlier; easier to process alongside imagery and to just fit in. And while some articles/parts of full sentences are missing (think 'There was a' missing from the first monologue line), it does read more easily – the imagery develops in a straight line. There's a single image and it simply develops it, rather than skipping about. Finally, in the very first words, the writing provides its own formal context by straight away setting out that it's a journal excerpt, not a speech (although it's used almost like a narrator's overlay). This gives a clear context for how to read what's there. Where do the reader and the writer sit in relation to this? We are not hearing a reliable narrator. How you write in your journal is a character insight in itself.

Here are some lines from a character in *Mutazione* called Ailin confiding a secret to the player character Kai. In the game, characters don't often talk for this long or with quite as many short lines in a row. But I made this decision here so that the confession Ailin is making would feel like it's tumbling out of her mouth, like a dam breaking on a long-held body of water. Also note that in *Mutazione* we used text-message-style speech bubbles above the character, so it needed to feel good and readable in an even-greater reduced width of line than a console or mobile screen span.

Ailin: Graubbie decided we should live on the mainland.

He was away so much, looking at places we could live, and building connections for trading or whatever.

And I was lonely, and confused, and Tung was just always there, to listen.

I've always thought of him as just this kid, you know?

But then this time, one night by the fire, he put his arm around me.

You know like people say, 'took me in his arms'?

Suddenly I realised this kid was not a kid.

He's man-sized. Bigger than man-sized, really.

And the things he said, they were just ... perfect.

Like he'd been listening to me the whole time.

It was just once.

He understood.

I think he understood.

And when I realised …

Well, I told him that was why we could never work – because of the baby.

I don't even know if he knows how many months it takes or whatever.

…
I'm awful, aren't I?

Pauses are written in using an ellipsis convention (…). I use a command I requested for 'interrupts' and had the character interrupt herself with many of the lines so the player didn't control the pacing like they normally do (and made sure that the meaning would still be there even if they didn't catch every line) giving an 'overflowing' sense. Line length is short. Imagery is simple (because there's no 'review' function, you can't scroll back through text in *Mutazione* when it's off-screen, and on-screen only about four to five lines are visible max), and the sentences are fairly complete so they can be easily processed. But, the rhythm of spoken speech is there too: in the shortness, the self-interruptions of new thoughts or developments, and her character – youngish, but older than the youngest in the community, she uses 'likes' and 'whatevers' more than older cast members, but has the articulacy of experience, and of running this over and over in her head.

So, that's what I want to offer you here, the idea of writing for reading like speaking. How do you need to adjust your writing for that mode?

Let's get into deeper exploration of some of the other explicit affordances of writing for games.

• Line length

Line length should fundamentally change the way you write. If you're writing for the full length of the screen, what will feel good to the player to read will be vastly different than if you're writing for a speech bubble. If you're writing into a system which is very different to how it will appear in-game, a good shortcut to getting a feel for what feels good for sentence length and for when you should start new lines (if 'spoken') or paragraphs (if not spoken) is to work into an A5, A6, etc. document, or even carefully sized cells in an Excel sheet.

• Testing and redrafting

Testing and redrafting have more to do with the practice rather than quality of the writing. Very often you will be writing materials before tools are even made to get writing into the game, or you'll be writing into backend tools which don't display the text visually or interactively as it will appear in game. You might also have to fight tooth and nail for good in-game testing tools which aren't hugely laborious. Do fight for them, because they will make your writing, pacing, and storytelling much better. But if you can't get them immediately, approximate them. Test a few approaches in mock-ups. Give yourself rules and word count limits. And mock them up in relevant tools like Twine, Ink, etc. to test your assumptions. When you're working with player pacing, and the competing attention-grabbing aspects of animation, other visual effects, audio, and possible VO, try to get the resources to mock up at least one full version of these things as soon as possible, and try several versions of writing for the same scene or encounter so you can set yourself useful rules about what works and what doesn't.

Another note: if working in a professional context with few resources, you may need to write every line like it's the line which will make it into the game. Sometimes because of the volume of writing, the lack of tools, or a lack of resourcing, writers aren't always given time to meaningfully redraft their work. You might spend a year working on story and ideas, but be given the tools to actually get writing with in only enough time to do everything once. Add to that the fact that indie game processes are often unreliably resourced; if the team is running out of money, it's just a factor of game dev that it's likely writers will be let go first (who are anyway most likely to have been brought on later, and only be there as a contractor). In some situations you may need to assume you won't get a chance to redraft or restructure. Hone your practice so you can glom on to character voice quickly. Always have a good overview of what each line and each conversation should do for gameplay, character, plot, or worldbuilding, and submit only when you'd be happy with it being read by the public.[2]

Define your workflow: How do you write? Who sets up the systems to make the writing appear? Should it be done in bulk in advance so the writing can flow easier? How do you plan out areas, scenes, content, character arcs, and plot in advance? What should be contained within each place/time/story beat? How do you piece it up for review? How do you accept, define the realms for, and implement feedback? How do you track bugs (from logic and text markup, to spelling and grammar)? How do you annotate it for animation, art, music, localisation? There are conventions for these things in film, theatre, and comics that aren't established in games; for each project you will define this with your collaborators (or join and learn a house style/tool).

---

[2] Unless you're a student or someone using a piece of work as a learning device or exercise (in which case 'the public' wouldn't matter), work quickly, messily, challenge yourself and seek feedback and reflection often. More on that in Part III.

What Is the Writing in the Game Supposed to Do? What Is Its Verb?

People often describe writing as having different verbs behind it – it's a way of asking, for example, what's the purpose of this line? The *modes* of writing in a work will also have a verb – something it should *do*. In a script you have stage directions. The front matter includes legal lines. Sometimes you might have commentary from people involved in the script, or diagrams to indicate the ideal or original staging. You'll also have the blurb, and maybe some promotional quotes on the back, an author's biography, and more. Each of these can be collected behind verbs like *direct, instruct, defend, inform, contextualise, describe*. It's just the same for the different modes of writing present in a video game. It's important to know how many modes you're working with, what voice you'd like to use for each, and what their verb might be.

Examples of modes of game writing:

- The game menu (settings, credits, etc.)
- Loading screen matter
- The game tutorial
- The in-game UI (including prompts)
- Ways of keeping track of progress (may or may not be a part of on-screen UI, i.e. accessed through a menu)
- Characters talking to one another
- Characters talking to themselves
- Any narrator voices you might have
- Credits sequence
- Marketing – online
- PR – press and partners

It's possible for a game – when written well and with consideration – to have different registers for many of these modes. For example, you might want to do something like this:

Neutral – developer speaking to player formally and with maximum clarity	Menu, tutorial text, non-universe UI matter, PR materials
In the register of the world (i.e. high fantasy)	Written content from within the world – books, signs, etc.
Individual voices within the register of the world	Characters, anything written or narrated by characters (journals, barks, conversations, cutscenes)
In the register of the contemporary writer commenting on the world	Narrator, loading screen matter
Casual – developer speaking to player casually, like an online friend	Credits sequence, behind-the-scenes materials, marketing

One of the trends I find most dispiriting in indie games is the common erasure of all of these modes into one self-aware-jokes-from-the-internet style register. So all the characters speak in quips the writer imagines are witty because they sound like the cadence of online humour,[3] or all with the same wry voice for each character, as if one person were telling the story and voicing everyone. The tutorial text takes on the same forced jollity, as does the credit matter, the Twitter account talking about it, etc.

Not to say that this is always the wrong approach, it's just not always the right one. The extremely popular *Night in the Woods*, for example, is – I feel – one of the reasons many people think this is 'indie game house style' when in fact it makes a lot of sense that everyone there talks like they're from the internet. In *Night in the Woods* the player deals with an unreliable narrator: Mae. Mae is a kid from the internet. A grown-up kid and high school dropout. Each character sounds like Mae doing an impression of them. No mom really speaks like that, except they do when you do an impression of them to your friends.

So, not all characterisation needs to be via naturalistic dialogue. Sometimes there will be only one or two registers for all these modes. But whatever you do, make conscious, form-driven decisions. And don't imitate your faves without critiquing why those decisions were effective and if they will be effective for you.

Then, in looking closer at the question of what is this writing meant to do, I like to ask what is the writing's *verb*. At a meta level, what is this writing meant to do for the player or the game at this moment?

- To flavour: add colour or flavour
- To drive: drive the activity or story forwards
- To situate: make the activity feel situated
- To worldbuild: exposition about the world of the game
- To instruct: communicate instructions
- To remind: remind the player of what to do or how to do it
- To hint: build hints or clues
- To develop: build characters and shape their journey (exposition, change)

There are probably a ton of other potential verbs, but that's a few immediately useful ones. This exercise can help you sort writing into different registers, as well as give you a means of reminding yourself if the writing you're considering should be e.g. consequential or light, opaque and intriguing or clear and explanatory, the focus or the background, and allow you to adjust accordingly.

And then finally, even more important, ask what is the story meant to do within the primacy of the game experience. Is the story the main character, a co-lead, or a supporting character?

---

[3] Which they may be – online in that specific context – but a game is not often shorthand between friends with shared context, it is a piece of work for exploration in many contexts, by many different people.

If the story is there to provide only a backdrop for puzzle solving, a lot more of what you do will be flavour; you won't want to expend resources on lots of character development and variability, nor on naturalistic character development or text effects. You'll want to look for things which enhance the puzzle-solving experience: delightful world details, funny asides, simple set-ups and pay-offs.

If the story is the lead, however, even the gameplay (such as puzzle design) should be driven by the story. Say you're working on a folk horror game with puzzles that gate progress through the plot. The puzzle should progress worldbuilding, character, or plot meaningfully. A writer should know what the puzzle is doing, as well as what the writing in the puzzle needs to do.

If you don't know the answer to these questions, then your brief hasn't been well set. You can work with the creative director or narrative designer/lead on this, but if you don't define it, you risk producing writing which is limp, uncoupled from gameplay, and maybe even distracting. (Also, check out the story-driven puzzle design matrix exercise in Chapter 15 for more thoughts on story-driven design. It might not be your job to design the puzzle, but it is your job to know what it does for and to the needs of the writing.)

Writing for a Player Character

Not all games have player characters. Sometimes you are a cursor on a screen, or the player is simply removed (think a mobile-based card game). But very often (and especially in story-driven games) there are one or more player characters through which the player plays the game. One of the bigger and more unique challenges of interactive media is writing for character(s) that the player uses to exercise their agency in the game world. Agency being the ability for the player's actions to affect the experience.

This challenge is different to how you write for other characters and for player agency in general. The player character has a different relationship to the player, and how that affects their writing needs to be a conscious decision.

Before you write for a player character, you need to ask a bunch of questions around authorship and agency: Are they player-generated? Are they a neutral vessel? Are they well formed with an authored journey? Are they shaped dramatically by the player's agency? Are they simply the means of the player's agency (a tool to explore the game with)? Are they essentially the 'same' person, but with choices that allow them to be the best and the worst of themselves? And what is character exposition when the player plays as them? Should the player feel like they *are* them in a closer way than other characters – like reading a novel in first person?

A quick note on agency vs. authorship: there is no good or bad end of this spectrum. It's just the question at the heart of the tension between artist and audience which has been with us since art and audience were invented: How do you balance the tight rope between agency and authorship for the effect you want to have? Are you writing structures for emergent storytelling? Or are you telling (authoring) a specific story where full agency would interfere in the effectiveness of its telling?

Think of an interactive playful event like a ceilidh/ceili, a Scottish/Irish folk social format for dance, storytelling, and music.[4] The format is a vessel for play, story, and dance. It's necessarily simple (like most folk mediums) in that there are basic dances, songs, and story forms, but as an interactive experience it contains much room for flourishes, individual and local interpretations, and reinvention too. Here, it's the structure and systems for play, dance, and story which are authored to enable emergent agency. But the participants' 'characters' are their own selves; roles are very general and loose so people can insert themselves, adapt, rework.

Think of an authored story, such as a conventional novel. The authorship is strong, detailed, and extends from structure to telling to characterisation – all of it. You have some agency but it's outside of the work, that is when you pick the book up and put it down, and how you read and take the story into your life after you have taken on what you want of it. You might take agency after the fact by writing some fanfiction, but the authorship of the original work is fixed and recognised. The content and structure are authored, agency is limited.

Neither of these is better or worse, but they do demand very different approaches to how you think about working with the different balances of authorship and agency. And if you're hired to a game as a writer, these decisions may have already been made or be the responsibility of a narrative designer. However, you still need to know what these decisions are in order to plot and develop (if relevant) your player character – how to find their voice, how choice affects them, and where on the level of player/author/game/fiction the character sits.

Do they comment on the world like a narrator? Are they silent, a vessel for the player? Are they on a single journey from A to B, and the player's role is to explore the space in between but not change A and B? Or are you being asked to work with branching ending character plotting or development? All of these would demand different voices, different possibility mappings for the writing, and different thoughts on how to structure and expose the character's development (if any).

So, what factors should we consider in balancing authorship and agency at the heart of the player character? How do you author the means through which the player exerts their agency within the game? Here are a few thoughts. Again, there are many more considerations, but here are some beginnings for thinking about how you author a character the player controls.

---

[4] A social gathering built around set folk music and group dance moves that everyone learns from a young age. Everyone knows roughly what to do, but also have room to modify, develop, and make their own mark on the songs and dances. They have local and cultural variants. The structure is a set of rules as a basis for play and interplay.

- *Genre and design conventions*: It's highly likely that before you come to a team as a writer, they will have decided the player modality in the world. They will have decided if you're first person (you see through the eyes of the protagonist, like in *Firewatch* or *What Remains of Edith Finch*) or third person (you see the character you play as like in *Wild at Heart* or *Knights and Bikes*); if you can play more than one character, as a party, or only as one; the kinds of action the player can take, the key mechanics, 2D or 3D, etc.; and will have in mind a certain game genre. But this doesn't mean you shouldn't think about how you write with or against those qualities.

  For example, Japanese role-playing games (JRPGs) often use a party system where there's a lead third-person party member you play most of the game as, but where you can also add others and use their mechanics to exploit the world differently. It's still conventionally a hero's tale, typically, but you will have other characters who need meaningful development. Within these conventions, the lead character's party members are really an extended toolkit. And the exploration will focus on exploration of areas, building of experience, boss fights, and cutscenes. Plot will focus on the player character, and while wandering empowers the player, plot points will be placed on mandatory battles or cutscenes. You don't have to worry about exploration being a place for character development. You can author player character fairly linearly in this context; your larger worry will be making the world and journey expansive enough to fill the genre's hundred-hour runtimes. You can work with or against these conventions, but in such an established genre you'll have to earn the 'against' in the mind of the player.

- *An empty vessel*: Characters which don't speak, or who don't change particularly, and have a single purpose like 'find home' or 'save X' are most often found in puzzle games. The story framing is a narrative support, and worldbuilding is a sandpit for the player's presence and ability to exercise agency, sometimes with a simple pretext for doing so. *Carto* is a good example of this. The player character doesn't speak (though they do communicate). The player's purpose is to solve puzzles by cleverly manipulating the map. The character's motivation is to get closer to reuniting with their grandparent by travelling across the map. The world is rounded out by the ability to converse with other members of the world. The sprinkling of humane interactions breaks up the pacing of the puzzle solving and makes the world-wrapping more compelling.

  If your character is a vessel, a lot of how they are shaped and will be pleasing is how other characters relate to them. It's common to give a silent character a kind of magical, mechanical, or alien difference which makes characters open up to them for some reason, or makes sense of their not speaking. You won't need to plot a hero's journey style arc for this character, but you will want to work out where else you will find the arc of change. Perhaps it is the landscape, the people you meet on the way, or the implicit importance of A and B which allows the player to insert their own feelings of change and accomplishment.

- *A character developed through pinch points* (cutscenes): Another very common means of balancing player agency with authorial control of the player character touched on in the first example is pinch-point or cut scene storytelling. You hand over mechanical agency to the player in sandboxes and then give them missions, tasks, or puzzles to solve, and then take agency away by either funnelling them to character development moments (mandatory story encounters) or cutscenes.

The agency is in collecting the needed encounters, clues, kills, etc. in the open area, and then (you hope) rewarding them with character/plot developments. As a storyteller interested in form-driven thinking, I prefer to provide puzzles and/or tasks which move the plot or characters forward themselves, rather than cutscenes. But it's nevertheless an often-used convention to separate mechanical agency from narrative agency. Pinch points don't have to be cutscenes; they can be battles or rooms you can't leave until you've had an encounter, or like in *Mutazione*, certain things you have to do to progress time. Think about how you will unite or align agency and authorship.

- *Player-generated personalities and/or journeys*: Does the player create the character themselves? Or do their choices for the character send them down many different possible pathways? This is a whole new ballgame: you might write several personality 'checks' for certain encounters, barks, or journeys (if you chose witty or wry character traits, then bark X is available); or work closely with narrative design and story programmers to create generative systems based on the choices made in creating the character or how the character develops through player choice. This is the kind of thing you tend to want to produce systems for because it quickly becomes an exponential writing task. Expect this to be a much more collaborative writing process; expect much more playtesting, balancing, and bug fixing. *Procedural Storytelling* is great for further reading on the complexities of this area (Short and Adams, 2019).

- *Amnesia and traumatic brain injuries, or, a person from out of town*: The game writer's friend. Part of the challenge of introducing the player to a new world is placing them in a character who in theory should know about it. You can use that dissonance to good effect, but if you want to voice a lot of hints through the player character's mouth (or those trying to instruct them), then often making them not know things is useful. Really this lesson is about thinking about if you want dissonance or harmony of knowledge between player and character – and to know what that means for your writing and the writing you have to lay around them.

- *Two sides of the same protagonist; agency is a quality not a virtue*: *Kentucky Route Zero* is my favourite example of well-founded characters who aren't changed through the player's choices for them, rather it's the character on a good day or a bad day, or the same character asking different questions. Their change (and those around them) happens in response to authored events; the choices are simply a means of exploring them through action.

Here's an example of a choice in *Kentucky Route Zero: Act I* (Cardboard Computer, 2013–2020)

1. Conway: Sure, I have an old friend who runs a bar, and they've got a real big stage. (go to bar-stage)
2. Conway: Sure, I know a furniture-warehouse you could probably break into. (go to furniture-warehouse)
   [bar-stage]
   Carrington: No, no, it can't be indoors. Impossible … (go to introduce-play)

[furniture-warehouse]

Carrington: This isn't some illegal drug party! (go to introduce-play)

[introduce-play]

Carrington: But I'm obliged you'd stop a moment to help me work this through. Let me explain my charge:

Carrington: I've dedicated my last twelve years to the design and orchestration of my life's great work: a grand, broadly experimental theatrical adaptation of 'The Death of the Hired Man' by Robert Frost.[5]

The minute decisions which make the conversations feel active and pacey for the player do not change the end result – see how it rounds back to the same place, the detour is 'colour', not consequence.

I'm in favour of spending as much 'cheap' agency as you can in games writing, to earn the 'expensive' agency that you might want to employ. Choices are not better if they're meaningful in agency terms, they're best if they're always *doing* something. And sometimes that's making a conversation feel active because you clicked something, or uncovering memory 1 or memory 2.

Player agency in story or character development isn't vital for a game to be a game. It's a quality you need to make a conscious decision about. This is narrative design, of course, but as a writer, you need to know this is what you're writing in the context of, and adapt the kinds of choices you offer and how you shape the possibility space of the outcomes.

Let's develop the idea of writing for choice a little more.

Choice Voice, Type, and Modality

Choice writing is something that most general (non-games) writing and story craft books won't cover.[6]

One thing to to consider when writing for player choice is the various affordances of consequence – both in actual implementation, and in player perception. I'd like to think all the choices written for a game matter (add to the intent of the work), but the amount of control the player has over them, and what they in turn effect, is often seen as the sum of how complex or accomplished a piece of interactive writing is. Sometimes it can feel like playing audiences will judge the accomplishment of games on how close they get to the 'real' world of choice and consequence.

But as a storyteller, sometimes abstraction rather than simulation, or linearity as opposed to branching, is a more useful tool for the story you are telling. The most important thing

---

[5] Interactive transcript provided by Eli Fessler (2020) at consolidatedpower.co/~eli/.
[6] Although we can draw plenty of non-games works which do involve choice. Consider Yoko Ono's instruction pieces or the Choose Your Own Adventure series of books (which is as a genre known as a 'gamebook', because CYOA are fairly active in protecting their trademark).

is to make *conscious decisions* about how you use choice, branching and variation. How a game works with player choice produces different results, but none of them are inherently better than any other. What's important is that those working on the story understand the implications of the choice for effect, implementation, and workload.

When asked this question about choice with regard to *Mutazione*, as I mentioned earlier, I describe it as using the *Kentucky Route Zero* model of choice – a game which does a wonderful job of colouring how the character plays the situation, but not letting you choose *who* the character is. In *Mutazione* I offer the player, are you attempt-to-be-articulate Kai or are you diffuse-the-situation-with-a-joke Kai? Either way, you're still Kai. The conversations branch; you might access different micro-reactions, memories, and stories, but they come to the same place at the end, serve the same kind of beat in the story. This allowed me to author a more careful overall pacing and structure for the story, and to build a community that felt fuller and realer because you, the player, *couldn't* affect some things.

One of the key themes for *Mutazione* was community, and you can talk about community more effectively when it's not there to serve the player, but rather the player is rewarded for exploring and listening to it. Tending to the community's story, rather than applying pressure to it, portrays community much more truthfully – as a collection of people as real and subjective as the individual's perspective on it.[7] I kept the feeling of *active* presence and pacing alive, though, by offering many short and easy-to-process choice texts to choose from, which (on choosing) expanded into fuller and sometimes surprising contributions from Kai. You choose 'Make a joke', and then get to find out how good Kai's joke is. The player still had the pleasure of discovery, without changing characters and outcomes unnaturally.

Choice type and design may well be outside of your remit as a writer (the job of the narrative lead/designer) but it is something which will be encoded into the story tools and game design and is something that will be defined either for or with a game writer. It's also something to which a game writer can and should bring flair.

When working with choice, your affordances move from 'mode and register' (Is the choice part of the UI, the game speaking to the player? Perhaps the character's unsaid lines?), to 'voice and perspective' (character, third person, first person) and 'choice format' (multiple choice? Change a word? A summary of what's said/of the approach which is replaced by the full lines?). Plus other affordances such as how many choices is typical (if you always have at least two, it would feel like something to be presented with a single choice only in a moment of difficulty), size of the space the choice is offered in (should you adjust character count or line length), and indeed, do you offer surprises (what if you offer the player a choice which ends up not turning out like the description implied).

---

[7] In my opinion, one of the most meaningful dialogue options I offered players in *Mutazione* is 'Stay quiet'. When someone is talking to you of their grief, or sorrow, or regrets, sometimes the most powerful act is to not to act but to listen. This also supported one of the other themes of colonialism and its harms. The White saviour trope shouldn't be reinforced by giving the player's 'outsider character' too much agency over the community's characters or the ability to fix everything.

Here are some bullet points which describe some useful questions you can draw on when thinking about choice:

- What is an appropriate line length and character limit for how they're displayed and for pacing?
- Is there a genre convention to work with or against?
- Do the choices control only one character's contributions, or are you choosing for more than one character?
- What are the affordances of the tools you're working in for writing and shaping choice, and do you need to request features?
- Narrator, character, game, or game designer speaking?
- First person or third person?
- What are the conventions about the choice types you want to offer – and can you subvert them pleasingly for certain effects?
- Do choices change from the version you choose and how they're printed? Is there room for surprise, humour, and pleasure in seeing how a choice expands after it's selected?
- How many choices is the player offered?
- How does it 'feel' to pick a choice for the player (on controller and PC)?
- Do you punctuate choices like the main game text?
- Do some choices need to be kept track of in documentation, variables, and marked up in systems? Should that change your workflow?
- How are you going to test the feel of choices? Through mock-ups?
- What are your 'cheap' choices (that don't change anything, just colour it), and where are your 'expensive' ones (that mean you have to branch the writing and/or account for the choice later, i.e. make the variability more complex)?
- Does the player choose different sentences, words, images, swap words in or out (this one is bad for localisation), or something else?
- Does the choice 'wait' or is there a timer on them? Can the player miss the opportunity to respond, and how does the writing accommodate that?
- Are the choices always words, or can they be actions, images, punctuation?

There's a reason that narrative designers are often game writers and vice versa – sometimes the space between design and story, narrative design, and writing is very close. But while the answers to these questions might be provided by a narrative designer, creative director, or story tools programmer, all of them are part of the landscape of how you should think carefully about your writing: the affordances of those formal decisions, the effect your writing has within them; what choice tells the player about their relationship to the characters, the world, and how it situates their agency in the story.

Once you have these design decisions pinned down for you, or through your work, your approach to writing choice isn't that different to an approach to *good writing* in general. As for how to develop good writing, well, that's what this book is about! Continue reading, and look out for the exercises on character development, voice, and naturalistic dialogue which will be used in and around choices. You'll work on that in the workbook part of this book (Part III).

If you want to read more about the potential *result* of choice – branching (which is, in my opinion, narrative design) and decisions that designers might make around how to deal with branching story structure – we're back to the excellent Emily Short. Her blog post 'Beyond Branching: Quality-Based, Salience-Based, and Waypoint Narrative Structures' neatly summarises contextual resources, before clearly and succinctly exploring branching storytelling narrative design (Short, 2016).

When Is Writing Not It?

Another saying we hear fairly often in other media is 'show don't tell' – in real life people rarely tell you how they feel directly. They might allude to it. They might avoid it. It might build up over weeks. Or they might betray it in their tone, body language, or actions. The same goes for worldbuilding and politics. The difficulty of game writing 'show don't tell' is that while it's a big interdisciplinary team, each person is *in* their discipline, and it can often be much easier to have an effect with what you have control over – the 'tell' of writing. You can, for example, plot a series of encounters which would build a body language subtext in order to show not tell two characters are growing closer. But what if there's no animation budget left, and even if there is, how many people do you need to communicate the intent to and convince it's worth the resources? Writing is a lot cheaper than animation.

So while a rule of writing can be show don't tell, you will need to work out whether naturalistic exposition is something you can afford, and if you can't, how to make it okay for things to be communicated through 'tell' (are the characters more cartoonish? do you have a commentary in a journal? does a narrator tell you what you can't see?). You can also try to establish a palette of things you will use often to enhance your writing and the gameplay experience, in which you can ask the team to *invest*. Perhaps you can't ask for a different bespoke animation every time, but what if you agreed to ten conversation animations for main characters, and a minimum of three for lesser characters? That might be more doable.

Building a Palette for Showing Not Telling

Here's another list of things – so many lists of things – from which you can build a toolset for writing that shows rather than tells.

Text effects: Do you want bold? Italics? Underlining? Attractive all caps? Even these things need to be encoded or implemented by the programmers, and unless you're working with a what-you-see-is-what-you-get tool like Yarn, will need you to agree to a markup like <italic>*this*</italic>. Also, think about the affordances of animation. I loathe all caps in games. I think all caps is a remnant of the-way-we-talk-on-the-internet, not suitable to reading writing like speaking. It's much more elegant to have animation or effect (bold and a five point larger font size, with a shudder on each word when it appears, for example). Maybe you can't afford that, but someone's going to have to implement an all caps font, so if you can suggest a palette of text effects instead, all the better. Here's what's immediately useful for projects I've worked on:

- Laughing
- Singing
- Whisper/scared
- Angry/shouting
- Something to mark up a different language being spoken (using a different font or colour)
- Italic/emphasis

Of course, it depends on the kind of story you're telling. But agreeing that the work will be done to provide a text effect for each of these (including things whether it applies to whole lines or only words wrapped by the mark up; or whether it changes pacing, font size, font weight, colour, appearance, character animation, and more) and agreeing how you will mark it will enable you to work with it long before it's implemented. You can write <singing> ♫ Song lyrics ♫ </singing> knowing that you won't have to come back and implement everything after the fact, and knowing that you can show not tell in the writing – you don't have to write 'Let me sing it to you' at the beginning of the line.

Pacing: While there's much about an individual's cadence of speech, thought, and pause which can be intimated through things like ellipses, commas, repetition, etc., remember that the designers are already making decisions about how text appears (letter by letter? word by word? do full stops give a longer pause than a comma?) which you can be a part of and in which you can make requests. Maybe you want to encode silent pauses (not related to punctuation) or interruptions where before a line can finish the system doesn't wait for the player's input to print the next one. How does choice feel in terms of pacing? Does the choice you made remain visible or disappear? If the player takes too long. does the choice time out and pick one for you? Bear this in mind.

Animation and expressions: When I came to *Mutazione* as a writer, almost all the animation was already completed. The creative director had a clear idea of what the plot was, so had specified what he thought the crucial movements, gestures, and expressions for each character would be. Animators were brought in, animations were done. But barely one day of ten game days of actual writing had been done. When I wanted to propose reworks, cuts, changes, and additions to make it all hang together better, I knew that we didn't have any budget for new animations, and so I made sure that all of my edits and additions used existing placements, expressions, and animated moments. That was a restriction I had to work with. If you're lucky, you will be in a process earlier and with a team that is eager to support the storytelling.[8] In that case, think about how you can propose a palette of animation which is effective and economical. Perhaps there are 'standard' animations for all characters (happy, sad, laughing, scared, angry, for example), and you have a limited budget of 'special requests' for high impact moments.

Game-Specific Formats of Writing

While many of the principles of good writing for games aren't that different than good writing of dialogue, narration, exposition, and genre found in other disciplines, there are plenty of game-specific formats of writing – or formats which come up a lot more in games and which you might be asked to produce a big volume of. Following are just a few examples of different formats that can come up.

Barks

In open-world games, or games where the player will run around a bunch or maybe often repeat a certain kind of scenario (like in a role-playing game where you will expect to have many fights with random-encounter enemies), you should expect barks to be a big part of the repertoire. There is a huge skill in writing barks and in designing the systems for triggering them intelligently (although one-size-fits-all might be the system you're working in). Barks are the things characters say in the in-between time to keep them active and alive for the player. Maybe there are a selection of barks for entering a battle:

> 'You'll be sorry!'
> 'Time to take you down!"
> 'Haven't you had enough, yet?'

Or while you're running around during a specific mission or chapter:

> 'I've got to find this [mystery item]'.
> 'Sure does feel like I've been going in circles'.
> 'This was not how I expected my day to go.'

You'll want to know the conditions under which barks are triggered (after a certain amount of time, if they're with certain characters, if they're in a certain place, only if they've done or said X, Y, Z, etc.). They'll ideally reinforce character. And, crucially, be as unannoying as possible after the player has heard them for the hundredth time. The most difficult might

---

[8] Not that my team wasn't. *Mutazione* was a complicated project developed through many stops and starts, grants, platform funding, and publishing deals over its development, which weren't ideal, but was also the only way it could have worked. I actually felt the most listened to and supported in working on *Mutazione* than I did in any other project I've worked on. It's just that we couldn't afford additional animation, so that was that.

be making sure that different characters' barks interact well. So, for these, you need to understand the systems design, as well as tackle the challenges of characterisation, dialogue, and possible repetition exhaustion.

Found Objects

One of the commonly used phrases for how games can use story is 'environmental storytelling'. Escape rooms and immersive/interactive theatre often use this too. Environmental storytelling thrives when players can navigate a space in a sense of 'trying to work out what happened here'. A common example might be graffiti on a wall communicating a 'national mood'. Or diaries lying around. More subtle things might be the books on someone's bookcase, trinkets which hint at memories, and other paraphernalia which hint at something without having to portray the event itself. You may find yourself working with narrative designers and environment artists to define these items, and then writing character reactions which underline (but ideally don't overexpose) them (if dealing in naturalism). Being able to use space, architecture, objects, and place for player exploration is one of the really rewarding aspects of writing for games.

Item Descriptions

Item descriptions are sometimes functional for gameplay, sometimes for story, and sometimes just universe/worldbuilding colour. You'll want to work out the voice of the descriptions (is it the game talking to you or the character whose inventory it's in's voice). You'll likely be working in a different UI to dialogue, so will need to know the way it will look (or guess at an appropriate line length and character limit). And you'll need to know if there are functional things that need to be communicated ('adds +3 resilience'), crucial hints ('a broken watch, stopped at the time of the explosion'), general colour/character ('love this record, Midwestern emo 4 life'), and if inventory item descriptions should change as you learn more (when you have three pieces of evidence about the explosion, the watch description could change from 'a broken watch, stopped at 3:37' to 'a broken watch, stopped at the time of the explosion').

Lore

I dislike the word *lore*.[9] It is unspecific and used to describe a few different things; sometimes slightly sarcastically to describe 'filler' worldbuilding which isn't actually necessary, sometimes the 'history' of a fictional world or series, sometimes unironically to mean 'worldbuilding background'. A book collecting religious hymns from a fictional world's

---

[9] I know quite a few game storytellers who also hate the word, but I also know some who use it happily, and it has also come to be a bit of a meme-y word in game circles. Use it critically and with caution. And when someone uses it, check in with them on what they mean.

religion is an example of lore: stuff which is absolutely not necessary to know for the story, but rewards players who love this stuff for digging deeper.

There are a few things I'll say about lore. Let's define it here as a word which describes worldbuilding and environmental storytelling through, e.g. diegetic books, poems, artworks, myths and songs. First, if you are producing work for a game in a professional context, always hire professional poets to write verse. There are far too many writers without training in poetry trying to write verse for fantasy lore. If you have no training in poetry and you're asked to write some, advocate for contracting it to a professional; some parts of rhyme, scansion, structure, and specific styles of poetry just cannot be learned by googling for an hour.

Second, if you have limited resources, do not get lost in building the world through background artefacts, or building details in documents you'll never refer to or need again. Plot, character, and central story beats are where you need to invest your time, and is a lot harder than the fun of getting lost in writing a book of rude limericks for stowing away at the back of the game's village pub. Good lore is essentially better described as a useful exposition for the story-world. And you should think critically with your game/narrative designers about pleasing places to situate this, or request clear instructions on how much of your time should be invested in it and the affordances those decisions offer you as a writer.

Remember especially that when writing books for reading in games you cannot expect to write it with a line length that would work in an actual book. Request a sense of screen span and font size to regauge what's reasonable line-feel on the screen (different for a PC than for a console, where you tend to be farther away from a TV screen).

Tutorial Text, Clues, Hints, To-Do Lists

This format of writing which is part instruction/reminder but could be in the 'voice' of the game, neutral, a narrator, or a specific character (player character or otherwise), and could be written for reading like spoken, written for reading in a separate UI (like a checklist), or written for display in the moment requires all of the writing for tone and line length skills we've already discussed. This text will likely need testing a lot more with people new to the game, or carefully thinking through in order to make sure that the crucial information you need to impart is clear, understandable, and instrumental (i.e. you understand what is being said, you understand how to do it, and when you do it, it's rewarded by progression or affect.). This kind of text is likely to be made closely in partnership with game designers. Again, make sure you know the voice and affordances of how it will be displayed.

Menu and UI Text

In smaller teams you might have programmers writing the text for menus and other user interfaces and not thinking twice, but a practised writer's eye can be very useful in checking if a certain voice is appropriate and in unifying the approach in these spaces. I worked hard with the *Mutazione* team to rephrase a lot of their initial garden mode terminologies and UI hints to try to find the best, most communicative phrases to make them align with the game and the tone of the UI and to make sure they weren't confusable with others. Sometimes the phrase the designer had developed didn't need changing, and sometimes I spitballed with them. I always made sure to check precisely what was being communicated and ask 'is there a reason why you didn't say X', because there often was, and it helped me zone in on the best option. You will also be dealing with character limits and localisation complications.

I'm certain that there are other types of game-specific writing that I might not have come across because of the kinds of game I've worked on (rarely high fantasy or science fiction, military shooters) and because I've not worked in the huge AAA studios. The most important thing to take from these examples therefore are these things to always be thinking:

- Voice
- Verb
- Visual affordances
- Dependencies

Who or what is speaking, and what is the voice of the speaker/character, object observed by the character, the 'game' or 'designer', or something else?

What is the primary role the writing serves? To develop the world? A character? To communicate an instruction, hint, or reminder? To make an interaction clearer? To teach? To show a relationship between two or more characters? To make the player immersed? Or to laugh at or comment on the genre/game?

How will the writing be displayed? How big will it be on the screen, and what size font will be used? What font will be used? A diary written in cursive will be much harder to read than a speech bubble using a serif font. Discover line length, paragraph fit, if you have colour and formatting at your disposal (bullet points even!).

Are you working with dependencies? Does this writing need to work no matter what the player knows before now? Or does this happen only if the player already has three clues? Is this an update of a previous line, and that the player can reference and return to? A line often repeated? Or a line that happens once and never again?

You need all of these things to be defined to write well for a videogame.

Loc, VO, Accessibility, Style Guides, Proofreading

Part of writing professionally is also making sure your writing fits into the necessary processes for publishing/presenting it publicly. That means understanding the processes the writing will go through, and making sure that the team working with your writing has given you the tools and considered the workflows necessary for that to work well. More on this in Part III, but it's worth touching on here, as you should think about your game as a work you want to be as high quality as possible in all the languages it will be published in. Sometimes your work as a game writer will be to support writers in other languages.

If your game is planned for localisation, then you will need to know how this process will be managed. You will have a much earlier 'content lock' to allow time for it to be translated. You will need a system for notation and export, for comment, and localisation quality assurance (LQA; people who test the game in the new languages, usually not the same people localising it). You will want to write a general guide for the localisation team(s) on characters' pace/style/idiomatic ways of speaking ('this character should use old-fashioned words and sentence constructions'), give a primer for anything that's of value ('we intentionally use the phrase "people who give birth" here so it's gender inclusive', or 'they/them pronouns translation should be replicated in consultation with a member of the LGBTQ+ community in your language'), and have a system for the loc team to ask you questions ('what line comes before this', 'does the single string "presents" here mean more than one gift or is it the verb "to present"', 'what does it mean when a character says "per ardua ..."[10] and then trails off'). You might contribute to decisions about if place or character names should be localised.

You will want comment, feedback, and review systems. And it will help you if you can annotate as you go or in passes as you finish bulk bits of writing. When advocating for resources, find out if you will be part of the loc process, and ask for tools, processes, and time to produce documentation. VO is similar in terms of needing to lock content early and to be able to produce a 'script' which has enough context for performance (which a good voice director will request). There are examples of localisation documentation and more in Part III to look forward to, so if that doesn't make too much sense yet, it will through example soon.

Accessibility is another thing to bear in mind – just as you work with text effects, line length, and animation – is someone also thinking about if there will be a 'on-screen description' voice to describe animations? Will you write that? What if someone needs to turn off text effects and increase the font size? We should all be advocating for resourcing greater accessibility features in our work on games – as a writer you can be a part of this by mocking up, testing, and building into your workflow considerations around it.

Finally: *style guides and proofreading*. There's nothing worse than a poorly proofread piece of writing. That means having a means of bug tracking and proofreading the work, and time to fix it. Maybe you want to print a script and have a professional proofreader go through it. Perhaps you need quality assurance (QA) to do a proofread pass and report spelling, grammar, and style bugs. For all of these things you need an internal style guide. For example, I won't accept 'Ooooh' in my game writing/studio's games, only 'Oh!' for surprise,

---

[10] This would be a great bit of show don't tell in British English, where the Royal Air Force motto is 'per ardua ad astra', Latin for 'through adversity, to the stars'. One old retired Air Force buddy to another, on agreeing to enter a difficult situation, might jokingly say '"per ardua" and all that'. But how do you have that make sense in Italian? Someone needs to know that it's an air force motto, look up the Italian one (virtute siderum tenus) and work out how to drop part of it into the conversation at that point. 'Lo sai come si dice: "Virtute..."' 'You know what they say, "Virtute..."'

and 'Ooh…' for wonder. Do you write laughter? (I also don't like this. Only sounds like 'Ha!' or 'Aha!' are allowed on my games.) Do you use British or American English? What about characters who might have some kind of dialect effect? What are your rules on capitalisation after an ellipsis? You will likely come up with more style guide notes as you go; keep a document so you can keep consistent, and pass that consistency on. It doesn't matter if it's not standard elsewhere; what matters is that you make a firm decision on what feels right, and have a means of recording, checking, and standardising it. These systems are built into a lot of other writing, but may not always be factored in by a game dev production process.

Documentation, Proposals, and Design Meetings

Games are often exhaustingly interdisciplinary and sprawling processes. When you are writing a novel or script alone, your documentation can be whatever suits you best, whether it be Post-its on a wall that keep falling down, or an intricate pin board of string connecting influences, newspaper cuttings, and notecards. When you are collaborating with others you need a process where the writing will be fitted into an overall design, where you need to attach it to markup, variables, characters, places, items, etc. You need to consider how design and documentation will fit into your process.

Good documentation, rules about how and who edits that documentation, clear specifications and communications, and research and reporting skills will be almost as important as your story skills in being a writer for a videogame. You will need to understand the intent of your director and designers (not always doing what they say, but listening to the effect they want and proposing your solutions). You will need to communicate your needs and to advocate for them with a level of certainty which is effective in a room full of people who think story is magical and doesn't require meaningful programmer resources. You will need to ask leads to define things like markup, provide you with line-length mock-ups, and communicate the tools and systems you'll be working with perhaps long before these things are completed or implemented. And you will need to have different strategies depending on if your team is part remote, fully remote, or all-in-office for communicating your needs and input.

Design documents (docs) are a common means of communicating proposals. At one to two pages max, they are a way of describing a new feature or approach, how it contributes to the overall design intent, what problems it might solve, and/or an example of the impact (who will resource it, what resources it might save, why it's necessary). As a writer, you will certainly need to be involved with reading or perhaps contributing to design docs, and you may need also to contribute towards worldbuilding docs and character proposals, or work on proposing changes to the plot, structure, or display of your writing. I have included more perspective and a 'real' design document from *Mutazione* in Part III of the book (but you don't need to skip forward now to continue to follow this section).

It's also worth noting that there are pitfalls surrounding documentation. It can be thrilling and enjoyable to build a world bible or a bunch of character descriptions, but be sensitive to the time pressures, and don't build documents because it's easy and nice for a writer to just be in their own doc typing away when there are more complicated but necessary tasks afoot which might involve more interdisciplinary negotiations and communication.

If you're unlucky enough to be working on a team without a producer or adept manager, you may find that meetings are poorly run – the loudest people talking over one another, with no clear preparation points, time limit, or intended outcomes or notes written up afterwards. To do your job well, you may have to do the emotional or material labour of setting an agenda, keeping people to time, and asking quieter members of the team for their thoughts, and at the same time request that in the long term this be solved by hiring someone, or a lead or manager taking responsibility for it.

You might also find yourself needing to define systems of collaboration and communication between your department and others. You might develop the spreadsheet into which different characters' barks are written, and request the support of a programmer to define a variable notation system so you can mark dependencies. You also might want to define that all changes to a certain sheet should go through you. Especially if it's a 'live' sheet (very commonly these days, Google Sheets are used as a direct input into a game engine like Unity as a 'live' import format).

You might need to learn version control tools. You might need to have a human system of locking editing of certain areas or content if there are multiple contributors working on a sheet or area, so that when you push your changes there aren't conflicts, which might be as simple as having a Slack channel where you write 'locking area X for edits'.

You will often need to find ways of making broken tools sufficient and will often be dealing with systems for writing which have none of the word processing features you're used to. I wrote much of *Mutazione* without an undo button, with manual save only, and, until the final year, no copy and paste. There were also bugs in the tool I worked in, which sometimes meant saves didn't take, and workflows which might have made sense to a programmer in setting it up, but when I had to select a character from a dropdown box for every single line I wrote, I quickly knew I would need to request being able to search the box by pressing a letter, or get a severe repetitive strain injury (RSI).

You will also be dealing with writing in the context of a wider game dev production process; uncertain funding and spiralling costs might mean that they wrap up your work on the project early, and writing you thought was placeholder will ship with your name on it. Or you might be asked to contribute towards milestone documentation so that the funder awards the company its next payment. Finally, you will also need to know how to respond to playtesting and QA. Playtesting isn't always the most useful way of judging if story, characters, and writing are effective. In that case, it's always much more useful to work with peers also working in storytelling who have the critical background and practical underpinning for expressing problems instead of voicing solutions. But tutorial text is worth playtesting and refining with non-games professionals, as is clue-laying, hints, etc. I go into this notion in more detail, including providing methods for feedback and reflection in Part III, so if this piques your interest, feel free to skip ahead and pick up this section later.

QA might be internal or working with an external company. You might use an issue-tracking piece of software to report, assign, and fix bugs. And bugs can be spelling mistakes, grammar issues, failures of markup and variables, balancing, or missing story information because you haven't considered a certain pathway through the story. You also might need to request that testing tools be built so you can test the game, and especially so you can test it without playing through eight hours to check one single conversation you rephrased a few things of. Testing tools can be an afterthought in many processes, but writing is its best when you can see how it will feel on screen and in context of animation, artwork, environment, etc. If your team can't resource testing tools, you may need to find ways to approximate it, perhaps mocking up things in a tool like Ink or Twine in an appropriate width and font, or just having a word processor doc open in the line length and font, just so you can at least get a feel for it.

Scope

One thing about writing in games is defining and understanding scope, and how it can balloon. If someone asks you to add something into your writing which they think seems simple, it's useful to be able to respond carefully about how many hours of work that would add. One of the most useful phrases I've learned to use is 'that's not a small change'.

Alterations in choice structure and variability can quickly balloon into huge amounts of writing or rewriting. You may need to request programming or narrative design solutions which could turn 100 hours of writing into 10 hours of writing, plus 10 hours of programming. Think of the difference between writing 'Hello [character name]' where the character name is programmatically printed, or where you have to write out the line for every character name the player could have selected. It will be the director's or your manager's decision about whether the 100 hours of writing is preferable (make sure you're paid for it), but your job will be to meaningfully express the scope of what you're asked to do, to make and alter time estimates, and to communicate when changes impact on you and the deadlines which have been set for you.

Project-Specific Vocabulary

A final note to think about is that because the process of game development includes the act of defining – everything from how 'up' and 'down' works, systems for time, to units of story, characters, variables, etc. – it's very common for a team to need to define internal vocabularies that mean nothing to outsiders, but which provide a necessary short hand for inter-team communication. You may name tools. You might propose or co-develop features. And in these cases, it's common to have to work out what to call it, and ideal if you can keep a project-specific glossary together somewhere so that people can communicate effectively, and join the team at a later point and know what's going on.

Here's some project-specific internal vocabulary from my current project which you wouldn't be able to understand without a specific definition and working on the project for a little while: screen span, interjection, observation, location (not the same as a place), node, 2.5D puppet, panel-based storytelling, log variable, room, debrief, secondary expedition character, language, song, radio, bubble. All of these describe behaviours, features, or discreet parts of the way the game is put together, displayed, written, or experienced.

One advanced note about these things is not to get lost in how you make the game work behind the scenes. Recently on our current project we realised that although the writers needed to know if they were writing an observation or a conversation, the experience wouldn't feel particularly different to the player. It was a useful definition of scope and content for the writers, but we realised we didn't need for that to be in the player's experience, and therefore the writing didn't need to feel different. When thinking about the need for project- and team-specific vocabularies, make sure you don't let them affect your writing when the behind-the-scenes form isn't what the player will see.

What If the Writing Can't Solve the Problem?

A writing duo (Matthew S. Burns and Tom Bissell) made a Twine game about this question; it's called *The Writer Will Do Something* (2015) and it's an upsettingly realistic portrayal of what it's like to be a writer on a team which doesn't have great story literacy. Check out matthewseiji.itch.io/twwds to play in browser and really bring home the point I'm going to make here.

Sometimes your writing won't thrive because what it actually needed was work from other departments which was never resourced. You might have needed narrative design and structural solutions to make a story work, but you never got them; you might have needed markup, an undo function, and a testing tool, but never got it. The font and display might be changed after content lock on the writing. Or the story you're being asked to write for might be antithetical to the central game mechanics ('write a story about how imperialism is bad and the main thing the character does is loot ancient artefacts').

In any under-resourced, interdisciplinary process it will be often very easy to count all of the features you couldn't advocate for, all of the things which there were never time to do, or the project changing radically without your brief being updated. We have talked about form-driven aspects of games writing, but if the form changes under your feet and you don't have the time to adapt your writing, well, sometimes that's just what happens.

Your authorial control in writing for games will be much, much less than writing for things like theatre, comics, fiction, or film. But remember that in collaborating in such a rich environment you will build other, rich tools for communication and collaboration. People will bring things to you to work with you could never have thought of. Characters you would never have drawn, but in finding a voice for them you end up with a sum greater than its parts. Story is often a neglected part in the machine of game making, and there are some structural problems there which can't be solved at the level of your current writing gig. But take care of your practice, take all of the considerations and affordances I've outlined here, and as you work, note what you learn, and what you wished you had known or asked for, and fold that into your next gig.

Games take a lot longer per project cycle than many other artforms, and so you will need to find ways to iterate on and develop your practice outside of your actual experience (peers, mentoring, talks, and articles). You may also want to develop your story and writing skills by completing exercises (I just so happen to have written a few for you in Part III), or by working with professionals or on projects in other disciplines.

Every game is a miracle of collaboration and communication. Every game would have been better if you could have had just another six months to work on it.

CHAPTER 6

Form-Led Design

What Is Form-Led Design?

Different art forms, genres, and design decisions all have a big impact on how a story is best told. 'Form-led design' is the act of taking a piece of content – a story, an effect, a question – and working out what form, structure and format will make its exploration most effective. One of the gifts from my own training as a playwright was the 'adaptation' module I did in my master's. Select a source, then transpose it into another medium, paying particular attention to how to best tell that story within the new one. It's such a rich way to think about how a medium should reshape a story for its best telling. I was then lucky enough to develop these first lessons by moving into a part of theatre called 'devising theatre'. This section is going to lead you through an example of how devising theatre operates as form-led design in order to illustrate what I mean when I talk about it, and how I developed it as a practice.

DOI: 10.1201/9781003182832-8

You should be prepared for this section to be a little more personal and to draw from very specific creative works. I've done my best to thoroughly describe them in order to illustrate how they have supported my understanding of how form can shape content (and vice versa), but remember that if a section of this book doesn't work for you, you can skip it or return to it later.

Devising theatre is a big part of the independent theatre scene in Europe and the UK. When you imagine 'theatre' you're probably thinking of a fairly old-fashioned form, in which a playwright has written a play that a director stages, performed by actors, who all pretend that the audience isn't there. Well, if you imagine that as the 'orchestra' model (composer, conductor, orchestra), devising theatre is a 'band' model of theatre. Devising companies start with something – a newspaper article, an issue, a story from someone's life, a text, a song, a concept – and work together (often using performance games, little rulesets to test out movement, improvised dialogue, etc.) to produce scenes, research, and ideas for parts of the performance, which they will iterate on, construct and design, and test in front of audiences until they have a performance they are happy to call a finished script/work. Like a band jamming together, maybe starting with a riff, adding in a beat, some bass, trying different lyrics out, changing sections, until what they have is a song.

Devising theatre is form-driven or form-led, because it rarely assumes what the output will be. Sometimes you develop a rule set in itself. One piece of devising theatre I'm going to talk about here is *Story Map*, which I worked on with the excellent Sheffield-based devising company Third Angel. *Story Map* was part of the project *What I Heard About the World*. *What I Heard About the World* was made up of two main parts: a durational research game (*Story Map*) and a staged performance (which took the full title).

What I Heard About the World was about how we fit the world in our heads. In the 'electric age' (as media theorist Marshall McLuhan phrased it) 'we wear all of mankind as our skin'. This is a phrase I have always gravitated towards as such a perfect means of expressing an era in which I can read of the deepest suffering in a civil war in Tigray, a crowdfunder for bewilderingly expensive healthcare costs in the USA, and a deeply personal tale of transphobia in the UK. All while sitting in my apartment in Denmark.

I feel stretched thin – the film protecting my nerves so taut as to be almost torn apart. I practise and re-practise my empathy, try to not be exhausted by this way of living, because if I become numb (to survive) I will only do harm, but if I turn away, I lose my compass. How do I practise good global citizenship? For me, that answer is stories. And storytelling. Recognising that the way we need to fit the world into our heads to survive is often by reducing it to story/type/stereotype, at the same time as – in the telling of stories – reminding myself that everyone is as real and complicated and heart-full and heart-less as I am.

What I Heard About the World's durational research performance *Story Map* is about that dance. It collects stories; the performance 'game' is a framework through which we invite and tell stories. The stories we ask for are 'true stories about fake things' – that is, stories about the stories we tell ourselves about the world. Over the duration of the performance

(12 hours, usually) we collect a story for every country in the world. As we do so it also re-presents the audience to itself, uncovering the storied journeys of diverse communities to that particular place in the world and in time.

The durational performance game is 12 hours long. There are four people involved: Jorge, Chris, Alex, and Hannah (me). The rules are Jorge calls the countries. Chris collects and tells the stories, and gives them a two-word title. Alex draws a comic-style line drawing character or symbol to illustrate them. The country name goes on a coloured sticky note (different colours per continent). The card icon and sticky note go on the map. Chris knows where every country in the world is on the map. And all of us have a backlog of stories if anyone in the changing moving audience doesn't have anything. The audience passes through; when someone joins, we explain the rules. People can stay for hours, or just ten minutes, or revisit throughout the day. My job is fact-checking. It's important that our true stories about fake things *are* true. I use Wikipedia rules and need two to three first-hand or paper-of-record sources before a thing goes on the map. At any time anyone can ask for a story on the map to be retold and contribute a story of their own. Over the 12 hours we fill in every part of the map.

> A true story about a fake thing: a 'stand in' for the truth, or a replica. In Siberian Russia, it's hard to protest. Policing is brutal, often criminalised and the weather is … well, Siberian. In 2012, 'Police in the Siberian city of Barnaul [...] asked prosecutors to investigate the legality of a recent protest that saw dozens of small dolls – teddy bears, Lego men, South Park figurines – arranged to mimic a protest, complete with signs reading: "I'm for clean elections" and "A thief should sit in jail, not in the Kremlin"'. This story about stand-ins, tiny replica protests, is both verifiable, and about fakes/replicas/stand-ins. It tells you a little about that place, and the ingenuity and politics of its people.

(Elder, 2012)

This durational interactive performance stands alone, but is also a 'research game' for a more conventional stage performance where Jorge, Chris, and Alex tell a selection of the stories collected, in a curated, non-interactive version of the show. They speak directly to the audience (as a stand-up comedian would). There's a globe on stage where they find countries on the map. There's also shelves crowded and overflowing with props, a big sofa, and a microphone – with and around which the performers find dramatic and playful ways of illustrating each story.

The thread at the heart of the stage performance is the storytellers' commentary on how we use stories to fit the world into our heads; not just for understanding, but also how stories reduce, ridicule, or are weaponised. In the West, we tell stories about many 'far away' countries which are either false, more complicated, or not that strange really when faced with our own storied selves. How strange is painting a donkey black and white because you can't afford a zebra, when in the USA, soldiers' families can be sent cardboard, life-size 'dads', effigies of their soldier father, so the youngest doesn't forget them?

If you start with the idea that you want to think about how we use and tell stories about the world, it makes a lot of sense that that idea could be investigated by the actual practice of collecting and telling stories about the world. It's like practice-based research. This is what I mean when I talk about 'form-led design'. The makers of *What I Heard About the World* picked a form to suit the question.

It doesn't have to happen at such a 'high level' as this; it could start at the level of 'do we make a novel, a video game, or a TV show of this story' (although sometimes you might find that your adaptation isn't working, because it needs to be reimagined for the new form). Instead, it's more that you should understand that what you put the story *in* is as important as what the story *is* you're telling.

Form-Led Thinking in Games

I use the term 'form-led' thinking with regard to game writing (and thanks for bearing with the detour) because I think part of excelling in any medium is not assuming that the medium is 'inherently' good at anything, but yet that it also will have certain tendencies, affordances, and expectations which you can work with for good effect, or against with the intention of producing surprise or friction.

This means that in this section we will, in many ways, touch on narrative design principles – which, in turn, as a writer-only, might be something that you have no control over. However, it's still important to writing. To properly define the limitations or brief for your writing (either for yourself, or to explain why something won't work to a non-story-professional), you need to understand how these affordances are defined by all of the game design decisions gone before. Interrogating your form/genre/game and its design priorities will be crucial in leading you to identify the best path forward for your part in it.

Understanding the form you're working in might also help you unpick when non-story-professionals are trading on expectations from a medium they're not working in. Film is a common example – we've already touched on all the 'hero's tale' assumptions around story structure which are brought to games, when TV or theatre (episodic, vignette, environmental) might be better learned forms.

Learning from other media and how they have used their forms with virtuosity is one of the most valuable ways I personally have learned about form-driven design. To wrap up this chapter I want to offer a little series of moments where another medium helped me see something about games writing and storytelling in a new way.

Form and Craft: What Game Stories Can Learn from Other Storytelling Disciplines

There are just five examples here. This is going to be a little chewier than other sections, and if it's not for you, that's okay, head on over to Chapter 7.

Dance

One of the things that live performance knows best is the magnetic quality of a body in performance. On film, someone doing the same thing over and over usually has to be cut differently or presented with a varying pace to be interesting (notwithstanding when the director wants to find interest in it not being so). On stage, someone taking their time to brush their teeth with the same amount of time and dedication as they would at home can be daring. Daring to take the space where a whole room of people has agreed to offer their attention in exchange for asking them to watch a slow, mundane thing. Dance holds much of that for me – adding to it the more expressionist and less written qualities of it. The history of dance has often produced some of the most interesting digital art experiments; something about such a purely embodied form being interested in the stereotypically disembodied.

Making repetition meaningful is the thing I take from dance. I saw a piece which was called dance, though perhaps also close to performance/live art. The performance consisted of a transmasculine actor beating a lump of clay under strobe lighting. It was a short piece. It spoke to the choreography of boxing, of the process of shaping and reshaping. Of the violence of being seen and not being seen. And what wrapped it all together was the heavy movement of their feet – the beat of their wrapped fists against the clay, the sweat that fled their forehead in the second they were lit for.

What I take from it to games: Sometimes when I am influenced by other forms it's not about taking a direct technique and putting it in a game, instead it's about seeing how well they lean into their own form, to think about what that would mean for the affordances of the one I might be working with. That work of repetitious movement was about effort, sweat, bodies, pain, intermittent visibility, and it all worked because of the performer's present, sweating body. Thinking about how we tell stories *without* bodies – and indeed, in the difficult space of often-uncanny representations of bodies and performances in games – I think about what holds the attention or moves the player when a tiny hint of a frown or the way a body shudders when it strikes clay cannot be found in the same way.

So instead, I think of the body of the player. I think about how I can use imagery or language that speaks to feeling a thing in their bodies, and I also think about – depending on the kind of game you're designing – the stories between the player and the people around them as they play and, more obviously, contemporary means of embodying effects; haptic feedback. The subtleties of which are really getting quite astonishing in current-gen game controllers.

Poetry

I have in fact been a poet. I have had poetry printed, commission for performance, and I've performed it. Fairly early on in my performance career, I used some minor project funding to commission a little workshop from one of my favourite poets – Hannah Jane Walker. Other poets I admire and enjoy you might also enjoy looking up are Inua Ellams, Ross Sutherland, and Harry Josephine Giles. My best experiences of poetry are all performed poetry. I understand and enjoy written poetry, but often in a more 'head' than 'feelings' way (probably because that's how I was taught to experience it in school).

When I lived in London I used to go to an excellent poetry/comedy event at the Bethnal Green Working Men's Club called Bang Said the Gun – they called it 'stand up poetry', and it was the opposite of what I strongly disliked about the US spoken word poetry which pervaded YouTube. If that stuff is to your taste, great! But for me it had the sticky rhythm of cadence over content (it was more about how you said it than what you were saying). Poets like the ones I noted earlier are making work which is funny, offbeat, surprising, concept-driven, and full of complex and unfolding meaning. Not meant to be heard like a song, but instead, like a piece of origami, delightful in its folded state, but also in knowing it was once a flat, blank piece of paper with intriguing writing on it.

Working with Hannah Jane Walker I learned some really useful exercises and tools to add to my writer-practitioner's toolkit, but one thing in particular stuck with me that I most often use when I talk to game writers: the difference between the page and performance, and how you use it to unfold meaning.

What I take from it to games: I have already spoken a fair amount about the difference between writing for speaking (film, theatre), writing for reading (books, short stories), and the space of games which is often writing for reading like speaking and is sometimes also spoken with voice over (VO). Hannah Jane Walker, in talking to me about the most important part of understanding the difference between page and performance said something along these lines (I am paraphrasing her):

> When you write for reading, you can make your meaning emerge on reading a sentence for a third or fourth time. You can allow an eye to make it to the end of a verse, and then reconnect it with the beginning, and then reread the whole again. The pace at which meaning unfolds and the way you can therefore fold it in to your writing can be much more complex, and part of the texture of the piece. When writing for performance, however, your audience can't return to what was said just a moment ago. The complexity of your writing emerges in different places, and in your performance, your introduction to the piece you're about to read, and more. The heart of poetry is surprising language. It's taking a thing you have thought of fleetingly probably many times in your life, but re-presenting it in a way that causes enough friction that the reader or audience stops for a second, and experiences it again.

That's what I mean when I say 'unfolding of meaning'. I mean thinking about the quality of the attention of your reader (How much else is going on? Can they reread passages? Can they experience a passage again? Is it written and voiced? Is it timed? Or can the player be distracted and pause their progress without hitting 'pause' directly?). Think of the quality of the attention of your player, then strike the register that's right for making the words unfold at the right pace; surprising when they need to be, in a way that is effective.

Ceramics

I am a massive fan of ceramics. And if I earned a lot more, I would have a lot more unique ceramics in my life. The lesson I would take from ceramics is more elemental than some of these other observations: it is the space between accident and certainty. What is it when what you work with is *chemistry*? One of the affordances of working with clay, firing processes, glazes, marks, hands, etc. is that you might sometimes have in mind a colour or an effect, but each instance of it will be emergent from the exact combination of chemical, material, and atmospheric conditions in which that item is made, glazed, fired. Sure, you know a raku firing will have a certain general effect. Or perhaps you're building a custom kiln in order to produce one particular firing environment. Or you're working with stoneware, because you know it will work a certain way, glaze a certain way, and wear a certain way. But you will never, ever be able to exactly predict the outcome.

What I take from it to games: I take a metaphor. A game only exists fully when it has a player. A player coming from a rich and complex context; politically, socially, geographically, and in the specific time and place they play your game. They are your unpredictable element – they are the chemistry which completes its firing. Is your storytelling still effective when it associates autumn with November for someone who lives in the southern hemisphere? (It will if it's set clearly in the northern hemisphere, but if it's meant to relate to the player, you break their suspension of disbelief in that moment.) What about when you offer the player a slur or cliché to speak. Does it mean the same to say it if they're someone to whom that slur or cliché applies?

Some things you cannot know or control for – if they're playing alone at night or with friends at a rowdy party. But the thing I think of when I think of ceramics that I take to games is the thought that 'player' is a material made up of people – not a testable 'Everyman', but people coming from extremely specific places and contexts. I personally prefer to write characters who are specific and complex and face humane decisions. To find the 'everyone' in the *circumstances*, not the characterisations. If you're writing a character that people are supposed to inhabit, however, that's a very challenging proposition. And you'd be wise to think about how you do 'glaze tests' – that is, how you playtest with women, people of colour, neurodivergent folks, disabled people, LGBTQ+ folks, people with different religious iconography, people from the global south, that is, the majority of people in the world who aren't White, cis, het, Western men.

Live Art

The most powerful experience in any artform I've ever had was at an event in Bristol called In Between Time. It's a festival that brings live art to sites all across the city of Bristol. They say of themselves that 'we bring people together around radical art and ideas to encourage new ways to think about the world and ourselves' (In Between Time, n.d.). I was pretty new to live art at that time, mostly aware of the Happenings and the era of people bleeding onstage. Encouraged by popular dismissal, I hadn't really thought about the work as being potentially moving; squeamish was as close as I got to a thoughtful reaction. But in 2010 I was privileged enough to see the last ever durational (three-hour) performance of *Hancock & Kelly Live: Iconographia*. Here is it described on their website:

> A 3 hour durational performance installation, during which Traci Kelly gilds the entwined bodies of Richard Hancock and a dead pig carcass with gold leaf.

(hklive, n.d.)

Here's how I experienced it: In the dusky light of winter in Bristol, I walked into the cool, stone space of the Circomedia Building, which before being a performance space used to be a Georgian church. 'Dido's Lament' from Purcell's *Dido and Aeneas* played. People stood around some kind of plinth in the centre. As I neared, I saw a woman (Kelly) in a black ball gown, black veil, black gloves carefully attending to something. As I moved through the people to see what it was, I saw a shivering duo. Hancock, naked, laid on the stone plinth, embracing a sprawling, stiff, dead pig. Kelly was moving around the duo, and carefully, laboriously, gilding them in gold leaf.

They glistened together with Vaseline, pink, naked. His shivers and cramps as he tried to stay still on the stone and cold dead flesh make the gold leaf that had been applied shimmer and break apart at the seams between them. They were in the process of becoming a statue – something between alive and dead. Hancock wasn't just next to the pig; he held it gently, tenderly even. And while Kelly applied the gold leaf with a careful eye, it was also something fragile and delicate.

Here's something written about it in a review for *Real Time Arts* by artist Folake Shoga, who also sometimes goes by the name Osunwunmi, as she did for this review:

> At this point I surprised myself – for I don't have that culturally specific Western sympathy for livestock – by feeling sorry for the pig. Then I felt the ways in which Hancock stood for the pig, and the pig for him, and both of them for all of us, tied to a hunk of dead meat and an inevitable end. The realisation was awful. I had to retreat. I went and sat up in the gallery where all that could reach me was the spectacle. I felt like howling.

> Although I can recall it to memory it was not a repeatable moment, since it was triggered by physical presence. Occasionally I went down to stand in the same place and feel the same thing, drawn by the intensity of it –we don't face such raw perception very often. Kelly inexorably and gently covered the intertwined bodies, stroking and burnishing as she obliterated them with splendour. Hancock breathed, and trembled under her touch.

(Osunwunmi, 2011)

It was a profound experience for me. I wanted to cry in that way when your feelings are too complex to express in words. The fragility of the man. The deadness of the pig. The gentle hand of someone I assumed was a lover. The making of a statue and a symbol in a place that had been and retained the architecture and stained-glass windows of a place of religious worship. It said things to me about liveness, and bodies, and love, and tenderness. Of death, and endurance, of memory and lifelessness. It also made me rethink my ideas of what art was and could be. Never again have I dismissed an art form, genre, or format on the basis of anything but its actual content.

What I take from it to games: I trust in my playing audience. I trust in them to make connections which are not spelled out for them. To feel – to fill the spaces in between what they are told with their own thoughts and experiences. I trust in my playing audience that I can write a soap opera well, with craft and formal intent, and while the name might put them off, if they can make their way to playing it, that layering and layering of the mundane alongside the humanely dramatic, taken together over long consideration, might – if I work with consideration and craft – turn into something meaningful and occasionally profound in between my words, and their hands.

Radio Drama

That last one was a bit of a rollercoaster, so here's a nice simple lesson to follow. When I was 22 or 23, I worked a short placement at BBC Radio Drama. I don't know if this is still true in the era of Netflix, but at that time BBC Radio Drama was the biggest producer of new dramatic content in the world. A new play every day and a new serial every week for several different slots in their various stations. I was doing a bit of everything, including getting to guest as a background performer on the longest running soap opera of all time *The Archers*, which was very exciting. But I also got great insight into how radio dramas run their writer's rooms and was able to hear quite a lot of really interesting insight from various directors and showrunners (in radio they're called producers). I don't remember quite who quoted this line to me – perhaps it was Vanessa Whitburn, perhaps another – but it's a phrase I hear over and over again in my head whenever I think about exposition.

A little context about radio drama: one of the long-running jokes about *The Archers* is that characters say each other's names much more often than they would in real life. How often would someone call their partner by their name on greeting in a field? In *The Archers*, it's a lot. Because if a listener is newish or if a regular listener needs the scene quickly set, sometimes Ruth needs to say 'Oh, hello David, how are the lambs?'.

But radio dramas, such as the famous *Afternoon Play* slot (approximately 45 minutes), can be a little more subtle and build themselves with a little more expositional panache. This is the particular line that a character, running their first Christmas as matriarch in the family, says quietly to themselves:

'Little crosses on the bottom, just like mother…'

I wish I could remember the source! There is a lot of knowing their audience involved in knowing why this works. Around seven million listeners a week tune in to BBC Radio

4's drama offerings. They skew slightly older, slightly more middle class, and, unlike writing for games or international TV offerings, you can be confident that the audience is predominantly British residents. That means that nearly all of the people listening will know about the tradition of sprouts as part of dinner on Christmas day in the UK. And many of them will know that the traditional way to have them cook well is to cut tiny crosses into the bottom.

There is nothing vital wrapped into the quoted sentence. It's a scene setter, a character developer, and a world detail. But if you don't understand it, nothing vital is lost. That's one of the lessons about exposition as well: if you build it gently, you need it in more places so if one point is missed, it's built elsewhere.

But the biggest thing for me is that nowhere does it say 'I'm preparing the sprouts for Christmas dinner'. The character could have shouted to the next room. Or said, '[Character name] where are you?' and had her shout back, 'In the kitchen, doing the sprouts!' But instead, here, we get the same in a much subtler, character-driven moment of exposition. And that matters in radio. It's a piece of clever exposition for an audience who cannot see the action except in their imaginations, but it's also a piece of exposition that understands the 'quieter' register it's working in. Radio is intimate and completed in the head of the listener. Often in intimate settings like cars, headphones, kitchens too.

When I think about this lesson as I work in games I think of several things: I think about the texture of writing for a game, with regard to register. It's not quite 'in someone's head' but it's not like film or TV either. The attention is often greater – active. You need to give the player input to hold that. You also don't control the 'camera' or the players' imaginative direction in the same way as other dramas, as often exploration belongs to the player. Exposition and time need to work together in a different way. And the player might be alone, in headphones, in that quieter space, or they might be playing with someone else, but rarely are you designing for the impact of a larger audience's attention towards a screen or stage – writing can be subtler. But then you're also – like radio – not able to have actors at your disposal. Even with contemporary cutting-edge motion capture, you will not be able to gather gestures and expressions, which can do a lot of the work of film and TV. So, then I think again about radio drama. And also why I prefer to work with more abstract character art, so the gulf between the writing and art and the player's suspension of disbelief is greater – so the player leans in harder to imagine the characters. The art style you're writing for matters. The register you're trying to strike should shape the way you write. And it's okay for things to be complex sometimes, so long as there are always other chances to understand it. You can either make things clear and said once, or complex and layered. Or strike a place in between. So long as you're making these choices in a form-led way.

I share these five examples to demonstrate how my life and practice is richer for having bridged to other creative disciplines, especially those beyond what we think traditional 'film', 'art', 'theatre', etc. are. Mainstream TV, radio, and film will always find you. So, spend your time seeking out the experimental weirdos; they'll make you better. If you're studying games at a university, make friends with people in other courses. If you're crossing to games from another discipline, you might want to try to find the weird and challenging spaces in games (perhaps *Avant-Garde Videogames* (Schrank, 2014) will give you the language to start your search).

Other Forms

Here are some other forms/formats to think of. Can you dig into them and think about your practice by thinking of what they do? Could you create a kind of scrapbook of notes every time you experience a work that moves you? How did it do that? What did it lean into? How did it surprise you?

- Installation art
- Site-specific art
- Gigs
- Children's theatre
- Puppetry
- Orchestral music
- Soundwalks
- Pervasive games
- Photography
- Musicals
- Devising and experimental theatre
- Podcasts
- Religious storytelling
- Animation
- Film
- Painting
- Books
- Sculpture
- Television
- Comics
- YouTube
- Streaming
- TikTok
- Pop music
- DIY music
- Durational art
- Science communications-driven art
- Gardening
- Architecture
- Many, many non-Western traditions
- Folk tales
- Craft and other working-class forms

Conclusions

The conclusion of this chapter, is, I hope, a thorough means of understanding the simple idea that games are a material, full of material practice and process-driven decisions. Many of these, as a writer, will be wholly out of your control, but if you take the time to understand them you might have a chance to advocate for better ones, and if you can't, you can at least produce writing that does the best with the brief you've been given. Remember that briefs are often badly written, and that you might need to listen to the effect you're being asked to achieve – not necessarily how someone without story craft assumes you'll have it (more on that in Part III).

And finally, remember that part of your brief will be tools and processes – many of which might be broken. You might be writing in home-spun tools without spell check, undo, or autosave functions. You might be given tasks in poor production processes which you fulfil, but then have to be cut entirely because the project is over-scoped or funding is suddenly in jeopardy. But if you equip yourself with the ability to be prepared for this, to communicate well, and to understand the material you're working with (in both product and process) you will at least be able to do your best.

When you're working as a small part of a team working on a game, sometimes the best you can do is the best despite poor processes and tools, and learn everything you can from each piece of work. Projects in games can often be much longer than many other artforms, and in that sense you can be robbed of the quick iterative practice-based learning you might do in theatre, poetry, radio, TV, short stories, etc. If you can, keep notebooks. Set a time each week or month where you can reflect on what you did well, what you want to improve on, what you learned, what you want to carry forward. It's rare that games processes make room for their employees, contractors, and collaborators to reflect on their craft, so take the time to make the space for that yourself.

In Part III there's more on 'setting your own brief' – tools (mostly forms, I'm a fan of forms as a means of brief-setting) which you can use to reflect and develop your craft. And also tools for reflection.

But for now, two final notes to round off the Theory part.

CHAPTER 7

A Note on Writing Comedy

While a lot of my theory has been reasonably high level – i.e. above that of deep dives into particular genre or forms – I want to take a moment to talk about one of the most mercurial types of writing which is the least well done, in my opinion, in most of indie games writing. That is, writing comedy.

I think we're used to thinking of humour as a kind of inherent trait or quality – someone *is* funny. But any professional comedian will tell you it's a craft you can hone like any other. And it is a specialism as much as verse writing is. So much so that you might sometimes want to advise that a comedian or comedy writer be on board to punch up script/game writing just as if you have poetry in the world of your game you might want to advise a poet is brought on board as a contractor specifically for the poetry. Take care to set a good brief for a collaborator coming from another discipline, giving strict line length and localisation context for a poet, or perhaps for a comedian explaining that a bark might be heard hundreds of times by the end of play.

DOI: 10.1201/9781003182832-9

There are a couple of books I personally consider the foundation of my comedy writing. One is a playwright's standard: *The Crafty Art of Playmaking* by Alan Ayckbourn. One of the most popular writers of comedies for the English stage in the 20th century, Ayckbourn's *The Crafty Art of Playmaking* is in general an excellent guide to everything from characterisation to dialogue, how to find comedy in darkness, and that comedy writing is a craft with essential principles you can learn.

One important consideration when trying to write comedy is *perspective*. Sometimes comedy is a kind of formula you can devise – like the rule of threes. Sometimes it is built of contrast – how someone sees themselves and the gulf between their self-image/image of the world, and how others see them/other events happen. Sometimes comedy is built of surprise – like the best poetry, but instead of the surprising turn of phrase turning the world on its axis to observe it properly, a comedy surprise shocks you into a laughter response. Comedy is other things too – physical, observational, etc. I give these examples not to be exhaustive or to draw a 'true law', but instead to show that comedy too has its own set of material affordances, forms, and ways you can work with it.

I've spoken about the affordances of games at length, and other media and genres have them too. Comedy is no exception. You have to locate where the comedy is centred or drawn from, its genre, what its register is, and how it emerges. Comedy could arise, for example, from a character who takes himself very seriously and considered himself a very capable manager of a hotel. The fact that he keeps doing things that spiral out of control and that make him look like a very bad manager of a hotel must be *someone else's fault*. You don't write Basil Fawlty as someone who makes the jokes; you write him as someone whom the jokes are made about, which makes him ever madder.

A lot of ineffective comedy writing puts everything in one place – the voices of the characters. It might take its *comedy* register – 'self-awareness' – and put it in all the characters quips, all of whom now sound the same. Good self-awareness register comedy examples I can think of situate the awareness in the voice of a helpful narrator (*Arrested Development*) or in a single character who is deeply self-aware, where few others are (*BoJack Horseman*).

I can't remember which Alan (Bennett or Ayckbourn) said it – and I suspect both probably have – but let's go with the source I could find:

> The best comedy springs from the utterly serious.

> **(Ayckbourn, 2002, p. 80)**

The point here is that humour, and the surprise or astonishment that underlies it, emerges from contrast: expectation and reality. Farces work only when the characters in them are taking those situations (and themselves) extremely seriously.

It is something of a contemporary fashion to use the 'Marvel wisecracking' method to inject a bit of lightness into games writing, and of course, it serves the same purpose as it actually does in the films – barks to fill the space (and the lack of characterisation) as a bunch of action happens. But it's very easy to fall into the space of allowing the cadence (rhythm) of humour stand in for actually humorous writing, or for piling all of your registers into a single place.

If you allow wisecracking to come from characters who are in actual peril, then you are choosing to undermine that peril. There is a difference between gallows humour (a humane reaction which in the right context can be funny) and allowing characters to continually make light of a dangerous situation, where the riffing becomes the only thing they do while they face death.

This also depends on your brief. Perhaps you're not looking to produce genuinely dramatic or funny writing. Perhaps the characters you're writing for need to operate on the same perspective as the player – they're not really in danger, just passing time being superheroes. If that's your brief, then so be it, write those Marvel wisecracks. But if you're trying to use comedy to contrast with drama or you're trying to make a story the heart of a game, not just the filler, then you need to understand where you situate the comedy, the dramatic irony (the difference in knowledge between the audience and the characters), and the perspective.

Think of something like *The Office*. Part of the success of the television series was the many sliding contexts of darkness and light. Cringe comedy relies on the astonishment that someone is *still doing something terrible even though they know it is but they can't stop*. David Brent (UK *Office*) takes himself extremely seriously, as do most of the other characters. When there are characters who exist more as an audience insert – who know that David Brent is ridiculous and can provide opportunities to dig into it further for the audience – the writers are careful to make sure that they have their own seriousness and their own blind spots. Tim, the hapless, shrugging, lost boy of an office worker is keenly aware of how unserious his job is and how ridiculous those around him are. But he is very serious about the reason he's there – to be near to Dawn. Every moment he's in the office, he's near Dawn, and that's better than not being there.

The many formats of 'a year in an office' give them all the situations they need. The comedy contrast of seriously silly people who take themselves far too seriously is underlined by the 'look to camera' documentary format (which implies seriousness! And more angst when you imagine these people embarrassing themselves for TV viewers). The cringe isn't constant, as they leaven it with the romance, that's before you even get to the actual individual characterisation and writing. Look at all those complex affordances having an effect!

Another book I often reference with regard to the craft of comedy is Stewart Lee's excellent *How I Escaped My Certain Fate*. In it, Stewart Lee footnotes in detail transcripts of his stand-up routines, sometimes you can read a two-page-long footnote about the use of a particular word. It's an incredible resource (so too on the art of live performance), especially on the technical craft of words, constructions, and rhythms. Also, because Lee's practice is as keen to push at the boundaries of the conventions of comedy, it means you get to see that in action and then read reflections on that process.

As a writer approaching comedy, the thing you can most usefully do (apart from reading comedy writers exploring their craft) is to think about *where* the comedy is situated.

Is it in contrast, in the juxtaposition of different cultures, values, or world views? Is it wisecracking, and if so, how and where do you find the weight to counterbalance the lightness? If it's situational, if a situation is ridiculous or farcical, then who is there taking it seriously?

Tragicomedy arises from things getting worse and worse in weirder and weirder ways. Think of the game *Kentucky Route Zero*; parts of it are starkly funny, but only because you recognise that it's because you didn't believe things could get this bad (surprise!). Comedies of errors rely on mistaken identities or lies spiralling out of control, but they're not about important things like tragicomedies are; they end with things fixed.

Fish-out-of-water comedy arises from characters used to one context being thrust into another, you can take the player with you if your 'old' context was similar to the player. Or you can make the player laugh at the character if they're from another very serious culture/ world. For example, the planet Risa in *Star Trek* is a pleasure cruise of a world. It's full of naked sparkling human wonders, beautiful weather, and relaxing beaches. It's a place Riker or Jadzia Dax feel right at home, but they end up comedy episodes because they take uptight characters like Jean-Luc Picard or Worf there, and challenge them to relaxation, indulgence, and idleness.

Pastiche can be a kind of comedy – where you take a form which takes itself seriously and laugh at the form itself. A pastiche is best done lovingly, by paying the form you're pastiching the respect of understanding how it works, before you present it as a pastiche. The form you're re-presenting also has to be known well enough for the audience/player to see that it's a pastiche.

There are many other flavours of comedy, but I hope just this small piece of the big picture allows you to see that we return to the overall theory principle that all writing is a craft, and that if someone gives you the brief of making a character or a world, all writing is probably going to need some humour, and when you think about how to insert that, you should do so consciously.

And think too about what you don't have that other comedy does: you don't have a laugh track like many situational comedies,[1] and you don't have physical stakes for performers, so physical comedy is a lot harder. *Untitled Goose Game* is probably the best example of a game pulling off physical comedy, but it's rare. You may not (if you don't have a voice-over budget) have intonation or timing in a conventional way. How are you going to use text effects to enhance comedic moments? And you don't have performers' facial expressions. How

---

[1] Actually I know someone who's working on a game with a laugh track right now and I really hope they keep it. It's really interesting as a texture in the storytelling/genre they're working in.

effective is a 'Tim' character in *The Office* if not only can they not do a 'look to camera' but the camera itself is in the timing and control of the player?

Finally, in writing comedy for your games you should in general avoid meme-like internet references. Memes are a format that dates extremely quickly. They're often funny because they come in a flurry of sharing, and most often because they're an in-joke for an industry, community, or interest group. Contemporary references will dull very quickly, rarely work for a global audience, and memes themselves are of our world. They are the worst kind of 'cadence of a joke more than an actual joke', and in general 'speaking like you're from the internet', using words like 'smol', 'snek', 'doggo' or 'birb' (small, snake, dog, bird) will only show that you spend far too much time on Twitter, make your game feel hugely dated very quickly, not be effective for a wider audience, and break any pretence that your characters live in a real world which is not you. It also comes with the territory of poor-quality dialogue where all characters speak with the same one-note jokey voice as the writer. There are very, very few games that do this effectively, although it's not impossible to do so when it's a comment on that culture (a pastiche) especially. But the success of those games for people who are very online has meant that people think that's what humour is. That single note when there's a whole symphony orchestra to play with out there if you look.

Just two Theory chapters are left: 'Further Reading' and 'A Note on Ethics'.

CHAPTER 8

Further Reading

As promised, here are some texts I recommend for developing your writing practice and why I think they could be useful to you.

Straight-Up Technique

These are books for reference. Written with clarity, often accompanied by examples and exercises to reinforce your learning, these books will help you build on particular areas of technique where you might find yourself struggling, and do so in a precise and dedicated manner.

I have three books to offer here and recommend you pick at least one of them to read after this book. You could identify an area you feel that needs the most attention in your practice in *Playwriting*, or to develop your practice in the context of other practitioners with the other two books.

DOI: 10.1201/9781003182832-10

- Stephen Jeffreys, *Playwriting*
- Nisi Shawl and Cynthia Ward, *Writing the Other: A Practical Approach*
- Ursula K. Le Guin, *Steering the Craft: A 21st-Century Guide to Sailing the Sea of Story*

Stephen Jeffreys's *Playwriting* is an absolute foundational text (after something like Lajos Egri's classic, *The Art of Dramatic Writing* (1946), which is good, but a little stilted for a contemporary learner to use as a first resource, I think). I have owned perhaps three copies over the years, as I've moved across countries and had to leave my book collections behind. It's an incredibly valuable teaching resource; there's always a chapter I can just point to precisely about characterisation, or dialogue, or structure. I first came across it studying playwriting at the University of Birmingham, and while a little stuffy, and very theatre-focused, it is also a gem of simple practical theory. You don't have to follow Jeffreys's rules, but there is value in understanding them before breaking them.

His chapter on dialogue in particular is something I recommend again and again when faced with new writers whose characters all sound the same or who write in fully-formed sentences and paragraphs. You may not want to end up writing naturalistic dialogue, but a lot of games demand writing for speaking (if accompanied with voice over) or writing as speaking but for reading (like in a script or comic). If you cannot compose natural rhythms of speech and characterisation, you will not write for games well.

Shawl and Ward's *Writing the Other* I provide as an antidote to the stuffiness of Jeffreys's work and also because Jeffreys is writing from the perspective of the playwright, usually a single author encouraged to 'write what you know', where the solution to more diverse stories has become the development of playwrights from diverse backgrounds and perspectives. Games writing is a larger, messier, and more collaborative practice, often working with large casts of characters and outside of realistic earth-bound settings; story worlds where you portray a whole world, not just a slice of it.

In this context, games can and should be examining the assumptions it re-presents from our world about race, class, gender, and sexuality, and we should be radically diversifying our companies, collaborators, and practices to make sure that games are made by diverse peoples. In this context, what does this mean to construct a character voice? To portray a Black character in a cyberpunk alternative present? Or to present a trans character in a fantasy world? Some of the answers to this is process-based, not creative. It's about producing entry-level training positions that radically shift the huge imbalance in the games industry which currently works in favour of middle-class, cis, het, White men. However, if you're reading this book, I suspect you don't have the resources to affect this kind of change (yet). In a small indie team, without the resources to take control of hiring practices yourself, you might find yourself writing for characters of diverse backgrounds, genders, and sexualities not represented on your team. You can perhaps lobby for the contracting of sensitivity readers. You should take time to listen to people from marginalised backgrounds talk about the clichés and stories about them of which they are tired of hearing. And you can also read Shawl and Ward's *Writing the Other*.

Writing the Other is a book which could be just as useful in developing the kind of empathy in a cis man which might enable him to think of women as people, enough to write them convincingly, as it is enabling a White writer to avoid stereotypes and clichés when constructing a Black character. The book is set out as a number of chapters noting common pitfalls, and with exercises in empathy, listening, voice, and with a huge amount of further recommended reading to deepen your understanding. When thinking about not just how to construct believable characters, but also how to make sure your characters are diverse and believably so, turn to this book.

This brings us to the final book on technique: Ursula K. Le Guin's *Steering the Craft: A 21st-Century Guide to Sailing the Sea of Story*. I once read an article in the *London Review of Books* that considered Le Guin's practice as explored through her own words and writing. There is a certain amount of bravado, I think, when she claims that she has no track with plot:

> 'I have never written a plot-driven novel', Le Guin said. 'I admire plot from a vast distance, with unenvious admiration. I don't do it; never did it; don't want to; can't'. She tended to write stories which include long journeys that loop back on themselves, where a hero thinks she's getting somewhere new but actually (if she's lucky) finds herself close to where she started out.

(Burrow, 2021)

Just because a work is not plot-*driven* doesn't mean it doesn't relate to, understand, and nevertheless understand what plot does. And for all Le Guin's rejection of certain tools and tropes, she knows and understands them with pure mechanical clarity, and takes you through the mechanisms of storytelling (in the context of novel writing) precisely, with theory, example, and exercises in each chapter. *Steering the Craft* is a book for those interested in literary device and the kind of writing that you might employ in games outside of dialogue (think, for example, of the modus operandi of a game like *Disco Elysium*, which reads like noir detective fiction, or the anti-colonial reinterpretation of *80 Days*, which despite its steampunk recasting, reads like a novel from the late 1800s).

Workbooks

I've got three recommendations here, each for a slightly different type of mind. They offer tools for developing technique a little more holistically than the 'straight-up technique' category, where you can flick to a chapter to shortcut learning on dialogue or narrator perspectives. Each of these books, instead, offers a practice and set of exercises which can be woven into your daily life.

There are three, because this is a very personal area of practice, and each of them will apply to different minds and sensibilities. For example, I know that Julia Cameron's *The Artist's Way* is very dear to some writer friends of mine, but I put off reading it for years because the name just felt so … *spiritual* (ick). I'm glad the writing of this book saw me finally look through it, and I feel like these three titles together have something to offer everyone.

How should you work with a workbook? They are usually about taking the amateur writer and giving them tools with which to become more professional – that is, not sit around waiting for inspiration to magically 'occur', but rather having deadlines and collaborators and needing to sometimes just sit down and work. That's not to deny the vicissitudes of procrastination and attention which are the part of any creative person's day; rather it is that my main definition of a 'professional writer' when contrasted to an amateur is not being paid or published – it is that a professional writer has a practice which builds a toolset that helps them adapt to brief, deadline, form, and style as required. They do not write at leisure. They write with discipline and self-understanding, whatever that means for them.

- Michael Atavar, *How to Be an Artist*
- Lynda Barry, *What It Is*
- Julia Cameron, *The Artist's Way: A Spiritual Path to Higher Creativity*

Which one should you choose? I am definitely a Michael Atavar kind of artist (I use the term here to include all people who create). *How to Be an Artist* is a plain, clear, and unsentimental handbook for giving you tools for starting, making, and finishing work. It is an A–B approach. I discovered this book myself when trying to put together some of my first lectures on 'creativity' for programming students, and for those of a mind which could be characterised as linear and ordered, and in need of minimal clutter, it's a natural pick.

I have included Lynda Barry's book because I often teach with it in parallel with Atavar – it feels like the very opposite of his work. *What It Is* is chaotic, highly visual, and describes a scrappy, mussy wayfinding, which gives non-A–B people means of honing in on wherever 'B' might be, and describing for yourself where 'A' is, wherever you left it. I owe the discovery of this book to playwright, TV writer, teacher, and watercolourist Emma Adams. Adams is a writer who often describes herself as working against the grain of her dyslexia, and Barry's book makes sense in her hands – highly visual, cluttered, and confident somehow that *everything* is illegible, so you might as well luxuriate in it before you tease it into the form of a story.

I have already described *The Artist's Way* a little. My friend, collaborator, excellent writer and narrative designer, and trained yoga instructor Char Putney is the person who should be credited for finally handing me a copy and making me actually look inside. Once you get past the cover of the misty mountains and cranes in flight (I cannot speak to the cover of your own copy), and the long fluffy subtitle, it's full of precisely the same amount of solid, workable, invaluable, professional, creative practices to pull into your writing life as the other books. It's just all phrased and framed in a way that will appeal to people who feel like their writing comes from their heart and soul, rather than their heads. If that's you, and you're looking for a place to continue after reading this book, start there.

Understanding Format

As someone who came up through devising theatre (as you've read at length), *form-driven* design has been and will be the lifelong backbone of my practice as an artist, designer, and maker – and a crucial part of that is recognising form and format and using the material of it to your advantage. For texts to accompany our considering of format, here are some places to dig a little deeper:

* Matt Madden, *99 Ways to Tell a Story*
* Raymond Queneau, *Exercises in Style*
* Scott McCloud, *Making Comics*

The first two examples are, similar to my offering of Lynda Barry vs. Michael Atavar, two approaches to the same playful challenge. Telling the same story 99 different ways. A story in which the plot, characters, setting, and story are the same, but the narrative choice (means of telling and presenting the story) are different. Madden's *99 Ways to Tell a Story* is a comics-based approach to (almost like a 'cover' of) the restriction Queneau sets himself in his much earlier *Exercises in Style*. If you're visual, go with Madden; if you prefer examples in writing or are a little more angled to learning through plain text, go for Queneau.

I also offer Scott McCloud as a resource here. *Making Comics* is one of those books which exhibits a medium's practice so clearly and with such perspicuity, and which has myriad things you can learn from as a game writer and collaborator in the space of games. Games deal in so many crossed disciplines and, for example, McCloud's basic art history of abstraction will hugely complement a better understanding of art direction (and the need to resist straight realism as a marker of progress). But it will also teach you a lot about storytelling without writing, and to think through when words really are needed.

I tend to find, after having run several worldwide entry-level recruitment processes for writers from any background interested in working in games, that those with the most 'natural' instinct for the affordances of game dialogue more often come from the world of comics than anywhere else. The line-length affordances of panel-based storytelling chime quickly and easily with on-screen text, but candidates from comics background are also often grounded by a foundation in art history and the aforementioned notion of what it is to make the abstract feel 'realer' than the real; something vital to understanding the qualities of storytelling with the virtual puppets of games.

Journeys in Writing Practices

Finally, this is the kind of writing about writing which is extremely personal; writers writing about their own practices and journeys, less with a view to drawing out rules and examples and exercises, and more as an exploration of their own story as a writer and how it relates to their work.

These can be incredibly valuable. Your journey as a writer will belong to you and only to you. Your 'way in' might involve fan art, university, working in journalism, theatre, comics, poetry written for open mic nights, a book of writing exercises, a free workshop, a diary, therapeutic practices, or just a wild leap you take one day. And that first step, at whatever age and for whatever reason you take it, will be much less important than learning to reflect, understand, and develop your practice as it grows. The most important thing about writers talking about their journey is that you read their journey not attempting to emulate it, but as an opportunity to peer into their practice and toolkit, and see how they constructed it.

- Various contributors, edited by Sherry Quan Lee, *How Dare We! Write: A Multicultural Creative Writing Discourse*
- Various contributors, edited by Kwame Dawes, *When the Rewards Can Be So Great: Essays on Writing and the Writing Life*
- Stewart Lee, *How I Escaped My Certain Fate*
- Anna Anthropy, *Rise of the Videogame Zinesters: How Freaks, Normals, Amateurs, Artists, Dreamers, Dropouts, Queers, Housewives, and People Like You Are Taking Back an Art Form*

I have offered two collections of essays and articles from a variety of writers from a variety of creative writing disciplines as my first two recommendations – really getting a spread of voices so that hopefully there's something here that speaks to as many people as possible. They include reflections on the craft of writing but also the life of being a writer, and both Lee and Dawes draw together voices from a more diverse set of backgrounds than your usual collection. Lee, in her introduction, sums up the kind of question this personal-practice reflection can offer:

> How did you get here? I ask my students. Not just, I skipped dinner, got hung up in traffic, but how did you get to this classroom, this particular class, wanting to write, writing? What is your timeline for your journey to become a writer? When I began my journey as a creative writer, I noticed there were no books about me – a Chinese Black female who grew up passing for white in Minnesota. So, I began to write myself into existence.

(Lee, 2017)

And I also offer a very personal selection as insight into me and my approaches as a writer: Stewart Lee's *How I Escaped My Certain Fate*, as referenced in the comedy section, is one of the best books on writing for performance I have ever read and left a significant mark on me. Formed of transcripts of his stand-up routines, matched with a frankly ludicrous number of footnotes annotating it; picking out how different parts of the routine were sparked, matured, how they played in different places with different audiences. Why the word *wool* is inherently funny. How his own practice is honed somewhere in between late '80s punk, devising theatre, 'alternative' comedy, and a grudging admission that sometimes you have to do TV because it pays for your mortgage. The sheer *craft* of the man. And the clarity with which he can speak of it.

I was not a huge fan of Lee's stand-up before I read the book, at which point I saw that for him the truest expression of his work is caught up in the process, somewhere between the words on the air, the electricity of the audience, the 50th time through a particular bit. The live redrafting that happens in performance is something I learnt instinctively through my own devising performance practice (helped substantially by peer mentors such as the excellent Alexander Kelly), but Lee's reflection on his writing is so … *savage*. It is a masterpiece through which I try and refract a similar approach to my own practice. Lee might not be the writer you need to hear from. But I recommend always looking for the account that might be.

Finally, we reach Anna Anthropy's *Rise of the Videogame Zinesters*. I offer this one book about the practice of DIY game-making particularly to all of the readers of this book who aren't coming from a games background, study, or player-level literacy. Games can often seem huge and impenetrable, and the games that make it to mainstream coverage are often billion-dollar monoliths. But games are an art practice with its weird, queer, experimental avant-garde, just like any other. Read this book to know that everyone can have a home in games, that anyone can make games, and that we need you.

CHAPTER 9

A Note on Ethics

We're going to finish the theory section by noting that when you write, when you build worlds and create characters and put words in their mouths, when you *tell stories*, you cannot do so without considering the ethics of how you do.

Who is there? How do you treat them? How are you adding to the storied understanding of a certain group when you write for or about them? What does your writing assume about humans, about history which might be unexamined, lazily developed by other lazy assumptions? Stories are how we fit the big world and its richness into our relatively smaller heads. They are how we imagine different worlds, different systems, different ways of living together. Stories are politics, histories, and social ammunition. How are you arming someone when you use a military metaphor instead of a non-military one?

There are three main areas, in my opinion, for consideration of ethics in games writing.

- What is the story/game?

DOI: 10.1201/9781003182832-11

- Who makes the story/game?
- How is the story/game made?

Think about the characters you build and the assumptions in your fantasy and sci-fi or historical universes. Does gender have to work in an alien world like it does here? Do you have to have cops in your fantasy space adventure? Who wrote the historical sources you're drawing on, and can you find alternative histories to draw on? And what about your characters? Sometimes representation is about inclusion, having visibly disabled characters (and a world which they could traverse), or LGBTQ+ or BIPOC characters. But sometimes a considered ethics of storytelling is thinking about what traits or characters *shouldn't* be present – including common storytelling tropes which aren't on the face of it hateful. If you have a character who is trans, maybe they shouldn't be duplicitous, and their transness shouldn't be a 'twist' (in fact, maybe it should just not come up at all). Even if other characters are supportive of it, it still reinforces damaging tropes, and centres the character in their transness, not their humanness. Likewise, a good design process should make sure some aspects of the game don't undermine others. You might write in an ethical reimagining of trade, but someone might design a capitalist-derived trade mechanic. (You also might not ever get a say in that, but I'm trying to be optimistic here.)

That leads us to *who is making the story*. Diversity consultants, and consultants who might specialise in areas of helpful worldbuilding research – like police abolition, or anarchist means of self-governance, or matriarchal societies, or gender-fluid traditions – can be an incredibly valuable resource. But if your team is made up of all the same types of people (typically in indie games this is White, cis, het, Western men), in the end, your storytelling and game will not be as good as if a diverse team is making it. Your audiences are diverse; a diverse team writing, designing, and developing a game will just do a better job at making it work for more people, giving more people room to interact with, understand, and see themselves in the worlds you're working to build.

Sometimes the best contribution you can make to a project is to turn it down and recommend someone with lived experience of the characters or context you're being asked to write for. Turning down work in solidarity is a very tough thing to do in a world governed by capitalism, and writers rarely have the luxury of being involved in hiring decisions, project management, or the founding of game studios. In that context, identify what is the most you can do. Ethics in games storytelling will be about choosing the least bad path as often as choosing the best.

Solidarity is a neat link to the final point – labour. Besides how the game is made, how you and your fellow workers are treated is important too. First, join a union. Unions are getting better at being aware of videogames industry working conditions; IT unions, arts and writers unions, screen and media unions. Find out who does what in your country, and ask them about if they work with games industry workers, what they can do for their members in general, and for games specifically. Perhaps you could join a union and develop their awareness of games by encouraging others to join with you. Unions will help you assess contracts and conditions, they can provide legal support, and they can advise you on rates and negotiations.

Second, consider how you're treated as a worker to be as important as how you treat your world and characters. In writing a book aiming to equip new game storytellers either graduating or moving across from other disciplines to games I would be remiss if I didn't note the often-severe abuses of workers that occur in the industry. Sometimes it's the kind of cissexism, racism, ableism, and LGTBQ+ phobia that exists in other industries, but sometimes it's a specific kind of 'crunch' culture or 'auteur' culture that pervades in games because of the structures studios grow from, the pressure of investors, or just straight up capitalism. It is also often worse for contractors like writers who rarely have rev shares, company shares, proper contracts, or aren't considered 'properly' part of the dev team. Here's the thing:

- You deserve to be respected, heard, and listened to as any other collaborator on the team.
- You deserve weekends, evening, and holidays.
- You deserve to be paid to do any substantial work in 'testing' for a role.
- You deserve to never be touched or commented on inappropriately.
- You deserve the right to practise your craft to an agreed brief.
- You deserve to not be shouted at, humiliated, or bullied.
- You deserve to never feel pressured to drink or eat anything against your will, comfort, or religion.
- You deserve to practise your religion.
- You deserve a means of reporting behaviour that makes you unwell or uncomfortable, safely and without fear of repercussions.
- You deserve a contract, and payment and/or revenue share terms on par with others with your responsibilities and seniority.
- You deserve the support of systems, structures, and good planning that prioritises people over product.
- You deserve to not be manipulated, gaslit, or guilt-tripped into conceding any of these things because you care about good story, games, or because you're told others are doing so, or because the team is a 'family'.
- You deserve managers and bosses with training or experience in management, not just 'vision'.
- You deserve credit on the game which fairly represents your work on a project, whether or not you were working when the game ships.

I have worked in places where all of these things have been missing. Most people in games have. Many are also working hard to change it. But in the meantime, there are some things you can do (apart from join a union).

1. *Read your contract and company handbook closely.* Look for clauses about overtime. Ask about other people's pay. Ask about how internal complaints are handled. Ask to whom you will be reporting, how your brief will be set, and how creative decisions will be made.
2. *Speak to other workers.* Ask other workers how they are compensated on similar projects. Peer networks will also be valuable in asking about studio conditions, structures, culture,

and specific red flags they might have heard about. Also look at who has recently left a studio and how often people leave. If the leadership is all White, cis men and the entry-level workers are mostly from diverse backgrounds, then either they don't promote diverse candidates or marginalised folks leave before they can progress.

3. *Seek solidarity*. Build peer networks, in common disciplines, and common areas of experience/identity. And offer solidarity in return. Advocate for improvements in process, hiring, promotions, and structures.

This is always, always easier said than done from the position of a single worker (hence, unions). You may feel like there are a hundred other writers ready to take a position if you don't. You may feel as a woman in a male-dominated studio that standing up for a Black colleague's right to work with equal dignity and respect will single you out for exclusion. How many of your bargaining chips do you want to use arguing for employing a sensitivity reader? Why should you argue for the inclusion of an accessibility feature, when so many other features have already been cut? It's not easy, but you should challenge yourself on how you act in circumstances such as these.

Ethics aren't the doing of things perfectly. They are not a product; they are a process of learning, thinking, revising, and doing the best you can with the power you have (and combining that power with others where you can). You of course should consider your safety and security when you act or advocate – though it's also often true that the labour of making a workplace accessible and fair falls on the most marginalised and precarious. I can't solve White supremacy, capitalism, cispatriarchy, Western imperialism, ableism, classism, or homophobia today. But I can tell you that you deserve everything on that bullet-pointed list and more.

This has relevance in a book on the craft of writing for games, because you should be careful to know the difference between your need to improve your craft within the confines of your brief, and when people or processes you're operating in are making it intolerable or impossible for you to practise it well.

Join a union, build trusted peer networks, and make room for difference in your stories, teams, and labour practices.

PART II
Case Studies

CHAPTER 10

Introduction to the Case Studies

If you've made it here after reading through all of Part I, then great work! That was a fair amount to process. You might want to take a break, reread sections, make some notes, or go for a nice walk before digging further. The book can wait; let your learning breathe.

This part is going to be relatively short compared to Part I (Theory) and Part III (Workbook). For this Case Studies part, we're going to take three indie videogames with great writing/ storytelling and use them as short case studies focussing on a single theme drawn from our Theory section. These are the thematic touchstones:

- Dialogue
- Adaptation and ethics
- Format

DOI: 10.1201/9781003182832-13

This part will work best if you play the games or watch a playthrough (ideally without commentary) of at least 30 minutes of the game.

These case studies will help us consider game writing affordances in practice, and in clear and well-known examples. After these practical explorations, we'll be in an excellent position to move to Part III, where we'll set up a number of exercises for you to learn how to start, develop, and perfect your writing practice.

If you would like to play or watch these case study games before reading anything about them, here are the games in question and some thinking points you might like to make notes on before you come to the relevant case study. The games are all available on PC, some also on console and mobile. If you haven't bought games online before, a game store like Steam will help you.

- *Life is Strange 2: Episode 1*
   Pay attention to characterisation and dialogue. How do you get a sense of the people, situations and relationships through their words?
- *80 Days*
   Read a little about *Around the World in Eighty Days* and think about this as an adaptation of that literary work. How is this adaptation original? What choices have the team made in adapting it? Pay particular attention to the NPCs, how they shape the world, and how are they shaped by your choices (if at all).
- *Last Stop* – 'Paper Dolls', Chapter 3: Imposter Syndrome
   What format is being used here and how does it help structure this chapter and make this part of the story effective?

CHAPTER 11

Character and Dialogue in *Life is Strange 2*

This is going to be a fairly straightforward analysis of a single scene and the characterisation and dialogue which is demonstrated in its writing. The scene is from the game *Life is Strange 2:*

Episode 1 is free on most platforms, which is why I'm selecting this episode in particular. I recommend you play through (or watch a playthrough) of the episode before digging into this analysis.

I'm being supported in this analysis by the wonderful resource that is the *Life is Strange* fandom.com wiki (life-is-strange.fandom.com), and we're drawing specifically from scene 5 set in the Diaz's garage where Sean's father is working on a car. This is the second time we meet Esteban, Sean's father, and it's a lovely example of exposition, for establishing relationships through subtext, and in allowing gentle player interaction to colour but not cast characters (allowing for a strongly authorial-driven mode of player interaction and storytelling).

DOI: 10.1201/9781003182832-14

A formatting note: where there are choices, I've italicised and centred them, and then placed the 'selected' choice in parentheses and italics. Bold text shows the character who is speaking. Italics also note stage directions.

We're going to go line by line. I'm going to crit each section, point out things I think don't work so well, as well as the things that do, and in this way we're going to think through how to crit, as well as consider it a useful example of character-driven dialogue in a story-driven game.

Let's take a look at the first time Sean and Esteban interact. First, the reason you've been directed to the garage is to collect a number of things ready for a party later that evening. Sean is in his late teens, and Esteban is a single father of both Sean and Sean's kid brother Daniel.

> *In the storage room connected to the garage, Sean finds a blanket stored on one of the top shelves.*
> *Sean (internal monologue):* I'm sure Dad won't miss one blanket for the night …
> *As Sean walks into the garage, Esteban is working under a car.*
> *(If Sean ate the chocolate)*
> *Esteban:* That you, choco thief?
> *Yeah. // It's me, Daniel. // (No answer)*
> *(It's me, Daniel.)*
> *Sean (putting on a high-pitched voice):* It's me, Daniel!
> *Esteban:* Cool. Can you tell your big brother he's grounded tonight? When you see him …
> *Esteban:* Hey! Since you're creeping around up there, can you pass me the wrench in the top red drawer over there?
> *Sean:* Sure!

One of the nice choices here is that the text immediately recalls a decision you made in a previous exchange where Esteban, Sean, and Sean's kid brother Daniel were in the same room together. You got to choose whether Daniel or Sean gets the last chocolate bar. What this does is immediately remind us of Daniel, and also Daniel's absence – this is father and oldest son together now, and their conversation is naturally going to be in a different register than it would be with a young kid around. Also note that the writers give the player a reason to move further into the scene – the request for the wrench.

> *Sean checks the drawer, but there is no wrench.*
> *Sean:* Uhh … There's no wrench here.
> *Esteban:* Ahh, shoot! Must be somewhere else then … Take a look around. I know I left it nearby … It's a 16 mm reversible flex wrench.
> *Sean (to himself):* Jeez … That was definitely my plan for tonight … So yeah …
> *Sean (to Esteban):* Hold on!
> *Esteban:* Sam came by the garage today. Told me to tell you hi for him.
> *Sean:* How's his leg?

> *Esteban:* Well, you know … Old fossils like us don't heal the way you do.
> *Sean:* Remind me never to get old …
> *Esteban:* Hey, it beats the alternative!
> (…)
> *Esteban:* Hey, son … where's my wrench?
> *Hold on. // So many tools …*
> *(Hold on)*
> *Sean:* Hold your horses, I'm on it.
> *Esteban:* Well, bring it to me when you got it.

The offstage character Sam here is absolutely unimportant. What's important is that it gestures towards a natural familial depth (there are lots of things beyond which the player will never see or know about their lives) – and that it's a relatively warm one. Esteban's friends ask after his kids, and Sean cares enough about his dad's friends to remember when they're ill or injured. The gentle back-and-forth is a little cliché, but most interactions between kids and adults – and especially in many father-and-son contexts where masculinity provides extra structures and rules – do fall back on cliché. Add that to the context of manual mechanical labour and you draw a situation of warm familial relationships, but also of masculinity. It's easy to see Esteban here as a single father doing his best, and Sean's openness to playing within it as something similar.

The player is offered a number of filler conversation snippets depending on how quickly they find the wrench and hand it over.

> *Esteban:* Hey, seriously, what's taking you so long?
> *Sean:* Hey, seriously. I'm not a mechanic.
> *Esteban:* Come on. Bring me anything, really.
> (…)
> *Esteban:* Hey! Did you get your English midterm back?
> *Sean:* Uhh … Yeah … I got a B.
> *Esteban:* A 'B'?! But … you were so confident about that essay you wrote.
> *Sean:* Yeah, I think Ms. Calloway is just prejudiced against Vonnegut …
> *Esteban:* But Slaughterhouse-Five is amazing!
> *Sean:* Hey, you don't gotta tell me! Tell her!
> *Esteban:* Next parent-teacher meeting … She's gettin' a piece of my mind. Prejudiced against Vonnegut …

The first interlude begins to very lightly draw Sean's difference from his father. We know from those three lines that he's not doggedly building himself in his father's image, and it's underlined by Sean choosing to mimic his father's phrasing. Twice, the line says 'I'm not you': in its literal 'I'm not a mechanic' and in its literary device, mimicking 'Hey, seriously'.

The second interlude, conversely, develops both characters along the same lines. Another easy exchange from a life lived together. At once, when a B is a disappointment, you learn that Sean is a good student, and also that father and son are interested in literature. *Slaughterhouse-Five* is a war novel, so it still doesn't stray too far from a certain kind of masculinity, but Sean is intelligent, diligent, and articulate, and his father – until this point characterised by fatherhood and fixing a car – is also offered a literary bent.

Just a note on the quality of the dialogue here: I would argue that there is a little too much formality to the structure of the sentences – a lot of yeahs and heys which I think detract from the naturalism of the speech – but its consistent in its approach which is the most important thing. And in general, it's fairly strong when it comes to how people form speech.

Let's take a look at what happens if you offer the right tool quickly:

> *Offer the right tool quickly // Offer the wrong tool // Offer the right tool eventually //*
> *Offer the wrong tool too many times*
> *(Offer the right tool quickly)*
> *Sean picks up the wrench from on top of the car and gives it to Esteban.*
> Sean: Is that it?
> Esteban: Hey, yes, that's the one! That was quick. So you did learn something from your old man after all ...
> Sean: Yeah, yeah ...
> Esteban: All right, just let me ... tighten ... this. So. Finally decided to come and join your old man under the hood, huh?
> Sean: Yeah, uh ... sure ...
> Esteban: I know, it's not your thing. But you gotta learn a trade. Art, athletics, engineering, I don't care ... As long as you put your heart into it.

You've now dealt with the motivation for being drawn into the garage, and just in case you miss the interlude on Sean's education, it offers a neutral way into the same conversation about Sean's direction in life, as well as a note on the differing aptitudes of the father and son. Esteban is still being drawn as a generally supportive father as far as he has the means to articulate it. Note that he calls it a 'trade' – it's a slightly odd word to use, as he immediately complicates it to mean 'vocation' but 'trade + complication with examples' is the vocabulary through which he can express 'vocation' and his supportive fathering.

We'll take a look at a slightly longer excerpt here:

> *What's the point? // I'm trying ...*
> *(I'm trying)*
> Sean: I'm trying ... I just ... Don't know what direction to go ...
> Esteban: You're only sixteen years old. You've got time to figure it out ...
> Trust me, took me a while too ...
> Sean: And ... You happy with it? I mean, your job ... living here ...?

Esteban: Of course I am! We're doing great. Maybe one day, when I retire, I'll go back to Mexico … To Puerto Lobos … But until then …

Sean: I've heard this one before …

Esteban: Hmm … I don't even know why I'm fixing you a sweet car for graduation. *You don't have to … // It's wicked.*

(You don't have to)

Sean: Well … You don't have to … I mean … It's cool …

Esteban: Are you sure you're my son? You don't want to visit Mexico … don't want to have a car … I can't even get you into Rush or Santana … Are you going to ride the bus for all your dates?

Sean: Like I'm going on tons of dates … Not when Daniel is cockblocking me over the whole time.

Esteban: He's nine. He doesn't even know what cockblocking is. He looks up to you, Sean. Try and help him … It's what family is for. Things are … kinda scary out there in this country right now.

Sean: Yeah. Oh … uh … By the way …

Esteban: Ha! I was wondering how long it'd take. You need money for the party tonight, right?

Sean sighs, Esteban is standing cross-armed but smirking.

This is a piece of writing which I think could be slightly improved by trusting its audience more. Twice they say Mexico because they want to be specific about where Esteban is from, though the voice acting is clear on this point too. My problem is in the first reference: the writing is *for* the audience. Sean knows where Puerto Lobos is; he even says 'I've heard this one before'. The second reference would have sufficed to do the job of specifying, but also keeping the exchange character-driven. That choice says a lot about who the writers think their audience is, and it's a choice I think they could have been braver with.

A really useful piece of further reading (or listening) here is the 'Explanatory Comma' episode of the *Code Switch* podcast, which discusses the practice of offering informational context for people who might not have that context at their fingertips. Co-host Gene Demby explains that this becomes especially complicated in a podcast made to centre people of colour, but which is broadcast on a channel which has a large White listening audience. At what point does explaining de-centre people of colour from the conversation?

> We do it to signpost that we're about to explain something, but we also do it so the people who know know that we know that they know. And explaining things is not a small thing. Like, how you decide whether to explain something or not tells you a lot about who a storyteller understands their audience to be. And the *Code Switch* audience is younger and browner than the NPR audience, and we want our audience to be different than the NPR audience more broadly. So we're going to have to make some different choices about the kind of things we explain and the kind of things we just leave to y'all to figure it out via context or to look up on Google.

(NPR – *Code Switch*, 2019)

Life is Strange 2 tells a story of a Brown, first-generation immigrant family in the USA. Throughout its telling, it foregrounds their racial codification in small-town northern America, from violent cops' reaction to them to the microaggressions of store owners. In this small dialogue moment, it feels to me like the writers chose to centre their White players. You could argue that they're aiming for transformational empathy in a White audience, but if even your stories of the Other are aimed at White players, then nothing is ever for Black and Brown players. That seems like the wrong way to approach diversifying storytelling under White supremacy to me, personally.

I also think the transition into the next choice is a little contrived. They could have just left a pause rather than have Esteban tease Sean for his sarcastic remark. But not all father–son exchanges are always super natural, so I can see the argument for it.

This leads us to the nicest piece of player-led characterisation in this scene:

> Esteban: Just be honest with me, no bullshit … Are you using this money to buy alcohol? Weed?
> *Yeah, probably … // Just Halloween stuff …*
> *(Yeah, probably …)*
> Sean: Uhhhhh I mean … Yeah. Probably. But … we'll be partying at a house and … nobody is driving home. I swear.
> Esteban: Well, everybody's gotta get home somehow. But yeah.
> You and Lyla better not get in any car with somebody who can't walk straight.
> *Esteban hands over some cash.*
> Sean: Holy shit, forty bucks! Really?
> Esteban: Yeah. Why not. You did a good job on the lawn … Plus … I appreciate that you didn't lie to me.
> Sean: Thanks, Dad.
> Esteban: Just be careful. That's all I'm asking for, okay? I know what kind of crazy shit kids can get into …
> *Did you party a lot? // Don't worry about us.*
> *(Don't worry)*
> Sean: Don't worry … We've got smartphones and stuff. We can call a ride if we need it … and I can always text you …
> Esteban: I try not to. Or you know, you could accept my friend request on Facebook, so I can keep an eye on –
> Sean: Oh my God. Okay, I have to go.
> *(Yeah, probably …)*
> Esteban: Now get outta here before I change my mind about that cash.
> And keep an eye on Daniel while you're home. Would you?
> Sean: All right.
> Sean: Thanks, Dad!

This is excellent characterisation through choice. Especially in how it uses the tension between role-play and affinity for characters to provide the player with choices they care about, even though they don't change the world – only the response you're given.

You can see how these player choices feel emotionally loaded: you warm to their relationship and you don't want to harm it by lying. But the player is also asked to role-play a teenager, so it also makes sense to sometimes be a bit teenagerish in your replies: to lie, or sulk, or be frustrated in your parent. What if the answer gets you in trouble? The stereotypical instinct to lie about doing 'bad' things (underage drinking, drugs) is also matched with the subversion of the stereotypical parent – the father is made more complicated and 'cool' through your telling the truth, but if you want to play a teenager and develop Sean as evasive, you can.

Then, we finish up with a moment of pure dadness:

> *Esteban:* Hey hey hey! Not so fast Seanie-boy … Don't you think your papito deserves a hug?
> *Okay // Oh my God …*
> *(Okay.)*
> *Sean moves forward to be embraced by Esteban's open arms.*
> *Esteban:* Okay, have fun. But … not too much.
> *Sean:* I won't. Promise!
> *Sean:* Bye! Love ya!
> *Esteban:* I love you too, hijo …
> *(If Sean said 'Don't worry about us')*
> *Sean (inner monologue):* Dad's a pain in the ass sometimes … But he's awesome.

In this final moment, the use of Spanish endearments is spot on. It doesn't matter if you've not heard them before; it makes sense in context and communicates character, even if it doesn't communicate literal meaning. I don't think you need that final inner monologue, to be honest, but the narrative design has made a choice to cultivate an inner voice for Sean – and it's useful later on to guide the player through small puzzles and open spaces, so it's worth establishing it before its entirely useful.

Key Takeaways

- Your exposition can make a statement about who you're centring in your audience, as well as your storytelling.
- Familial relationships do often adhere to a stereotype or format, but to turn from stereotype to character, consider how you will complicate your characters, and demonstrate that through dialogue-driven exposition.
- The characters speak in non-grammatical sentences, they hesitate and truncate naturally, use common contractions, and in the use of Spanish the father is developed as a first-generation immigrant.

- The tensions of father and teenage son established by the setting, situation, and initial meeting in the previous scene all allow the writers to draw tension from the choices they offer – tension that resolves into character development, investment in the relationship, and which asks the player to think about how they want to play. Are they role-playing or are they storytelling? It doesn't matter which the player chooses – just asking them to choose brings them further into the story.

Further Reading

A reminder that you can find the incredibly rich resource of fully transcribed scripts, choices and consequences online on the *Life is Strange* fandom.com wiki.

- https://life-is-strange.fandom.com

I also want to recommend the two-day dialogue writing workshop exercise plan that I've set out in Part III of this book, which offers several means and resources for understanding and better developing your dialogue skills. In particular I reference:

- The 'Dialogue' chapter from Stephen Jeffrey's *Playwriting*

But a lot of the learning there is by listening, doing, and group reflection. So, feel free to skip to that workshop for more practical resources to work on your dialogue skills if you're hungry for more.

I also reference the NPR *Code Switch* episode 'Sometimes Explain, Always Complain'.

- Transcript: https://www.npr.org/transcripts/782331005
- Audio recording: https://www.npr.org/2019/11/23/782331005/sometimes-explain-always -complain

On the theme of how *Life is Strange 2* handled the theme of racism in the contemporary USA, I also recommend this essay published on *Polygon* by Patricia Hernandez (2020):

- 'My Mom Crossed the Border in Real Life. I Only Cross It in a Video Game', https://www .polygon.com/2020/1/21/21070333/life-is-strange-2-episode-5-border-wall-interview -immigration-michel-koch-raoul-barbet

I've also written more about how we think about who our players are when we make games for a keynote address in 2019 at the Freeplay International Games Festival.

- 'The Player is a Material Made Up of People', https://www.youtube.com/watch?v =3gm97EKoypU&ab_channel=FreeplayIndependentGamesFestival

CHAPTER 12

Ethics and Adaptation in *80 Days*

80 Days is 'a massively branching anti-colonial steampunk adventure' (Jayanth, 2016a) based on Jules Verne's novel *Around the World in Eighty Days*. It's available on mobile as well as PC and console, so should be pretty accessible to most people reading this book. There are also many no commentary playthroughs on YouTube if you just want to take a look at the kinds of mechanics, writing, and choice-making at play.

For this short case study, we have an incredible first-hand resource to support the question of ethics and adaptation in *80 Days*: a 30-minute GDC talk from 2016 titled 'Forget Protagonists: Writing NPCs with Agency for *80 Days* and Beyond'. I'm going to quote directly from this talk by *80 Days* writer Meghna Jayanth, but it's still worth watching or reading the whole thing.

Instead of closely studying the text as we did previously, here I'm going to offer you the writer's first-hand insight into the kinds of decisions they made as a lens through which to view your playthrough. It might feel surprising to go from the extremely specific line-by-line

DOI: 10.1201/9781003182832-15

analysis of the first case study to this largely thematic and high-level one, but both of these case studies demonstrate theory in practice. One at the micro-level of line and specific written choice, and the other at the level of ethos, attitude, and character and worldbuilding as a meta-strategy. We don't always get first-hand knowledge of writers' decisions and intent in writing for games, and it would be foolish not to make use of it when we do.

In 'Forget Protagonists', Jayanth in particular considers the characterisation and writing of non-player characters, or NPCs, and the agency through which the game protagonist Passepartout interacts with them as both a means of worldbuilding, but also of fulfilling the necessary updating of the context of the story to an anti-colonial adaptation (and to that of a steampunk reimagining).

Often the process of working as a writer on a game – whether or not you're working on existing IP – will be some kind of a process of *adaptation*, as it's likely that you will be adapting story work that has already been laid out in your brief by a creative director and/ or by an art team. Considering how you take that material and process it for the ethos of the game and game's storytelling is often about listening to this brief, but not their assumptions about how to tell that story. Instead your work is to understand the intended effect, and then use the formal tools you have to execute that.

Whenever you've invited to reimagine an existing world or IP – i.e. '*Eighty Days* but steampunk' – as a writer you should also consider what other assumptions are wrapped up in the original text or source material, and make a decision about how to comment on them or rework them, so as to produce ethical and considered storytelling.

For *80 Days*, Jayanth came to a proposed adaptation of Verne's *Around the World in Eighty Days* and with the Inkle team added to the adaptation an ethical brief, formed of what parts of the story they *didn't* want to uncritically adapt: primarily, the idea that these White protagonists traversing a world where they are privileged foreigners with a colonial perspective shouldn't have everything they're own way. That the world of the game wasn't just theirs for the taking.

As Jayanth (2016a) explains:

> Fundamentally [the book is] about two white(ish) Europeans going around the world on a silly bet […] a chewed over story of a white dude coming into a native culture and saving the day. But that was exactly the story we didn't want to tell […] we developed strategies to give our NPCs life, agency and integrity.

Game devs can often make assumptions about player agency, choice, and how NPCs and the environment exist – for exploitation by the player and the protagonist – that in themselves aren't actually necessary for a game to be a game. Indeed, *80 Days* is a much better piece of writing and game storytelling because it takes time to separate player *supremacy* from the idea of player *presence*. Jayanth (2016a) describes player supremacy as a

> […] kind of structural centrality, these assumptions about what it means to be a game protagonist and have agency can lead us to unwittingly reinforce unhelpful cultural

and social norms. To keep making the same game protagonist over and over again – because we are mistaking variations on a theme for variety.

Jayanth therefore makes decisions about how the NPCs respond to the player, using their reactions to underline that the player is playing *through* whiteness and masculinity. But, it's still interesting, and it's still good writing: each NPC adds a different brushstroke to the worldbuilding painted by your interactions with the game, whether or not they do what you want them to.

> What that boils down to is that Passepartout – in a traditional choose-your-own-adventure sense – actually goes around the world 'doing' very little at all. We limit his actions and his power – but NOT the player's agency.

> **(Jayanth, 2016a)**

The player's choices can paint a world through negative responses, closed-off spaces, and problems that can't be solved – and do so much more effectively (i.e. to paint an anti-colonial steampunk world) than unquestioned agency would do. When the player's choices are refused, ignored, or shut down, they paint Passepartout in relief. In writing NPCs which are varied to the point they might offer differing opinions and accounts, and are able to tell the player no as equally as yes, the writing is able to create a much more real and grounded-feeling world, where the player has to 'lean in' and make up their own mind.

As Jayanth (2016a) explains:

> NPCs are a key part of the worldbuilding. We explore wider political, social and cultural themes through personal concerns and entanglements – the world feels complex because the way our NPCs think about, react to, engage with the world is complex and often contradictory – this is a much more elegant and natural way to unfold backstory, politics, plot.

> So in *80 Days* almost every single NPC has a slightly different opinion of the Artificers' Guild, they have their own biased and particular perspective, and that's what the player experiences. Worldbuilding through NPCs in this way actually makes the world feel more coherent and alive than offering the player a journal entry or a singular, definitive perspective — it gives the player the space to make up their own mind, rather than having their mind made up for them.

Sometimes player interaction isn't encoded in systems, but emerge in the space between skilful writing and its layering and interpretation in the player's mind. A crucial takeaway here is that Jayanth has

- Reduced player agency for better storytelling
- Created a more vivid world by having characters disagree about it
- Adapted the source material using a considered ethical stance
- Understood that writing in games doesn't need *affect* for the agency to be *effective*

- Added a steampunk angle to the Victorian register, which gives room for these changes to feel coherent because of their incorporation into the twist on the genre

As Jayanth (2016a) makes clear in her account:

> With *80 Days* [we] went in wanting to be respectful to other cultures, other peoples and characters – and that resulted in compromise. Balancing agency in a game as you would difficulty or challenge can not only be a question of design, storytelling or mechanics but also a question of *ethics* – giving NPCs agency can genuinely be an ethical imperative.

As a final point for this short case study, the ethical choice and the drawing of many and varied credible characters[1] is all possible because it's founded on a great deal of research. As Inkle note in a blog post introducing the game, Jayanth founded characters and their situations on real-world politics and events of the era (Inkle Studios, 2014). That makes the situations and the worldbuilding not just well-founded, but allows the fantastical twist to produce a more effective commentary on actual events than the novel written contemporary to the era. *80 Days* therefore uses the practice of adaptation to not just reflect on the source material, but the contexts and assumptions from which it arose.

What makes the characterisation credible (and the story compelling) is the writer's choices on what of that research to make accessible to the player. As Jayanth (2016a) summarises, she doesn't have characters ever tell all of those stories, but they all underpin how the characters act:

> Part of doing the research is also – as writers and creators – asking ourselves whether this is our story to tell. In *80 Days* some NPCs stories are simply NOT FOR Passepartout — they are not for the Player — they are not for strangers, tourists or outsiders, and that's okay. That can actually be a good thing. This is a question that we should ask ourselves when we are writing games and designing NPCs — how much of this is for the player? How much of this is for the protagonist? If we want to breathe life into our NPCs, there has to be something left over for them — something that is just for them, and not in the service of player, protagonist or plot.

I strongly recommend taking this lens and playing or replaying a journey in the game, bearing in mind everything that you've learned about the writer's approach. Look for those moments where NPCs keep things for themselves, where Passepartout cannot change events, and for how the world is painted through characters' comments, rather than narrator description.

---

[1] While this case study isn't focused on dialogue and characterisation, they are also very good in this game, as is the pastiche of the Victorian novel.

Key Takeaways

- All storytelling has ethical implications.
- Adaptation offers you the chance to reflect on the source's context as well as its material.
- Choice and agency are part of the material of storytelling in games – and you can make decisions against the grain of players' expectations for better storytelling.
- NPCs build your world in how they react, the stories they tell, and in what they withhold as well as what they offer.
- Characterisation can be derived from disagreement, silence, and lack of effect.
- Strong critical research is a part of worldbuilding and ethical writing.

Further Reading

A remind of Meghna Jayanth's GDC talk and transcript:

- Video: https://www.gdcvault.com/play/1023393/Forget-Protagonists-Writing-NPCs-with
- Transcript: https://medium.com/@betterthemask/forget-protagonists-writing-npcs-with -agency-for-80-days-and-beyond-703201a2309

You can also explore the fandom.com wiki for the game to find lots of great systems details:

- *80 Days* wiki on Fandom.com: https://80days.fandom.com/

'Multiple Middles & *Mutazione*' is an extended piece of writing by me on using the soap opera genre and anti-colonial ethos in the 'multiple middles' structure and quality of choice in *Mutazione*. You'll find me tackling similar questions about NPC agency and the legacy of colonialism, but in a very different form and genre.

- 'Multiple Middles & *Mutazione*': https://gutefabrik.com/craft-multiple-middles/

One of the problems of White supremacy is that when it does ask people of colour to speak, it only asks them to speak about their experience of being marginalised under White supremacy. In that context, I recommend this wonderful collection of textbooks, essays, book sections, and online articles from writers of colour writing about craft.

- 'Writers of Color Discussing Craft': https://www.de-canon.com/blog/2017/5/5/writers-of -color-discussing-craft-an-invisible-archive

Finally, the following four texts offer wider reading on politics, ethics, and colonialism in games, literature, and society – a relevant context to accompany a deeper critical understanding of the writing in *80 Days*. A couple of these are academic texts and fairly expensive, so remember that most public and university libraries will order in books for you.

- Mary Flanagan, *Radical Game Design*
- Frantz Fanon, *Black Skin, White Masks*
- *Storytelling: Critical and Creative Approaches*, edited by Jan Shaw, Philippa Kelly, and L. E. Semler
- *Locating Postcolonial Narrative Genres*, edited by Walter Goebel and Saskia Schabio

Bonus exercise: Why not read the original novel from which the adaptation was drawn, and an adaptation in another medium in order to consider both the source material and another approach to its adaptation? You could also run a small group discussion on adaptation with the game, the book, and a third media's adaptation as the starting point.

- Original text: *Around the World in Eighty Days*, Jules Verne (1873)
- Radio adaptation: *Around the World in Eighty Days*, BBC Radio Drama adaptation directed by Janet Whitaker (1991)
- TV series adaptation: At the time of writing, there's a new BBC adaptation due to be broadcast at the end of 2021 starring David Tennant as Fogg, Ibrahim Koma as Passepartout, and adding a woman journalist, Abigail Fix, played by Leonie Benesch. (There is a Detective Fix in the original, though I've no idea if the character plays a similar role in this new adaptation.) This could be a valuable comparator.

CHAPTER 13

Format and the Heist in *Last Stop*

We're going to finish up Part III by taking a look at Variable State's *Last Stop*, a game which takes three interweaving stories through several chapters before bringing them together for the trio's dénouement. We've gone from micro-case study to macro in the past two, and here we'll settle comfortably somewhere in the middle to consider the use of the heist format in structuring the 'Paper Dolls' version of Chapter 3: Imposter Syndrome.

Last Stop traces three central characters in contemporary London through six initially unconnected chapters before bringing them together in a chapter seven dénouement which involves all three story threads. I strongly recommend taking time to look at this chapter of the game before reading on. While you play through Chapter 3: Imposter Syndrome or watch a playthrough, here are some initial higher-level observations to reflect on:

DOI: 10.1201/9781003182832-16

- *Pay attention to the rhythm of the choices*, the way the choices are presented. It's a game with a lot of player input, and the choices expand from very short options to more complex lines, offering two points of choice unfolding, and more reason for the player to keep paying attention.
- *Choice length* is very short; line length is comfortable, screen-width dialogue.
- The *dialogue* itself is excellent. Extremely well-cast voice actors add to it by implying class and character through accents, but everyone is extremely well observed. From an 8-year-old child and her dad, to teenagers, a yuppy, and a secret agent and her ambitious rival. Each character has a clear register, background, context in London, and feel different 'on the page'.
- *Take a look at the time-out function* and the pacing that it offers the writers. Even if the player isn't paying attention, the pacing won't drop out – this supports the comedy and drama where needed.
- *Meta-pacing*. The developers are also confident in how they pace the chapters themselves and seem very happy to drastically vary the lengths to the needs of the storytelling. Opening chapters can be long; later chapters take a matter of minutes as you only need a single beat to progress the plot in the direction needed.
- *The extremely realistic characterisation, dialogue, and voice over*, as well as extremely well-observed design, architecture, class relations, etc., all lay an extremely solid background for the eventual extraterrestrial twist, making the resolution feel much stranger and affecting – because of the 'realness' of what came before.

Now that you've watched a playthrough of *Last Stop*'s Chapter 3: Imposter Syndrome for the plotline 'Paper Dolls', or played through it yourself, we're going to consider how the game is supported through its use of *format*. Remember that 'form' means the shape of something, and 'format' means a commonly used framework or shape for a story.

A General Note on Format in *Last Stop*

Last Stop's multithreaded narrative is given weight and orientation in particular because of its use of recognisable format – both in making the naturalistic and paranormal feel grounded (the player may not know what's happening but they know the *shape* of how it's being presented), and in giving the player a clear narrative handhold with which to navigate the interweaving plot arcs.

The core characters and their stories could have been much harder to follow if they were all operating in the same kind of format (that of the beginning and eventual end: paranormal thriller). Instead, Variable State's story team split up the storylines by both a macroformat[1] and subchapter formats like in 'Paper Dolls' Chapter 3's heist. While the player may begin by

---

[1] *Macro* when added to *format* just means 'the highest level'. It's the opposite of **micro**. I don't know if it's terminology anyone else uses, but it's useful in this context to separate the level of core-character plotline format, and per-chapter subformats. Writers are allowed to make up words.

not quite remembering who the characters (named in parentheses) are, they always know *what kind of story they're in*. The macroformats are

- 'Paper Dolls' – a buddy/body-swap comedy (John Smith)
- 'Domestic Affairs' – a spy thriller (Meena Hughes)
- 'Stranger Danger' – a particular British kind of paranormal mystery, like *Attack the Block* or *Doctor Who* (Donna Adeleke)

The 1980s prologue (which features none of these core characters) also prepares the player for the idea that the prologue might need to relate to that to the 'present day' chapter stories somehow, and prompts you to start looking for how they might come together. Using the macroformats to separate them firmly gives the player a starting point, a handhold. Kicking it off with a prologue tells you that these chapters are very likely to be drawn from or moving towards a similar point. You feel structurally oriented as a player.

These three macroformats also immediately produce an interplay which supports the higher-level pacing of the story. Allowing the player to choose which core character to follow in what order (per each chapter) is, on the face of it, a simple offer, but it is an interestingly empowering one. Variable State cleverly hand the agency over what a satisfying-feeling next-chapter choice might be to the player.

In considering this choice, the player is doubly empowered: not just in making a choice, but in making an *informed* choice. Because of the use of strong TV and film genre macroformats, the player generally knows what they're getting as an experience with their choice, even though they don't know the plot specifics. In being able to make such a strongly informed decision on if they want to transition from, for example, a dramatic storyline to a comedy one, the player is invited to *think* about their relationship to the stories, the characters, and what they feel like following the previous action with, imbuing them with agency at a story structure level. It's a device that not only lets the player decide what will feel good for them (customising pacing), but also invites them to *lean in*, to think about what they care about or are interested in.

Perhaps a player immediately wants to follow up on the previous cliffhanger with more of the same, maybe they want a comedy interlude, or they can't wait to see what kind of mess teen kidnapper Donna has got herself into. The macroformats of comedy, thriller, mystery empower the player to build their own pacing and lean further into the story by being offered pause to think about how they relate to it.

In choosing well-known TV/filmic formats, the writing has to deliver on that promise – that means *more focus on producing pacing* in each chapter. For this reason, the Variable State design team use a lot of the language of TV/film camera framing: lighting, varied camera angles, and swift and regular scenecuts. This visual work and swift scene-change and perspective-change approach maintains pacing where otherwise player interactions might not be enough. Their in-dialogue choice format also plays a role in maintaining pace. Let's use this opportunity to focus on the Chapter 3 heist subformat and specific examples of the writing in action.

The Heist

In 'Paper Dolls', Chapter 3: Imposter Syndrome the player plays as John – a middle-aged public-sector worker, who's a single father, living in public housing in (what feels like) East London with his 8-year-old daughter. In previous chapters you meet his acquaintance Jack – a young yuppyish tech professional from the north of England, who sometimes gets John's mail. John and Jack are presented as chalk and cheese: John public sector and Jack private. John is photocopiers and phonelines, Jack is programming and videogames. John is middle-aged, unwell, and portrayed as having an unhealthy lifestyle; Jack is a lean runner in his 20s.

The more you have them side by side, class and geographical backgrounds also feel contrasted; John has a 'local' London accent, but Jack is from the north. And while it's clear John is barely scraping by in his increasingly gentrified neighbourhood, Jack is the reason it's being gentrified. This characterisation is set up by accent, language, location, the kind of work they do.

Body-swap comedies work best when the swapped characters are very far apart in perspective, because the essential conclusion of a body-swap comedy is to understand the others' perspective: 'the grass isn't greener, it's just different, and now I understand where you were coming from'. By the time we reach Chapter 3, they've swapped bodies, come to terms with the weirdness of it, and are trying to work out how to survive in the meantime. As a player, we're ready to begin the process of not just acknowledging their differences, but also finding common ground. That's important not just for the conclusion of the format, but also because the warm burgeoning friendship between the two will provide the emotional underpinning for the eventual decision about their fate that the player will face at the end of the game.[2]

Chapter 3 of 'Paper Dolls' is the most successful piece of storytelling in the game (in my opinion) because it uses a subformat to both shortcut the process of character exposition for Jack (with whom we're less familiar – we start the game as John) and their growing closer. It does so by combining the metaformat 'body-swap comedy' with the subformat 'heist' to produce an excellent piece of comedy writing. The writers use the contemporary version of 'explain the heist as you commit the heist', which is the paciest form (lots of cutting back and

---

[2] Spoiler: Jack – in John's body – has a heart attack. John, in Jack's body, realises he has a solution and can return them to their right bodies. If he does so, he'll be saving Jack, but putting himself in his old body, which is in a coma in hospital, with no recovery guaranteed. There's also his daughter to think of in the matter. When making this decision it matters that the writers make the player feel Jack and John care for one another, as well as the player cares for them, because it adds weight and consequence to the feeling of the decision.

forth from planning to execution), and in a comedy setting this allows for a lot of prep to go wrong and comedy to arise from immediate set-up and bungled pay-off.

Comedy arises from several sites in this chapter – from character, format, and pastiche. In character terms, there's the slightly surreal-minded 8-year-old daughter commenting on the plan as they make it around the breakfast table (think a Phoebe presence in the television series *Friends*), to John's self-awareness (Chandler) next to Jack's supreme confidence that they're going to pull it off (Joey). The chapter's longer segments at Jack's office also contain a parody/pastiche of a videogame company, a videogame practice, and a videogame stealth sequence – all of which add to the lightness and provides other sites for comedy outside of the faster-cut set-up/pay-off sequences.

The aim of the heist is for John to convincingly impersonate Jack for a single day without arousing suspicion. Because it's a comedy, the obvious outcome is that they'll fail amusingly – this also means the player knows they can't really succeed. The process of going through it is – for the player – a chance to get to know Jack, the pleasure of taking part in playing out a well-known format, and a coming together of the swappers by the end. Because it's a comedy, it has to go awry, but this failure brings them all closer together; they are united through failure. They both get fired.

That failure also unites the characters in an additional and interesting way: as workers. In the initial thematic set-up of John struggling under the boot of a gentrifying London you have – before now – seen Jack as the person pushing him out. There's no doubt he *is* part of the gentrification of the area, but through this chapter we understand that while Jack might live in fancy non-council apartment, he still rents, and while he works in tech, his position is still precarious and exploited.

In exploring Jack's workplace (and the circumstances under which John gets him fired – refusing to work unpaid weekend overtime) you realise that their apparent class differences aren't as great as they might appear at first; both of them are exploited and maltreated by their bosses. One boss is a petty tyrant of old, the other is 'your buddy, a team player, we're all a family here'. There are two generational models of the exploited worker and renter class here – they can find solidarities as well as differences.

Let's take a moment to consider the first five minutes of Imposter Syndrome on paper. The whole chapter is only about 20 minutes of runtime, but to take a look at just how pacey it is, let's consider a smaller part of it. I typed this script up myself: I'm loosely breaking it up into 'scenes' – shifts in timeline or location – and offer stage directions as well as dialogue, but I may have missed something; apologies if so. The choices are centred and the one chosen is in bold.

Scene 1
Establishing shot outside the flat. Onscreen title reads: '06:35 John's Flat'.
Scene cuts to three people at breakfast. Molly, and the body-swapped Jack and John sit around a circular table. Jack (as John) explains the heist.

Let's hear it // What's the plan // Run me through it

John (as Jack): So, what's the plan?
Heist music begins and continues throughout.
Jack (as John): The only way this is going to work is if we imitate each other exactly.
It's got to be perfect right so good that even my own mother wouldn't know the difference.

Jesus // He's loving this // Non-issue

John (as Jack): Oh, for heaven's sake…
Molly: Let him finish, this sounds fun!

Scene 2
Begins to fade out // fade in as voiceover continues.
We're now outdoors, zoom in on Amy warming up and running off.
John (as Jack): First order of business: 7:30 a.m., run with Amy.
John (as Jack): Amy's got a mind like clockwork. She is a stickler for punctuality. If you're even a minute late she'll suspect something's up.

Scene 3
Cut back to the blacked-out background version of them around table; camera pans round as they talk, keeping the scene moving.

He's exaggerating // That's me done for // Oh, come on

John (as Jack): Right, and if I am, she'd automatically think I'm an imposter?
Jack (as John): You don't know Amy.
*Molly **(teasing):*** Jack loves Amy!
Jack (as John): I do not!

Moving on // Finished? // Wasting time.

John (as Jack): Can we get back to this please?
Jack (as John): Let's review the itinerary.

Scene 4
Cut back to Amy warming up
Jack (as John): 7:30 a.m. Run with Amy.
Cut to Mario's coffee and espresso shop.
Jack (as John): 7:50. Visit coffee shop.
Cut to zoom on coffee.

Jack (as John): 7:52 order skinny caramel macchiato, no foam.
Cut to Jack consuming beverage.
Jack (as John): 7:53 consume beverage.
Cut back to the kitchen table.

Scene 5

Kill me // *Flatten me* // Finish me

John (as Jack): 7:55, jump off London bridge!
Molly: 8:15, buy Molly a new mobile phone?
Jack (as John): Okay, now who's messing around?

Scene 6
Smash cut to Hogarth Park; onscreen title announces '07:24, Hogarth Park'.
Cut to John (as Jack) waiting in the park; play can run into next scene.
Amy is stretching as John (as Jack) approaches.
John (as Jack): So, I meet Amy. How do I explain what happened yesterday?
Smash cut back to breakfast table.
Jack (as John): First, you have to put her completely at ease. She's a bit of a detective, or
        something, so don't be nervous, alright? She can smell fear. Just be super casual.

Something endearing // *Something wholesome* // Something Northern

John (as Jack): Okay, so I'll just go up to her and say…
Smash cut back to the park, John (as Jack) is talking to Amy.
John (as Jack): Alright, love?
Amy: Pardon?

Scene 7
Cut back to breakfast table.
Molly: Dad, no …
Jack (as John): Try and bring it into the 21st century, yeah? Look just distract her somehow.
        Talk about something she loves.
Molly: We're out of cereal!

I'll pick some up after work // Cornflakes? // My fault

John (as Jack): I'll pick some up after work.
Jack (as John): Focus! Look, Amy's a big theatre nerd, she could talk for hours about various
        plays she's into. It's incredibly boring.
Jack (as John): She's also been saying she fancies a holiday. Distract her with that.
John (as Jack): Holiday. Theatre. Got it.

Scene 8
Smash cut back to park.

Musicals // Holidays // Plays

John (as Jack): So, seen any musicals lately?
Amy: What was the deal with that pisshead the other day? How come you're hanging out
    with fat middle-aged blokes.

Fat? // *Forget it* // Pisshead?

John (as Jack): Oh, him. Don't worry about that.
John (as Jack): But since you asked, he's actually a great guy. You know, salt-of-the-earth type.
Amy: So, are we going for this run or what?

I'm just misunderstood // *Thinking man* // Meat and potatoes

John (as Jack): He's a thinking man's man, you know. Got a lot about him. Got a lot to offer.

Scene 9
Smash cut to running interaction (stamina bar).
Onscreen title reads '07:30 Run with Amy'.
Amy: Keep up if you can.

I feel great // I can actually run // Regular Mo Farah

John (as Jack): Wow, I feel great. I've not been able to run like this in years!
Amy: You spend enough time on the treadmill.

Self-absorbed // *Pretty vain* // Jack is a bit ignorant

John (as Jack): Yeah, I guess that is pretty vain isn't it?
Amy: Well, you're no role model, but I wouldn't beat yourself up too bad.

Role model? // *Tell me more* // Jack's skeletons

John (as Jack): What do you mean? About me not being a good role model?
Amy: Enough with the chit chat, you're giving me a stitch.

Come on // Just tell me // I need to know

John (as Jack): Come on, let me hear it. What is it that makes me such a bad person?
Amy: Bad person? You're harmless. I just said you don't set a good example.
Amy: You're just like me, you're a total workaholic, and a massive geek.

Not a criminal? // *I'm harmless?* // Massive geek?

John (as Jack): I'm a harmless dork. Well, that's a relief.
Amy: Yeah, sure.
They finish running.
John (as Jack): That was great! I feel fantastic! So, when can we do this again?

Amy: What's going on with you? You alright?

I feel great // Do I sound different? // Sorry

John (as Jack): What do you mean? I've never felt better! I'll call you tomorrow.
Amy: No, it's fine, I'll call you. Take care of yourself, okay, Jack?

Just look at all those cuts, changes, overlaps, and registers the writing is hitting. What do you see immediately from looking at it on paper?

There's obvious economy in the choice style they're working with – in both how it's offered and the variability of results. In order to prioritise pacing, they need less consequential choice (you don't want players worrying too much about the impact of what they say), and they need it to be scanned and chosen quickly (hence the very short choice texts). These choices are often not even branching at all – several of the choices fit the same outcome. What's important is that the player is acting, leaning in, and playing 'as' the character *very often*. The rhythm of the writing and choice-making encourages the player to be a direct part of the rhythm-making of the heist, and to derive pleasure from producing the comedic juxtapositions between the plan, and reality.

Told without the heist format, this wide variation on locations, times, number of things to remember to be a satisfactory imposter (and the fact that you would need to remember those things for a much longer if playing in 'real time') could have produced slow and stressful storytelling. In using the format 'planning the heist' plus the master format 'body-swap comedy', we know precisely how to read these events, always know what we're supposed to be doing, and therefore feel free to enjoy the comedy juxtapositions.

This kind of comedy is difficult to achieve in games, often because of the importance of pacing and camera control. Here, the planning/executing aspect of the heist format offers a clear reason to offer fast and frequent cuts, and shows the player the steps to follow just before following them (or choosing to mess it up on purpose, because it's funnier). By pulling the player in through their contribution to successfully paying off the set-ups, it becomes almost like a *Rock Band* heist comedy; press the buttons at the right time, and it will sing.

All in all, this is a prime example of how format is useful in storytelling. We all know how an audition format works. A courthouse scene. A wedding. The shorthand that exists in format can give us ready-made stepping stones with which to construct surprise, reversals, character development, pacing, or other narrative satisfactions that those familiar with the relevant format will be able to access with lightness and ease. In *Last Stop* – when combined with crisp dialogue, rapid choice placement, a time-out auto-select function which keeps choice moving if you're not paying enough attention, fast cutting and varied camera angles, and format-relevant sound design – this chapter comes together to produce a light, effective, and enjoyable plot beat which feels genuinely amusing to play.

That's it for this case study detail, but I wanted to leave you with a scene-by-scene breakdown which I took time to write out so you can get an even clearer overview of the structure and pacing of the chapter beginning to end. I didn't transcribe all the text, so you can see more clearly how the plan/execute structure works.

'PAPER DOLLS', CHAPTER 3: IMPOSTER SYNDROME

Scene 1

Establishing shot outside the flat. Onscreen title reads '06:35 John's Flat'.
Scene cuts to three people at breakfast: Molly, and the body-swapped Jack and John sit around a circular table. Jack (as John) explains the heist they need to pull off: that John (as Jack) – a public sector office worker – needs to get through a day of being a convincing videogame developer. First off, run with Amy.

Scene 2

Begins to fade out // fade in as 'planning the heist' voice over continues.
We're now outdoors; zoom in on Amy warming up and running off.

Scene 3

Cut back to the (blacked-out background) table; camera pans round as heist set-up continues. Questions are asked, quips are made.

Scene 4

Heist set-up narration continues.
It's described in military precision.
Cut back to Amy warming up.
Cut to Mario's coffee and espresso shop.
Cut to zoom on coffee.
Cut to Jack consuming beverage.
Cut back to the kitchen table.

Scene 5

Breakfast table banter.

Scene 6

Cut to Hogarth Park; onscreen title announces '07:24, Hogarth Park'.
Cut to John (as Jack) waiting in the park; player can run into next scene.
Amy is stretching as John (as Jack) approaches.
Smash cut back to breakfast table and crucial details for the Amy interaction.
Smash cut back to the park, John (as Jack) is talking to Amy.

Scene 7

Cut back to breakfast table.
John (as Jack) asks further questions.

Scene 8

Smash cut back to park where John (as Jack) meets Amy.

Scene 9

Smash cut to running interaction (stamina bar).
Onscreen title reads '07:30 Run with Amy'.
John (as Jack) tries to find out more about Jack from Amy.
They finish running.

Scene 10

Cut back to the breakfast table.
Heist set-up continues; now it's the journey to the office(s).

Scene 11

Cut to tube train.
Onscreen title: '08:33 Lie to Shaz'.
Zoom transition.
Outside the tube station, goodbye to Shaz.

Scene 12

Cut back to breakfast table.
Heist set-up continues; now it's the office.

Scene 13

Smash cut to outside the office.
Onscreen text: '08:51 Jack's office'.

Scene 14

Cut back to breakfast table.
Commentary on how to heist the videogame studio office.

Scene 15

Cut to Jack's desk, then zoom back to reveal the receptionist's desk.
Shows Sonya walking in through a glass door.

Scene 16

Cut back to breakfast table.
Heist set-up continues.

Scene 17

Cut back to John (as Jack) approaching the entrance of the office; he sneaks a look.
Onscreen text reads '08:35 Sneak past Sonya'.
A stealth section follows – pastiche.
Sonya spots him.
They have an awkward discussion.
Derek, the boss, makes an appearance (is set-up).

Scene 18

Back to the breakfast table, where Jack (as John) explains what he needs to know about the scrum meeting he'll run.

Scene 19

John (as Jack) does a bad job of running the scrum meeting.

Scene 20

Cut to general office scene; John (as Jack) gets a taste of the game they're working on.

Scene 21

Derek, the boss, calls John (as Jack) into his office by shooting a nerf gun at him (character pay-off from earlier set-up).

Scene 22

Derek asks John (as Jack) to 'crunch' because of a publisher visit (overtime without pay).
John (as Jack) is shocked and refuses to work on a weekend – he has Molly to look after, after all. They argue.

Scene 23

Exterior: John's tower block.
Interior: Jack (as John) enters the flat.
Jack (as John) admits that he was fired.
John (as Jack) admits that he was fired too.
Disaster! They decide to eat a cheesecake as consolation.
Zoom out from the apartment as they quip back and forth.
End of 'Paper Dolls', Chapter 3

Key Takeaways

- The use of the heist format provides a recognisable structure with which to develop the body-swapped characters and their buddy-comedy development.
- Regular but inconsequential choice gives the player a part to play in producing the pleasing rhythm of the fast-paced storytelling, but keeps writing carefully scoped and the player's choice-making time tightly paced.
- Excellent dialogue, characterisation, and voice acting allow the storytelling to focus on the fast pacing. You feel in safe hands in knowing who people are, when they're talking, and what the register and perspective of each character is.
- Overall, the fast pacing, growing solidarity of the characters, and pleasing rhythms of the player interaction work together to a produce a lightweight, easy-to-follow comedy chapter, which in turn compliments the other more complex and darker threads inhabiting the same story space.

Further Reading

Here are a few ways you could expand your thinking on format. First up, one of the clearest writers I've read on structure at work in storytelling is David Edgar.

- David Edgar, *How Plays Work*

Then, pair that serious thinking with one of my favourite movies that crams in so many formats in one (sport, double date, road trip, meal out, dinner party, wedding, New Year's Eve – more!).

- *When Harry Met Sally* (1989), directed by Rob Reiner, written by Nora Ephron

And here's five actual heists: two contemporary movies, two TV episodes, and one more 'classic' heist. Watch at least three of these and consider how the older example feels compared to the more contemporary ones. In what moment does the affecting and otherwise complex *The Farewell* suddenly find itself behaving like a heist movie? How does *Hustlers* frame and comment on the heist genre? And how do the long-running TV shows make use of or pastiche the format?

- *The Farewell* (2019), directed and written by Lulu Wang
- *Hustlers* (2019), directed and written by Lorene Scafaria
- 'Badda-Bing Badda-Bang', season 7, episode 15 of *Star Trek: Deep Space Nine*
- 'Pink Champagne on Ice', season 4, episode 19 of *The Mentalist*
- *The Killing* (1956), directed by Stanley Kubrick

This is the end of the short Case Studies part of the book. I hope that these three short glances at dialogue and characterisation, NPCs and ethical storytelling, and the use of format in a game's storytelling have given you a useful foundation for applying some of the theory of Part I.

We've taken a deep dive into theory, seen it in application in these examples, and now we're going to move into the final part of the book. In Part III we look at means of providing you with questions, tools, and exercises for developing your own practice.

As ever, if you've been reading for a while, now is a good time to make some notes, take a break, make a hot chocolate, or go and look at some nice trees.

PART III
A Practical Workbook

CHAPTER 14

Introduction to the Workbook

This part of the book is what I'm calling a 'workbook'. Consider it me offering you a look into my old grizzled toolbox; a bunch of tools which are hard won, hand worn, and fit perfectly in the palm of my hand. But just because they work for me, doesn't mean they will work for you too. You should weigh each one in your hand, see if you like the heft of it, and if it doesn't work (1) that's okay and (2) remember to ask yourself why. You will learn as much about you and your personal practice by considering why something that works for someone else doesn't work for you. Maybe it's too formal (after a decade of working to brief, I tend to like to set up each stage of a process with restrictions in order to form my own), or perhaps the form works but the headings don't. Do you need to start in a different space? Do you need to draw to think? Do you need fully formed characters before you can hear them speak? Or can you hear a voice and shape a character around it?

DOI: 10.1201/9781003182832-18

Before we get to the tools themselves, here are some foundational questions, the answers for which will prepare you for the task of listening to yourself as you get a feel for what works for you and what doesn't.

Know Thyself

Writer, know thyself. In building your practice in writing for games (or any medium for that matter) you will do so best if you also build your self-knowledge. From what hour of the day you're most productive, to how much procrastination is a necessary part of your process. Do you need pen and paper? Do you need to doodle? Do you need Wikipedia deep dives while thoughts percolate? Do you need peers to bounce ideas off of? Do you need silence, music, or the background hum of a café to do your best work? You may not always be able to work in your best-case scenario, but knowing what it is allows you to make the best compromises.

Here are some questions and principles to pose to yourself; you may want to pull up a doc, a notes app, or a pen and paper to think out loud about these things.

How Do You Learn?

Very early on in the book I spoke about how everyone learns differently. We tend to shape formal education around a one-size-fits-all model (not that good educators aren't trying to redefine and repurpose it for more learning styles), which leaves a good proportion of people leaving education thinking that learning is remembering and exams. But there are many other kinds of learning, and the best way you can grow is to understand how you learn best.

Perhaps there was a certain point in your life when you learned something (it doesn't have to be school; it could be sports, or a videogame, or a recipe) and you really felt like you were *excelling* – in that moment it was very possible that you were also being taught in a way that worked for you. Was it a drama teacher encouraging you to read Shakespeare out loud rather than in your head? Or a tennis instructor moving your arm through the whole swing of the racquet to correct your technique? Perhaps you follow recipes on video better than in a book?

Now think about yourself as a writer. In what way do your instincts lean? Visual? Auditory? Written? Perhaps you learn best by copying (covering) other works (fan art, fanfic) and unpicking how they work by trying them yourself? Perhaps you like formal exercises, boxes to fill out, neat pieces of process to tick off? Perhaps you like to be left alone with a free-roaming brain? I can't name every form of inspiration or process here, but I'm certain you have an instinct for this about yourself. Take a moment or two to think through this question: *How do you learn?*

How Do You Work?

You are not a brain on a stick. You are a fully embodied human *being*. Not just a human *doing*. Your environment, body, material conditions are all part of you being a writer. And you need nourishment. That might be meditation, yoga, sport, walks, reading, time with friends and family, rest, sleep, food, water, time of day, lots of small tasks or one big luxurious task, stress levels, sound levels, ambient temperature, space to spread out, lots of collaboration or lots of alone time, and so on. If you are malnourished in any of these areas, it will be harder to work.

Part of your process should understand your needs as a body, not just a brain, and if they are hampered, for example, by a noisy office, get those noise-cancelling headphones. If you work best in collaboration with others but you have to work solo on a project, you might need to construct a back-and-forth dialogue with yourself, reach out to peers in exchange for the same for them, or ask for 'idea bouncing' time with a member of your team as part of your process. Knowing how you work best allows you to get closer to optimal in other people's processes. And usually, the answer is paying attention to things that aren't work, like sleep and exercise and leisure time. So, tell me: *How do you work?*

How Do You Reflect?

You cannot learn, and you cannot do good writing, without some means of reflection and crit. Critique (a kind of active reflection) helps you learn from the work of others; personal reflection helps you learn about your own process and work. When I bring interns onboard at the company I run, I encourage them (by buying them a very nice special notebook and pen) to write a little at least once a week about what they learned. Early in my career I had a notebook of things I wouldn't accept/do again (this may seem a little negative but it was useful for me). In arts education, you're very typically taught that evaluation and reflection is a part of the learning process, but it can be easy to leave this part out of 'real' life.

I encourage you to think about what *would* work in your practice as a means of reflection. Is it a diary? Is it discussing exercises with a group of peers? Is it a game equivalent to a book club? It doesn't matter as long as you're taking time to think about what you did, why you did it, what worked, and what didn't. Or what another maker did, what effect it had on you, how it had that effect, or how it was unsuccessful. As time moves on you will discover the terrible power of looking at the stories you see in the world the way a mechanic looks at a car. You will hear the tone of the engine that sounds wrong, you will anticipate the electrical failure before it happens, and no one will want to be around you and a car except other mechanics.

I've done enough with that metaphor. But think, how do you best reflect? It doesn't have to be in one way – perhaps you enjoy reading critical analyses and also find a weekly work diary useful. Perhaps you need peer-mentoring relationships and to listen to masterclass talks to reflect on your practice. Perhaps you need solo structure – like an article writing project – or a group structure so you're held accountable. There are many ways to reflect; you just need at least one.

Knowing this about yourself will not only help you learn, work, and develop, but it will also help you identify whether things aren't working well because of you or because of things

177

out of your control. Reflection can help you sift through an experience and with a little distance and perhaps discover that there was no way for you to succeed this time. The lesson then is to find the most ethical way of acting within a state of failure.[1]

So, tell me: *How do you reflect best?*

Pathfinding

Many of the people I have taught and mentored as they try to move into games storytelling are people who are bridging the tricky gap between education and practice. The task of mentoring them seems to me to mostly be about reassuring them that they don't have to go from a world of structure to a world of formlessness, or from a world of teachers to a world that feels directionless. Instead, bridging from education to practice is about building a teacher in your own head; a voice that will counsel you, help you reflect, and help you build the structures or environment that you need to progress.

Many people will have some idea of 'what they want to do' – usually it's a job title – but very few will be able to secure that position straight away.

So, what can a pathway there look like? Perhaps you could look up that job description on a couple of company websites, and split up the experience and skills into a number of steps/ other positions? Or look at the portfolios and CVs of others in that position. Never fall into the trap of modelling your pathway on someone else's, however. It's most useful to think of your progress as a number of pathways you could take – some well-trodden, others might be yours to uncover – and part of striking out will be cultivating a self-mentor, an inner voice that you can check in with, with which you can set yourself exercises, form peer-crit groups, plan, and learn and reflect with.

Here are three principles of pathfinding I often find myself presenting to people at the beginning of their journey:

1. Don't be afraid to change direction.
   Listening to yourself includes listening to your discomfort – with people, process, and roles. Maybe the person you thought you wanted to be turned out to not suit you? That's such a valuable realisation. Don't pin success on the place you imagine you want to end up; pin success on the process of pathfinding itself. As long as you're moving forwards, that's success. I offer you this question: *How will you check in with yourself about your direction?*

2. Are you a scout or an A–B person?
   Some people can see precisely where they want to be, break it down into steps, and then follow the steps to reach it. Well done for these people. They should write one-, three-, and five-year plans, and follow them. I call these people A–B people. Things can

---

[1] *Star Trek* fans will recognise me gesturing towards the incredibly helpful Kobayashi Maru metaphor here.

feel a little easier for an A–B person, who will always go into a mentorship or a position knowing what they need. I am an A–B person, and while A–B people can look very 'together' from the outside, it's not the only way to pathfind in your practice and career.

Some people's brains don't work like that; they might not know what they want from life, or where they want to be in one-month's time, let alone five years. I call these people 'scouts' – like in a game of *Civilisation*, where you send someone out to uncover the map: it's okay to try a direction, find out it's not for you, then try another. When I support A–B people, part of the work is teaching them something that scouts are already good at: it's okay not to know. If you're a scout, the way you're used to pathfinding is to strike out, then check in with yourself.

The key to both of these processes is self-reflection. If a scout can trust that they're a scout and that it's okay to be so, they're often better at self-reflection, because every step on their pathway is a moment to check in: what did I learn, how do I feel, continue this way or try something else? A–B people can be excellent at the initial burst of self-reflection – where do I want to be – and what might that look like as a series of waypoints, but then build themselves a ladder instead of a pathway, and end up at the top of it before realising that's not where they want to be. Maybe you're a mix of these; that's okay too. Perhaps the metaphor doesn't work for you at all. The essential question here is intended to help you think through what kind of voice you need to build in your head, and if you know how you learn and reflect – applying that with your inner mentor as you build your path.

How do you pathfind?

3. Don't underestimate the value of your peers.

You can certainly shortcut/complement your learning, reflection, and pathfinding through external mentorship. People a few steps ahead of us in life can often offer reassurance, tools, and insight – but never underestimate the value of peer mentorship. Your peers – whether those also switching industries, those graduating with you, or those entering work–life with you on other terms – are the people who will grow *with you*. You can learn together, crit together, reflect together, all in a space of hitting the same hurdles at the same time. Pooling your experience, connections, and learning with your peers will be easier because the advantages will be totally mutual. What's more, as you move further along your practice pathway and begin turning work down, you will be able to suggest your excellent peers in your place.

When you go to events and are encouraged to network, it can be as useful to find kindred spirits in the same place as you as it can be to find people further along their pathways. So, here's your next question: *Who is walking their pathway alongside you? How can you connect with them?*

Practice Is Not Career

Here's the piece of advice I think is the most universally useful thing I say to early-stage practitioners:

Your practice is not your career.

That is, your practice and development as a storyteller is in your hands. The people who hire you, on the other hand, are in control of your career.

Of course, they feed into one another, but if you see success as a practitioner in a job title, you will always be fighting for something that is in someone else's hands. However, if you think of your practice as yours, it can be much more empowering. You can tend to your practice even when your job is completely unrelated. You can also steer less related jobs towards developing your practice. You can build peer-crit groups, attend game jams, set yourself a year's curriculum of exercises which uses an evening a week to build portfolio pieces and practise your skills, or you can spend time learning from practitioners online.

You don't need anyone's permission to be a storyteller.

There are degrees of privilege at work here. For example, if you have no savings, are caring for children, and live with a chronic illness, your time, energy, and priorities will be very different to someone whose rent is being paid by a family member, is childless, and not living with illness or disability. So, part of tending to your practice is absolutely assessing at what pace you can work and where it can come. Sometimes that might look like a day job where you steal time to work on your own things.[2] The systems of labour and how they intersect with health and caring responsibilities are monumentally fucked already, so I encourage you to fuck it right back.

But as a larger principle, in working out how to tend to your practice, ask yourself these questions:

- What is sustainable? (Plan weeks off, listen to your body, accept it's okay for it to take time and that you might move at a different pace to your peers.)
- What do you need to develop? (Is it skills? Portfolio pieces? Experience? Work out what you can tackle first and what might need to come later.)
- How can you exploit the work you do get? (It exploits us, so how do you exploit it back? If you're hired as an intern and they only give you admin tasks to do, why not ask if you can have a monthly mentoring session with someone in a role you're interested in? Why not ask if you can shadow some meetings? The worst someone can say is no.)

You may also find that you can create opportunities with your peers. If you work on a small self-contained project with another peer you will learn more about team work, collaboration, communication, and end up with a portfolio piece. If you form a company with peers, you don't need someone else's permission to release a game. If you are doing a game design degree, please recognise how privileged you are to have your main occupation be this thing. Use this time to find collaborators and try to produce works. Maybe you will

---

[2] I know plenty of writers who do this and, honestly, wage theft is so rampant I consider this a pretty righteous practice.

find yourself able to form a company with the help of university biz-dev resources, and (in Europe at least) seed funds and grants for young businesses.

Let's form the conclusion to this section as a number of questions (feel free to add to them):

What are your practice goals?
    What kind of storytelling are you interested in?
    What skills do you need for that?
    What do you need to develop?
    What can you develop right now, and how?
    What needs to come later?
    What time do you need for that?
    If you were a mentor, listening to these answers, what advice would you give?

What are your career goals?
    What size of studio do you want to work for/with?
    What is important to you about your work?
    What culture/environment is important to you?
    In what kind of culture/environment do you thrive?
    What genres/types of work are you interested in?
    What experience do you need for the roles you're interested in?
    If you were a mentor, listening to these answers, what advice would you give?

Before we move into the 'tools' chapters, take your time to just reread the questions posed in this introduction. Knowing the answers will enable you to shape your pathway into your practice with much more confidence, and they will help you reflect on the tools I'm going to offer with a little more self-knowledge. Trust in yourself, it will help.

Tools

The rest of what I'm presenting in Part III of this book is a number of tools – exercises, questions, and methodologies – that have been useful to me in my practice as a storyteller. I have numbered the exercises sequentially for ease of reference, but you don't need to complete them all or in order.

I'm presenting these tools and exercises under three main themes:

1. Tools for starting
2. Tools for developing
3. Tools for finishing

This sounds very neat, but really in practice you will sometimes come to a piece of work which is already started and you need to do your best to finish, with little time or resources to develop. Or you might use a 'tool for developing' to start with. Or find that 'tools for finishing' is just a bunch of questions, not exercises, and what's that about anyway?

A toolbox isn't always a neat thing, and mine certainly isn't. Learn from how you react to these things, file them somewhere differently if you need, and if this loose collection of tools seems to have something missing, fill in that gap from somewhere else.

CHAPTER 15

Tools for Starting

Everyone starts to formulate a story in different ways. Some with a world; some with characters; some with a theme, feeling, or question. If you're brought in halfway through a game dev process (highly likely) you may already have the key player verbs, genre, and world chosen for you, and have to shape the story around those affordances. In that case then, instead of just using these tools for 'starting' something, consider that they might also be useful tools for you to develop and understand what might be missing from your brief as started by someone else.

But for ease we're just going to call these 'tools for starting'.

1. Seeds (characters, world, or story),
2. Form-driven design – cultivating soil for your seeds
3. Character
4. Other character techniques

DOI: 10.1201/9781003182832-19

5. World sheets
6. Applied story: story-driven puzzle design
7. Brief setting

I tend to have a quite form-based practice. So, I'm also going to remind you of other approaches that I've noted before. If this stuff doesn't suit you, take a look at

- Lynda Barry's *What It Is* (for very visual people)
- Michael Atavar's *How to Be an Artist* (very similar to me, but more of it, really)
- Julia Cameron's *The Artist's Way* (more spiritual, freer and instinct-driven practice)

Seeds

What if you have no idea at all? You're in the remarkable and once-in-a-career position of being given carte blanche to do what you want. Some storytellers are full of ideas and just need support in developing them. But many people struggle with the empty page; that's where defining your *seed strategy* can come in handy.

'Seeds' are the tiny ideas, words, concepts, or strategies which get your creative cogs turning. What works best will be personal to you and the way your brain works. You may even already have seed strategies but not know about them. Here are a number of seed strategies that I know of:

- Collage making – Cut, stick, and build from a collection of magazines to make characters, places, or worlds.
- Blacking out lines and words in a newspaper, magazine, or book until you have a fun line of dialogue or story.
- 'Like X but Y' – Smashing together existing stories/genres/locations/characters. 'Like *When Harry Met Sally*, but queer, and set in the Italian anti-fascist punk scene'. Make yourself a Frankenstein monster of a story. Transpose characters. Steal with abandon. Change names and details until it's something new.
- Images, scraps, and moments in your notes app – Encouraging yourself to note down every time your brain amuses itself with a line, memory, image, etc.
- Julia Cameron's Morning Pages (Cameron, 2016) or other stream of consciousness techniques – Let your preoccupations rise to the surface. Wake up, put pen to paper, and *just write*, write about whatever, if you can't think what to write, write the word 'and' until you have something to say. Write to yourself, someone else, or something made up. If stuck on where to start, turn on the radio, or look on Twitter, or pick a line from a book by your bedside and write that as the title, then write from there. Set a timer for one, three, and five minutes, and see where you get each time. Collect them at the end of the week, and then look through them for cool lines, ideas, thoughts, images, or themes.
- Cuttings – Interesting stories from newspapers, screenshots of tweets, etc. kept in a scrapbook or folder on your computer; organise it how you like.

- Create a biscuit tin or book of scraps – Whether images, words, themes, and pull them out until you feel inspired.
- Exquisite corpse – Character seeds gathered from hundreds of photos, magazine cut-outs, and postcards. Go to charity shops and vintage shops and buy old postcards, photos, or read the inscriptions in books and base a character on them. Cut up a hundred heads, outfits, and backgrounds and pull them together until you meet someone you can hear the voice of, etc.
- Oblique Strategies – Brian Eno's Oblique Strategies offer means of turning ideas on their head for when you feel stuck. You can print these on cards (or buy them preprinted) and pull one out as a seed for a new direction.

The idea is that you discover the best means for you of accelerating ideas for a story or game. Maybe it's a scrapbook, maybe it's your folder of interesting news stories, maybe it's one of the aforementioned strategies adapted to your own needs.

It's worth saying I don't think I've ever – in my entire game writing career – been in the position of starting from scratch, but it is very useful as an exercise nevertheless, and it's also useful sometimes if you're stuck halfway through a story. Pull out a seed, strategy, or scrapbook, and let it guide your mind.

Here's a list of word-based seeds that I print, cut out, and put in little tins to use in writing workshops. Sometimes I add to them, but there seems to be enough here that someone always finds something. It's okay to pick a seed up, find it's not for you, and put it back. I offer these as an example only.

The sea
A sad fox
An antique suitcase
Red Riding Hood
Mermaids
A bird that fell from the nest
A religious medallion
The Golden Gate Bridge
Rooftops
City parks
An ancient ruin
Your 'go' bag
A refugee camp
A run-down spaceship
A game you used to play when you were a child

Your favourite book
A specific geometric shape
A confession
Commuters
A busy badger
A well-known book from your childhood
A children's playground
Silly monsters
Punching Nazis
That day in nature
A specific person
Why can't this fly?
Seven bad mistakes

Exercise 1 (2 × 0.5 days)

Pick a short form of creative writing you work with easily and instinctively, such as a one-page short story, two-page script, short poem, four-panel comic, one-page pitch for a longer work, etc. The idea is that it's a format you don't need to think too much about. You're going to create many of these – at least five.

On the first half day: Pick three to five of the seed strategies listed earlier (and feel free to invent your own), try to make sure there're some big variations (i.e. visual and written), and prepare a number of seeds for each strategy. Take your time with the prep. Spend some time gathering seeds thinking about what feels light, exciting, and sustainable for you.

On the second half day: Whatever short form of writing you've chosen, produce a plan or a quick draft of a new piece using each of the seed techniques you've prepared. At least one new idea per seed strategy. Pick from seeds until you have an idea for a theme, character, poem, scene, or design proposal – whatever it is you're working on. Develop them in ways that feel natural – make notes or draw sketches or whatever works.

It's okay to use more time after the exercise to finish any pieces you enjoy, but this exercise is about *starting*. The point here is working out which techniques you like the most. Work quickly and messily. Don't focus on the works; focus on what gets your brain moving most pleasantly. Spend the end of your half day reflecting on what suited you best and why.

Form-Driven Design

The form is the soil you will plant the seeds of your story in. Some seeds won't grow as well in certain soils (although sometimes you don't get a choice on that either). Let's say you have a seed – a story you want to tell (or retell) – and maybe you feel like you know how you want to tell it and what that means for the writing, or maybe you have no idea. Either way this form-driven design exercise is an excellent means of thinking through both; a tool for assessing the best way to plant and nourish a seed.[1]

This is definitely narrative design. But sometimes doing narrative design exercises will help you understand how your writing decisions will fit in.

Exercise 2 (0.5–1 days)

Pick a seed from the previous exercise or pick a well-known story which is fairly archetypal – something like a folk tale, religious story, or fairy tale will work best. The idea here is not to worry about the sweep of the story, but how the form will allow it to flourish. We're going to design nine different games based on the same seed.

Take the Form-Driven Design Sheet I've put together (see later), and put it into a document you can work into. There are three columns. On the left is an 'aspect' of form which could drive a piece of storytelling. You will be thinking about how to tell the story as if the game was (formal aspect)-driven.

So for example, starting off by thinking about how if it was an audio-driven game would mean thinking about that story beginning with audio. Does it conjure a certain genre or technique, or do you hear a certain kind of sound when you think it? Begin building the idea around that. But in the next row, you're asked to think about an art-driven game, starting by imagining an art style that suits that seed, and exploring the different directions your mind will move in. Each direction should *foreground* that formal aspect.

Then in the final column gather all your learning from this book's theory (Part I) and consider what this might mean for the writing. Line length, game voice, choice, agency, text effects, how much writing, how will you show not tell, etc.

You should end up with many widely different videogame ideas formed around the same seed. Some won't be interesting, some will be intriguing, others might feel like a burst of lightning you want to pursue immediately, but keep on working at the new ideas, don't get sidetracked.

The crucial thing for you here as a writer is that final column. Think through everything we've said about voice, line length, naturalism, tone, genre, and more. Have some fun coming up with the different form-driven game ideas, but think carefully about how that should change the writing brief.

It's totally okay to skip formal aspects which don't work for you, and to add ones that you think would be fun or interesting to work with. Also, feel free to add half a day to prepare the exercise – research and develop your exercise sheet and prepare your seeds in more detail.

---

[1] No, I won't leave that metaphor alone.

Along with the sheet, I've also prepared the following example as though I had selected the seed 'The moon'. I'm writing fast and free and not redrafting anything here.

Example seed: The moon

Example form completion

- Formal aspect: Sound
- Idea description: The moon immediately associates itself with the night – for obvious reasons. I think of owls hooting, I think of insect wings, the rustling of trees, and all those things which are louder at night, all the noises that you hear because of the absence of the day. I begin to think of a game which you navigate by sound, perhaps echolocation, like a bat. Let's also have a collection mechanic, where you have to collect different things from the world by identifying them by echolocation. We should visualise the echolocation nicely, a bit like sending out probes, which colour the world you're exploring. And let's not forget that our seed is the moon, so let's have everything lit by moonlight colours, and let's have a cycle of the moon be the structure of the game. Bat tasks, echolocation, and 28 game-days to complete it in.
- What this means for the writing: A 28-day structure of storytelling. A night-time setting. Because we're starting with sound, and the feeling of quiet, we probably want the writing to be spare and also subtle. How cartoonish are these animals? We should work out if they're animal-animals, that a human is guiding, or if they're people-animals, who might have archetypal characters. What threatens the bat? And what does it value? Let's think of characters or creatures that could challenge its journey. This is writing which should be supportive of a strong mechanic. Let's get a handle on how and why echolocation is challenging and rewarding, and how the skill tree escalates before we know how precisely the plot needs to support it.

Form-Driven Design Sheet

Formal Aspect	Describe the Idea	What Does This Mean for the Writing?
Sound (starting with the sound the seed evokes, or a particular genre or artist)		
Art (either a using the style of a particular artist, or a movement or type of art, e.g. pixel art)		
Aesthetics (to separate this from 'art', check out the MDA game design framework set out by Hunicke, LeBlanc, and Zubek, 2004, to define this, but if a category doesn't make sense to you, skip or refine it)		

Mechanics (the main means the player has of interacting with the game, like 'jump' or 'run' or 'plant seeds')

Gamefeel (focus on the tactile experience of the game – pacing, difficulty, juice)

Character (it's character-driven)

Player (maybe something special about where the player is, how they use their body to play, or how they play with others)

Location (where the player is when they play this as well as where it's set)

Hardware (Is this a mobile game? An installation work? On console? Uses a custom controller?)

Genre – comedy, romance, soap opera, horror (pick one or try many)

Character Sheets

You may be getting the feeling 'wow Hannah sure likes to build a table to do her thinking in', and, well, you would be right. The process of working out what interesting questions to answer is much more useful to me than a blank page. Instead of making things up, all I need to do is answer the questions! This is why we're going to try to do something very much like the form-driven design exercise, but for character design.

A character design sheet is useful because it quickly turns into design proposals, can be easily filed and referenced for people to collaborate on, and you can fill in the details you've already been given in a brief or by a character artist, and develop the rest of the character into something more interesting by filling in the gaps.

If you don't like my fields, try thinking of other fields you can add. A lot of this is basics, but the fields which can provide interesting contrasts are the crux of it for me: have secrets which could undermine goals; have dislikes that clash with the plot or other characters; have primary character traits that are undermined by recessive ones.

For example, take a character whose dominant personality trait is 'eager to learn', but recessive trait is 'rebellious in the face of authority'. Perhaps learning will win out, but if the person they're learning from thinks they are in a position of authority, conflict will emerge. There you go, instant character!

Where does this work in a game development process? Consider the possibility that the characters you've been given to develop are a bit stereotypical. This method is a quick way to weed out stereotypes and usefully complicate them. If you see there, plain on paper, that you've got a female character who is physically weak, young, emotionally intelligent, and with the goal of healing and helping people, then time to rework it or work in some counterpoints to make her more interesting. Another way of avoiding stereotypes is to take the character art and write the most stereotyped version of that character. Then write the anti-version of that.

Here are some exercises to do with the character design sheet – you can do them all or pick whichever you prefer:

Exercise 3 (2 hours)

Try filling out a character design sheet for a well-known character or two to start with. Then ask, Why is this an interesting character?

Exercise 4 (2 hours)

Try creating two new characters of your own design to make an interesting two-person script. Consider their relationship as well as their single characters when working on this. If you're stuck for a starting place for a character, use a quick word-based seed strategy, a single line from a poem, a quote in a newspaper, the writing on the back of an old postcard, etc.

Exercise 5 (2 hours)

Try filling out the character design sheet from some pieces of archetypal character art. Search images online as starting material for this with words like 'wizard', 'witch', 'alien', 'hero', 'heroine', 'drag queen', 'prophet', or look for genre fiction book covers. Imagine you've been brought on to a project and all the characters are already visually designed, and that the character art you've just picked from your search is your starting point. Develop their character sheets, finding those interesting contrasts and contradictions. Do several if you have the time. And try to think about making two or three characters work together interestingly.

Further reading. Remember to reference Nisi Shawl and Cynthia Ward's *Writing the Other: A Practical Approach* as a great primer for some key stereotypes to avoid.

Character Design Sheet

Question	Answer
Name	
Origin/geographical background	
Age	
Gender ID, racial ID, sexual ID, etc.	
Role/job	

Talents/strengths	
Weaknesses	
Goals	
Secrets	
Likes	
Dislikes	
Treasures	
Fears	
Dominant personality traits	
Recessive personality traits	
Other notes	

And here's an example completion for a character design sheet, from a long-ago prototype I worked on, which doesn't have any identifying factors for the project in question:

Name	Captain Marina
Community/origin	Traveller, itinerant, regular on the next ship going somewhere interesting.
Age	62, a very good age for the world.
Gender ID, racial ID, sexuality, etc.	Her racial background is mixed Mediterranean and Indian subcontinent. Bi, cis.
Role/talents	Not actually the captain, she just calls herself that, like, actually uses it as a self-ascribed nickname. Extremely good at navigating, negotiating, and diplomacy when she's motivated to be. Very undiplomatic when she doesn't have anything to gain. Deeply charismatic.
Secrets	She lives with chronic pain (hip joints in particular). Addict to whatever means she can get her hands on to medicate the pain. Lost her only child (at 13, who wanted desperately to be a traveller) a long time ago. Her and her partner decided to part ways and always be travelling in their memory.
Goals	Just wants to be constantly on the move. Also enjoys surrounding herself with smart people in order to be able to disagree with them. Likes to be surrounded by younger people in general. Wants to be in situations which involve smarts and luck to get out of, is tipping over into the dangerous end of this.
Likes	Winning arguments, having the last word, having a full belly, tea, homemade alcohol, not having to stop and reflect.

Dislikes	That her ailments and perceptions around her age makes her unable to enjoy and use her sexuality in the same way as she used to.
Treasures	A locket with a thin rock slice inside, painted with a portrait of her long-lost family. Portable distillery kit. Scrap of fabric – never explained.
Dominant personality traits	Cheeky, puckish, likes to test people, wily, careless with others' emotions, charismatic, usually gets what she wants.
Recessive personality traits	Aggressive, impulsive, unsure what she ultimately wants.

Other Character-Creation Techniques

This is a very 'me' approach to character creation, so if your brain works a little differently, this is where I'm going to offer more ways to think about character creation. Theatre practitioners can be of particular use, visual materials, too, as can theory on character archetypes; it depends on how your brain works.

So, here are a few more techniques for character creation. But remember that you will still need to document them for other members of a game dev team; you may still need to produce a form.

• Things – Start with an item of clothing, a childhood toy, etc.

Exercise 6 (2 hours)

Go to your seeds tin, or a website of childhood treasures, or Pinterest boards (i.e. pick a seed strategy) and pull out *things* – something a character could treasure and/or use regularly. Pick three to five things and build a person around them in a way which feels instinctive to you – a diagram, a list, a voice, a drawing, etc. Ask yourself why this thing is important to them; is it attached to a memory, or turning point, or person who shaped them? Use the things to form a character; make them important in interesting ways.

• Improv – Start with a Mike Leigh-style approach.

Mike Leigh is a devising film director who works with his actors to build characters around people they know from their past. It's a kind of curated improv, where you pick a few people from your past – maybe school, university, a friend's ex (it's better to do with people you don't know so well anymore) – and write down what you know about them, then develop their characters, adding events that happened to them in the present day. The idea is to build the fact with fiction, until you've got someone you know well enough to place in a new plot/story-world, but also know their foundations well enough to know how they might act/speak/look.

Further reading. Devised and Directed by Mik0e Leigh (Cardinale-Powell and DiPaolo, 2013).

Exercise 7 (2 hours)

Pick someone memorable from your early school life or youth. Write down everything you remember about them. Create some headings or other structure that suits you. Then imagine three fictional life events which affected them and changed their character between then and the adult they are in the years that passed since you knew them (or at least ten years on). Change their name. Change where they grew up and note how that reshapes the character. Write a description of them aged 32 as if you're trying to describe them to a stranger. Do not use any identifying details for the original person.

- History – Start with a historical figure.

Cultivate a folder of articles or shelf of books and comics which profile characters from history around the world. Dig into them until you find something interesting; pick and choose aspects from them, build others. Rework it until you have something original.

Exercise 8 (2 hours: 1 hour research, 1 hour working)

Look through a newspaper (online is fine) until you find a profile of someone historical or an obituary from a little while ago. Do one hour of research on that person, keeping notes. Use this as a basis for a character with a new name, age, job, gender, and location, working out how those changes affect the character.

- Seeds – Start with an evocative line from a poem, novel, or play. Build a character from that seed.

Exercise 9 (2 hours)

Use one of the following seeds to draw up a character. Whether it conjures a face, a person you know, an image, memory, or object, follow that seed until you have a sketch, description, or character form completed.

- 'Touch has a memory'. —— John Keats
- 'Home is what you take with you, not what you leave behind'. —— N.K. Jemisin, *The Fifth Season*
- 'His heart is a gnarled knuckle now'. —— Inua Ellams, *The Actual*
- 'Ah, mija! There you go! Rivers flow. A body of water that remains stagnant is just a cesspool, mi amor! It's time to move, flow, grow. That is the nature of rivers. That is the nature of love!' —— Ibi Zoboi, *Pride*

- 'I took a deep breath and listened to the old brag of my heart. I am, I am, I am'. —— Sylvia Plath, *The Bell Jar*
- 'I am my best work – a series of road maps, reports, recipes, doodles, and prayers from the front lines'. —— Audre Lorde

When you've done one or two of these exercises, make sure you take time to reflect and think through what you felt worked best for you, and if there's a combined or wholly different process that could work better – you're building *your* toolkit here, remember.

World Sheets

More sheets! World sheets are really not that far off the character sheet method, but are an example of how if you find something that works for you – lean into it. It's also worth finding ways to really *limit* yourself on worldbuilding, wringing out *precisely what you need to know* and nothing more.

As I've touched on before, worldbuilding is a big old storyteller trap. It's the easiest part to do because it's endless, unstructured, and something you can do in luxurious solitude. The best thing you can do for your worldbuilding is to formalise it – make it so it's only as big as it needs to be, and so that it's well-documented in a way that allows you to add to the things you need to know, in a working document that people actually use.

I'll share my world sheet in a moment, but it's worth noting a few other methods of world generation or development before I do.

1. *The Quiet Year* – A pen-and-paper tabletop role-playing game (published by Buried Without Ceremony) where you play as a community in the first quiet year after a crisis. The instructions invite you to invent the terrain, resources, and scarcities together with the people you are playing with. I strongly recommend anyone interested in collaborative worldbuilding, or worldbuilding in general, take a look at this game. You can do it solo as a world-creation exercise or with others to begin working out a world together. Find it at buriedwithoutceremony.com/the-quiet-year (Board Game Geek, n.d.)
2. Start with 'real' places – Just like the character-generation idea of building on a historical place, use a real place, or several real places and their relationships (i.e. London vs. Paris), and work out what the 'London' of your world is and where is its 'Paris'. Write out what makes London, London, and Paris, Paris. Change details until it's interesting or new.
3. Visual methodologies – Whether Pinterest, collage, or collaborating with an artist. Find art of a place or several places. Think through what the layers of architecture, layout, and terrain would mean for resources and the people who live there; the tensions of class, labour, and technology which might be at play.

But here's the technique I use: another form. Again, it's about finding interesting tensions. I start with communities, but maybe you might start with the whole world/region. You can design your own forms by simply changing the terms or questions.

Exercise 10 (2–4 hours)

Pick two of the three starting points listed earlier and create at least one place sheet for a fictional city or community, using each starting point, dividing your time like this: spend one hour preparing, and one hour working per method/place.

Make sure your second place is an interesting contrast to your first place – you're aiming to set them in the same world. So, think about the tensions between them which might make them feel interesting to visit.

Place Design Sheets

Name of Community
Summary
What is it built on? (What is the environment/weather like? Architecture?)
Age of community (perhaps who it was founded by)
Make-up of the people (Young? Predominantly Black? United by a political or religious belief? Or mixed in ways X, Y, or Z?)
Role/talents of the people in the wider world
Secrets of the past, present or future
Goals of community
How do outsiders perceive the community?
Technology, labour, and class?
Resources
Scarcity
How is it organised? (What are its politics? Religions? Conflicting or overriding beliefs?)
Cultural notes
Key figures/characters
What unites people?
What divides people?

And here's one filled out for a prototype on which I worked as part of a funding bid, but now looks very different and doesn't contain this community.

Name of Community	Trash Island
Summary	Trash Island is a community built on a floating trash dump, based on the Great Pacific Garbage Patch.
What is it built on? (What is the environment/weather like? Architecture?)	Trash Island is floating community built on a great mound of trash. The island inhabitants have no control over its movements. Weather changes with their position, and the architecture is of a 'long faded brightly coloured plastics' variety. Very different to the wood/stone of most other communities.
Age of community (perhaps who it was founded by)	Unknown/from the beginning of the end.
Make-up of the people (Young? Predominantly Black? United by a political or religious belief? Or mixed in ways X, Y, or Z?)	As varied as the colour of the ground they stand on. It attracts people who wish to vanish, let go of their tethers, or live more day-to-day. There is, however, a very strong hierarchy on the island, and a 'ruling family' who has been on the community – as far as anyone knows – since the end.
Role/talents of the people in the wider world	They are a people who can make anything from anything, and keepers of strange old words and colours. You never expect them, but you always check in with them if they appear nearby.
Secrets of the past, present, or future	There is a succession struggle in the core family of the internal hierarchy, of which the Matriarch is head. Niamh, the child chosen to learn from and become the Matriarch's successor, wishes to leave the community, not stay on a place ever-on-the-move.
Goals of community	Simply to maintain their way of life, whether through rules and hierarchies (they have to be careful about their internal community justice, as they welcome many outcasts from other communities) or through trading for what they need to survive.
How do outsiders perceive the community?	The moving island gives them an itinerant reputation which combined with the trash makes them looked down upon by some people – at best unreliable and mercurial, at worst too strange to be taken seriously.
Technology, labour, and class?	Strict sense of hierarchy to do with how recently arrived you are, and how close to the centre your dwelling area is, newcomers often establish floating outcrops, and the island grows in that way. Technology is many and varied but always scavenged, a lot of people fascinated in older materials end up here. People keep what they produce and trade 'fairly' as assessed by the island trade arbiter. Arbiter has been known to take bribes. Central family takes 'gifts' in exchange for the security and community justice they argue they provide – there is a tension there.

Resources	They have a great deal of ancient non-degradable materials which they repurpose and therefore trade in precious and strange items – but you never know when they will be nearby. It moves slowly and seasonally with the prevailing currents, and is rumoured to have been in the frozen north for a generation, and still prize the pelts they (say they) got there. Their wide reach also means they have broad information on the world and are sometimes sought out for that.
Scarcity	Natural resources, materials, food, and soils aren't found on trash island, so wools, natural cloth, wood, and ground-based foodstuffs are scarce. They subside on seaweed cultivation, and trained seabird fishing, but a lot of their trade is for food.
Cultural notes	There is a local tradition of experimental musical instrument building and every year there's a great concert where they exhibit their work.
Key figures/ characters	The Matriarch, the Arbiter, the heir, and an outside-edge agitator who's interested in using the heir's reluctance to overturn the Matriarch's family and set up a different order.
What unites people?	Their itineracy and that most have been drawn to the island to escape something else.
What divides people?	This brings together so many different cultures and experiences and languages that there are a lot of clashes.

Applied Use of Sheets: Story-Driven Puzzle Design

The examples I've shared so far for 'how to start' are for pretty independent story-only contexts, a situation which is fairly rare as a writer in games. It's much more likely most of that work will already be done when you're brought on board, and it's also likely that your role will need to cross over with a number of disciplines and collaborators. So, we're going to take time here to draw this learning together into a more practical application.

This exercise is a much more detailed and specific example of the places where writing and storytelling will cross over with design in game dev, and guide you in thinking about how you can use these form-based approaches to help you start and collaborate on producing story for game design features.

We're going to take a look at a means of thinking through collaborating – as a writer – on a puzzle. And on making that puzzle's design story-driven, rather than parallel and unconnected to the story.

This is another area which is going to look a lot like narrative design – and much of it is. But often you'll need to understand the narrative design to derive how your writing will work with it, to understand the *motivations for your characters* and the *mode* of your writing.

The first part of this section is going to set some context for the exercise and give you some resources for understanding the narrative design underpinnings for a piece of story-driven puzzle design. Then the second part will help you draw up a brief to inform your writing.

It's rare that a game dev process will ever be as well organised as this, but thinking through it formally here will help you draw on structures when you're not provided with them – again, helping you request a better brief if it's not given to you, and allowing you to advocate for story if you need to. It might just be advocating to be in the room where the level design is developed or to receive updates on it, or it might be that you need to communicate that there's a narrative design vacuum in the process, and step into it or ask who's taking care of it.

First: context. One of the most clear-headed explorations of story-driven puzzle design I've read was in a series of blog posts by Frictional Games. I recommend reading in particular these posts:

- 4-Layers, A Narrative Design Approach (Grip, 2014)
- Puzzles in horror games. Part 7 (Grip, 2009)
- The Five Foundational Design Pillars of *SOMA* (Grip, 2013)

Most formal videogame design processes in studios above a certain size will have a creative vision for the game which articulates 'pillars'. This can mean slightly different things for different studios, but in general they are the key values around which all the design operates. If a feature or piece of work doesn't add to or develop one of the pillars, it's probably not something that should go in the game. In this case study we're going to assume that you're working on a project that uses the five foundational design pillars of *SOMA* (a survival horror videogame released in 2015).

In Part I, I asked you to think about the relationship of the story to the player's agency and what that means for the quality of your storytelling. Well here's the pillars of SOMA as a possible answer to that question:

- Everything is story.
- Take the world seriously.
- The player is in charge.
- Trust the player.
- Thematics [*sic*] emerge through play.

(Grip, 2013)

As a brief, these pillars tell you that the gameplay is story-driven. That the tone of the game is that it takes itself and its characters seriously (naturalistic). That the player's agency/empowerment (ability to explore, feel mastery of, and effect the game world) is the highest priority. And that they want a level of subtlety which doesn't signpost things too heavily – the mastery should feel fairly won. Then finally, the themes of the storytelling should emerge through the action.

How could you apply this to story-led puzzle design? I would suggest this means that any puzzle presented to the player in the game should *contain interactions that make narrative sense*. A puzzle should offer the player actions that, as Grip puts it:

- Move the story or characters forward.
- Help the player understand or develop their role.
- Are coherent with the storytelling.
- Are not just there as padding.

(Grip, 2014)

For Grip, that means that when designing puzzles, they *avoid repetition* so that the player doesn't get comfortable with the systems they engage with and begin to see them as ordered rather than organic, which changes your relationship to the game (some puzzle games excel by being systems-focussed, but in a story-driven setting you need to take an approach more akin to the one described by Grip):

Repetition leads to us noticing patterns, and noticing patterns in a game system is not far away from wanting to optimize them. And once you start thinking of the game in terms of "choices that give me the best systemic outcome", it takes a lot of focus away from the game's narrative aspects.

(Grip, 2014)

Agency is important, otherwise it can feel like player-facing padding. And Grip develops the idea of 'agency' beyond moving parts in a puzzle, focussing of variation as a means of developing varied pacing:

In order to make the player feel agency, there must be some sense of achievement. The challenge needed to evoke this sense of accomplishment does not have to be skill or puzzle-based, though. Here are a few other things that could be used instead: memory tasks, out-of-the-box thinking, grind, endurance tests, difficult story choices, sequence breaks, understanding of the plot, exploration, navigation, maze escape, overcoming fear.

(Grip, 2014)

And for Grip, *story is important*, otherwise it can feel like game-facing padding. For that reason, he advocates for the principle that they *attach each puzzle to a story goal or plot point* in order to maintain the player's connection to the story. Examples provided are mystery (discover the unknown), uncomfortable environment (which drives you to want to escape), or character conflict [what affect will the player's actions have on the character(s)].

Before I reach the exercise here, an aside on the puzzle genre: if you're new to videogames, I recommend you definitely build yourself a list of well-known games in different genres and watch YouTube playthroughs of them – or play them yourself – because each genre has a lot of affordances, variation, and established languages. Not only are there different kinds of puzzle game, but there are a fair number of individual kinds of puzzle to be found in adventure games and story-driven puzzle games. I've summarised some of the most well-known puzzle types I can think of in this short and non-exhaustive list:[2]

- Reveal (hidden information revealed by action)
- Item use (key in lock)
- Hidden lever/mechanism (a switch)
- Code breaking (deciphering information)
- Timing (right timing of actions)
- Maze (navigate an environment)
- Order of operations (right combination of actions)
- Privileged information (i.e. knowing a password)

So, having laid all of these contexts and principles let's take a look at an exercise in how, if given the task of 'do some writing for this puzzle in the context of these principles', you could start by setting a narrative design brief in order to understand how your writing should fit in.

Exercise 11 (1 day, or 2 × 0.5 days)

Design a puzzle for a story-driven puzzle game using the following form.

Assumptions:

- You are working under the design pillars set out by Frictional Games.
- You have been asked to be part of a small team of one programmer, one level designer, a 3D artist, and you – a writer, to come up with a puzzle that works within those pillars.
- Your proposal will need sign off from a creative director.
- Take a well-known nursery rhyme, film or TV show, or fairy tale, and imagine that is the 'world' in which your puzzle is set.
- Choose a part of that story – a particular beat in the story – and devise a puzzle the player might experience in that moment that would be coherent and compelling.

For example:

The Little Mermaid story beat: The point at which she chooses to give up her voice for legs.
Red Riding Hood story beat: The very beginning Red Riding Hood, establish the character of Red herself.
The Hunger Games story beat: Katniss Everdeen goes into the forest where she is forbidden to hunt and begins to think about her father.

---

[2] If you can think of others, well done, but do not @ me.

For the first half days do research and note taking, reread this section, read the further reading suggestions, take a look at some online examples in no-commentary playthroughs. Make notes about how you want to approach the exercise.

For the second half day design the puzzle. Combine the form-driven design 'how to start' methodology and pillar-based thinking in a multidisciplinary design context to answer the questions in the Puzzle Design Form. Work in any order, filling out the answers that are the most obvious first.

Puzzle Design Form

Puzzle name (you need to be able to communicate about it with the team)

Story beat (describe the story form and content it needs to hold up)

Narrative intention (how should it move the story or characters forward and define how you fulfil your pillars)

Puzzle description (you won't fill this out until you have a clear idea of the puzzle proposal)

Puzzle type (try out a few; what feels like it fits best?)

Puzzle items (this will be valuable for the art team; they might request fewer or less complicated assets)

Player objective

Player action(s)

How does the puzzle relate to the player's role?

How does the puzzle hit or relate to the story beat?

How should the player feel?

What hints would you give the player? (Diegetic? Non-diegetic?)

Puzzle principles (How it interacts with the principles of the game, other puzzles, etc. Does it break the sequence of other puzzles? Add to the skills for later puzzles? Interact in other ways?)

Other notes (perhaps references to influences)

What this means for the writing (Line length, monologue or dialogue, head voice or spoken out loud. Should writing be sparse, be triggered by objects or interactions, be timed, or be triggered by the player? Read back through Part I: Theory for more considerations you might think of.)

Exercise 11a (0.5 days)

Use the Puzzle Design Form to produce a one-page design proposal, followed by a one- to two-page script or spreadsheet of writing for the puzzle. This could be an excellent portfolio piece.

Exercise 11b (0.5 days)

Bearing in mind the variation and repetition pillar, design the next puzzle the player will encounter. What beat is it attached to, and how do the two puzzles together develop and serve the design pillars?

Following is an example of the Puzzle Design Form filled out for an imagined horror game set in a remote Scottish island, where the player is trying to escape a pursuing mythical creature. It's loosely based on a puzzle design I did for something I worked on about five years ago. I'm not sure whether the work is being used in that unreleased game, so I've changed details and settings so it's not identifiable. It's something I did in five minutes to demonstrate how I wanted to work with the puzzles in a level, so it isn't thrilling, but it suffices to demonstrate what I mean by the headings in the form, and how you can use it to think through story-driven puzzle design. I've left out some of the headings, as I would expect you to, in order to find what I needed to support my thinking.

Puzzle name	Seek Sanctuary in the Kirk. Short name: Seek Sanctuary.
Puzzle description	Landslides have recently caused damage to the kirk. The door is locked. Scaffolding covers one side of the building. On exploring the side of the kirk, the player discovers scaffolding, and sees affixed to it the sign "No unauthorised access, alarmed" (handwritten in local dialect). You find a chain you can unhook that will lower a ramp that allows you to climb up to the scaffolding and access the kirk. The alarm is activated. The sound attracts the creature – currently thought to be a rabid dog. To solve the puzzle, you must realise that you need to run away – if you stay, you will be killed. When you return after seeking a separate hiding place, the alarm has run out of power, and you can now access the kirk.
Puzzle type	Order of operations.
Puzzle items?	Key assets: Scaffolding A sign that reads *No unauthorised access – alarmed* (or similar, handwritten in local dialect) A chain to pull A metal staircase that lowers when you pull the chain An alarm with a primed, active, and inactive state
Objective	The player's objective is to escape the area on their way to the harbour. They may also want to access the people they thought they heard in the kirk in Act I, thinking that they may be able to help.
Narrative intention (how does it move the story forward)	The player moves to a new area (the kirk), which will masquerade as hope, but turns out to reinforce and develop the plot against them – their Samhain whisky tour has turned into something rotten. In entering and exploring the kirk they begin to understand that the creature isn't a rabid dog, and the religious setting provides a spiritual underpinning for understanding that the situation might be supernatural. Going into the kirk is crossing a threshold of understanding and into supernatural rather than mundane horror.

Player actions and consequence	In Act I the player will be attracted to the kirk by apparent singing and lights – further signposted by a comment if you approach within a certain distance. In Act I you can try the door and find out it's locked. On testing the door, the singing abruptly stops (lights go out?). Progression will be unlocked when 60% of the clues in Act I have been uncovered. When the kirk is unlocked the player character will comment on the sign and the pull-chain – they can approach the scaffolding around one side of the building, and can choose to disobey the warning to climb onto the scaffolding by pulling the chain to lower the walkway, in turn setting off the alarm. To solve the puzzle, they must evade the monster somewhere they can reach more quickly that the kirk window (involves too much climbing). Let's discuss what nearby features could be used for this.
How does it relate to the player's role?	It should make them feel like a trespasser. In going against the stated rules. The transgression onto religious ground should also mark the crossing of a threshold from the mundane to the paranormal.
Relation to meta-story	Implicates the kirk in the mystery of the previous Samhain disappearances – sets the player up with the foundation of a paranormal conspiracy in order that they need to uncover the connections between those disappearance in later areas to eventually solve how to escape it themselves.
How should the player feel?	The player should feel like the kirk offers sanctuary against the frightening pursuit of what they think is a rabid dog. Possibly also that there might be a priest or congregation with comfort or explanation within. They should also feel some degree of trepidation, as they are entering a place of worship through a route which is unorthodox and warned against. It needs to feel like an unnatural threshold.
Writing notes	This is a pretty anti-intuitive solution (run away from the thing to access it), so we need to playtest the clues for the right mix of exposition but pleasure in uncovering. The bulk of this work will be through inner monologue; let's produce a number of line alternatives which can be drawn at random so that several playthroughs (as you will likely need to die at least once to solve it) feel rewarding.
Hints?	Most clues delivered as inner monologue by the player character unless obvious assets/environment. Before 60% Act I clues: • The player character should comment that there appears to be a light on in the kirk. • The player should wonder about reaching the priest 'they're always around', 'they'll know what's going on here'. • Strange singing and perhaps a light which stops abruptly if you try and knock on the door. • Further fruitless door knock hints that it might be useful later.

	• After 60% Act I clues: • The player character should wonder if there's another way in after 80% of clues are reached, or 60% plus a time threshold (basically don't let them wander too much). • On proximity encourage the player to reinvestigate. • After dying once, add in a clue before pulling the chain, about it being a risk to attract the monster, and wondering if there's somewhere else to hide. • After dying two times offer a more obvious clue.
Questions or discussion points	I'm not totally satisfied with offering the answer so plainly, but I think it's a nice solution. I wonder if we should work out how to flag the place of refuge more plainly – and what should that be? A nearby tree? Or some other kind of retreat?

If I were to produce example dialogue for this proposal as in Exercise 11a, I would probably draft into a spreadsheet with columns set out in the following table. I would set a line length limit, think about the different stages of the puzzle and concentrate on the inner monologue lines.

Puzzle stages:

- Lines from before the clue threshold is reached which tell you it might be important later, and on reacting to the singing/lights going off.
- Lines to bring you back to the kirk after threshold is reached.
- Lines on proximity and seeing the scaffolding, sign, and chain.
- Unsuccessful lines, after death lines, and puzzle-solve lines.

Example Columns

Line ID#	Trigger	Character	Line Content	Line Char Count	Conditions	Priority or Random
1234	Proximity: Kirk	Jane Doe	Is that … singing?	17	<60% clues	1
1235	1234	Jane Doe	It is!	6	1234 = true && <60% clues	n/a
1236	Proximity: Kirk	Jane Doe	There's a light in the kirk.	28	<60% clues	2

Brief Setting

Hopefully by this point you can see that all of my forms are essentially a means of brief setting. In unstructured creative environments, setting your own brief will quickly tell you what you know, what you need to know, and give you a structure to reach out to the people who've asked you to work with them to fill in the gaps if you need to.

Fairly often in videogames you're brought in halfway through a project and are asked to write but aren't given a good brief. Setting a brief early on and agreeing to it with the creative director or your line manager also allows you to hold them to account, and gives you means to ask for resources and comms if you need them. It gives you something to point at and say 'you asked for this effect, but what you're asking me to do won't have that effect, this will'.

Part I of this book will have hopefully equipped you with a number of headings you could use on a brief. And it can be as broad or detailed as you need, but the key to setting a good brief is knowing how zoomed in or zoomed out you need to be (is this for a single scene or feature, or is this for the whole world you're building).

To set a brief, all you need to do is draw up a form (or start a series of bullet points, or whatever suits you best) and set out headings/questions.

Work out what you know. What you don't know yet. And work with your collaborators to either make requests, or ask to be told what the plans are, so you can do your job well.

Here are some possible headings for a full-game writing brief:

- What is the story meant to do? Drive the action? Support the action? Be a backdrop? Support the puzzles? Drive the puzzles?
- Interactivity/agency – Is there player choice in the story, how does the player choose, how many choices are there, are there multiple middles, endings, or linear plot beats?
- Time – How does time work, and how do you gate story encounters?
- Who's in charge of narrative design and/or making sure other design decisions are understood and reinforced by the writing?
- How is the story told? (Environment, items, dialogue, monologue, narration, barks, etc.)
- Pacing – How do you make sure the story is well-paced?
- Exploration and expressivity – What is the player's freedom to explore and express themselves beyond the writing?
- Naturalistic, cartoonish, archetypal – What style of dialogue is appropriate for the effect they want?
- Art and animation – Style, aesthetics, integration into the story system. Will animations interrupt dialogue or run alongside it?
- Text effects, italics, etc. – What tools do you have to express tone?
- VO and loc – Is this planned and how does it affect your deadlines?
- Character limits – Do any of the UI recommend certain character limits?

- Game mechanics – What are the main verbs the player will use?
- Game genre.
- Story genre.
- For reading only, or for reading and VO?
- Ensemble, party, or protagonist? Who's in the story?
- First person or third person?
- Whom or what do you control?
- Are there words?
- How are they written (using what tools)?
- How are they displayed – What is an appropriate line length?
- What are the documentation standards and how much sign off are you expecting?
- What ESRB/PEGI rating do you need to aim for?
- Values of the team – Are there any key creative values you need to know about?
- Scope – How many hours should this experience last?
- Planning and project management – How long do you have for each phase of the work, and is it enough?
- Replayability – Should it be replayable? What rewards the replay?
- Sequel? Do you need to know what happens next?
- Audience and intention – What do you want the player to feel/experience?
- Team – Who are you working with and signed off by?
- Ethos/ethics of the game and story.

You don't have to present this to anyone else, but knowing the answers will help you make your writing the best it can be and help you find answers where they're lacking.

Here are some examples of headings for a brief you might use for a single scene:

- Who's in it?
- When does it happen?
- Where does it happen, and what's there?
- What leads in to it?
- What leads out of it?
- What is the writing *doing* (giving clues for a puzzle, developing a relationship, letting the player branch the action, etc.)?
- What has changed by the end?
- Is it optional or mandatory?
- What does the player/character know? Are there any variable checks you need to bear in mind (i.e. certain things in the inventory, or the possibility the game could remember details you can reference, like whether or not they chose to save a cat in a previous scene or if they met a third character before).
- Should there be a choice/multiple middles/multiple outcomes?
- Should it set any variables?
- Is it A, B, or C plot?

- Why is it fun/funny/engaging/compelling? Why does the player care?
- What's a rough appropriate line count/run time? (It's always 30%–50% shorter than you think.)

Come up with an answer to all of these and reference your character and location sheets, then all you need to do is (in your imagination) put the characters in the place, in a situation, and let them talk. Write down what you hear them say, then cut at least half of it, and you have a scene.

Of course, sometimes your brief is '10 × 1–5 word barks for Character X to say when running around Y location' – but that's a good brief! You don't really need to do much more to better define that. My earlier examples are pretty expansive, but hopefully the detail helps you pick and choose what works for you.

Exercise 12 (0.5–1 days)

Pick three games of any genre and on any platform that have writing in them – it's good if they're pretty varied. Pick a scene, moment, or exchange no longer than five minutes (shorter, ideally) from each. Pretend you're the creative director who has imagined that scene. Write a brief for that moment – aimed at a writer. Do this for each game you picked.

Exercise extension 12a (1 day)

You can do the same with each whole game if you like, but that'll take longer. Take half of a day to research and take notes, and write up a brief you'd give a writer coming on board before there's a word written for the game.

Exercise extension 12b (0.5 days)

Once you have at least one brief, think about different ways you could fulfil it other than how the writer did in the original example. Make notes and plan a one-page proposal to the imagined creative director on how you'd approach it, focussing on writing choices, and adding what other support and decisions you might need.

CHAPTER 16

Tools for Developing

If starting is hard, it is at least something you can work on solo. As soon as you're on a team working on a game, the point at which you are developing the storytelling is the point at which your work suddenly has to reach much further, be communicated to far more stakeholders, and change and be changed by the work of many others. You become a small part of the whole, you have to receive and offer feedback, you need to actually write and rewrite. You need to diagnose problems; make proposals; and deal with changing scope, sudden cuts, and the possibility whole swathes of your work might become redundant overnight because of the strains of even a well-run production process.

In this chapter we're going to focus on the skills of developing your writing/storytelling in a videogame context. We'll take a look at crit, feedback and playtesting, developing characters and worlds, editing, diagnosing what's wrong, and tools for collaboration.

I'm also going to take this opportunity to remind you that we're quite a few suggested exercises in and there are going to be quite a few more. Don't get overwhelmed! You could

DOI: 10.1201/9781003182832-20

do all of these exercises, and after a while the products of them will begin to feed into others. But these are mostly for you to pick and choose from. You could build a small curriculum for you and a group of peers. You could plan a year's worth of monthly exercises. Or you could just use each exercise as a thought experiment for how to think about things as processes and devise your own exercises. If you feel overwhelmed, put the book down, and come back to it later. These are tools, you don't need all of them, you don't need any of them – you just need to work out how you want to relate to them.

Here's a detailed summary of what we'll focus on in this chapter — some with context and short exercises, and some with more expansive exercises, like the two-day dialogue workshop with a number of tools to help you write better character-driven naturalistic dialogue.

1. Critical response theory – a critical mindset and how to take feedback; also touching on playtesting and when it isn't useful
2. Prototyping and how tools shape your thinking
3. Developing character voices – a two-day dialogue workshop
4. Developing story
5. Learning to edit
6. Diagnosing what's wrong
7. Advocacy, diversity, and representation
8. Tools for collaboration – design documentation
9. What happens when you don't get what you need from the tools, features or additions that you asked for
10. Writing is cheap

Further reading. I recommend checking out the middle of Michael Atavar's *How to Be an Artist.* It's a whole book of exercises and provocations, and is where I've drawn my 'tools for starting, developing and finished' framework from. The middle is all about developing writing.

Critical Response Theory

As you set out to tend to your practice over your lifetime, a crucial part of your developing it will be developing a thorough understanding of how to apply and receive feedback.

You will not improve as a maker unless you employ and can accept critique. And in cross-disciplinary contexts you may also find yourself needing to set boundaries and frameworks for others in order to receive useful feedback. But offering crit/feedback isn't always a part of games education, so how do you cultivate feedback?

I'm going to share the most useful framework for critique that I've come across, but the point is not to apply the whole process, but rather to understand how and why it works, and turn to it when you need. Which could be as simple as saying 'don't pay attention to X and

Y, they're placeholders, please tell me what you think of Z, and if it will be okay for the art department's workload, and fulfils the pillars of our game satisfactorily'.

Liz Lerman's Critical Response Process is something I came across when I was a devising theatre maker. As part of the devising process, you will often have 'work-in-progress showings' where you take a week or two's work in the rehearsal room to a general or invited audience, and try it out in front of them. You'd immediately get a feel for structure, pacing, and audience response in the room, and then in a post-showing discussion, you invite the audience to offer feedback. Liz Lerman's process is a means of structuring a feedback session for the most useful feedback possible and in preparing the artist to receive it in the most useful mode.

There's a book, *Liz Lerman's Critical Response Process: A Method for Getting Useful Feedback on Anything You Make, from Dance to Dessert* (Lerman and Borstel, 2003), and a very well-resourced website which expands on it (lizlerman.com/critical-response-process), and I encourage you to dig deeper beyond my simplified explanation here.

Roles

In considering how to manage feedback, it's important to consider the roles in both mediating it and in receiving it. You need to be in the right place for receiving feedback – both in process and in your mind. So too does the person offering the feedback need to be in the right mindset to support development and direct change. In this process there is also a facilitator, though often the artist or creative director who's offering feedback in the role of 'responder' could also structure the feedback. These are the roles in Lerman's framework:

- The artist
- The responders
- The facilitator

The Artist

The artist (for us, specifically, the writer in a game design team) needs to be ready and open to offering their work in progress. That means that they understand the context of the feedback (where they're at, what they hope it will discuss), that they have questions they want answered, and that they also know what they don't want feedback on. They need to be prepared to question their work in conversation with other people. This role is not to be underestimated in terms of preparation. It's asking yourself things like:

- What is it I'm showing and how can I present it usefully?
- Who do I invite to look at it?
- What questions do I have that will help me right now?
- What isn't it helpful to discuss right now?
- How can I prepare myself to listen usefully – to understand what is useful criticism, and what might be more taste-related or tackling something I haven't addressed yet?

- How do I separate suggestions which misunderstand the craft from the fact that the writing perhaps isn't having the desired effect, and how can I use my craft to better it?
- If that happens, how do I guide the feedback towards experience and not solutions?
- How do I give myself space to reflect on what I disagree with and what I think is worth considering? (It's still your work.)

The Responder(s)

These people/this person will offer feedback, and should be willing to follow the frameworks for the feedback set up by you or the company. They may be stakeholders, collaborators, a director, or perhaps a particular player demographic. It's useful to consider who is a most useful responder for the stage you're at. Are they peers (more articulate at early stage feedback, but not the majority of your audience)? Are they your target audience (and how can you support them to feel articulate)? Are they new audiences or target ones? They should know why they've been invited to offer feedback, feel comfortable about what they need to do, and how the process will work.

They also need to be resourced appropriately. You may do an exchange of feedback with a peer, students should expect lunch/mentoring perhaps, and you may pay people 'off the street' for their time. A creative director or colleague is on work time.

The Facilitator

This can sometimes be the artist/developer, though it's sometimes better if it's a 'neutral person' (i.e. not the person who directly made the work). It's the facilitator's job to keep the process in step, and to use the process to frame useful questions and responses from the responders. You may not want to use all these roles and structures, but remember that if a feedback session isn't going well, it might be because the facilitation needs more attention.

Then Lerman offers four stages or forms of feedback – you can go through all four; or consider what's useful, relevant, or interesting to you about the stages and how they work, then apply them as you need.

The Four Stages of Feedback

The following 'stages' of feedback are what the facilitator leads the responder(s) through after they have sat with the material for a period of your choosing. They are particularly arranged like this because they stop responder(s) offering opinions straight away that could make the artist react defensively, which would hamper the discussion, and because they direct the responder's thoughts in the most useful directions and then open it up for feedback and questions that might not have occurred to the artist.

1. *Statements of meaning*: I usually summarise this as 'how did the work make you feel'. You might want to use a different phrase for a different genre of game or type of responder, something like 'how did it feel to play' or 'how do you feel like the scene was successful/adhered to our pillars', but generally this question is about the overall

effect of it. It should give you a useful impression of how the material works. The word *feel* is important because it's subjective and unconnected to judgements. 'What did you think' might tend to focus on problems and perceived solutions, which eventually can be useful, but first up it's useful to understand the effect it's having, not the effect people think it should have. It's also an easy way to begin (not technically challenging – everyone has a subjective experience) and gives a neat framework to understand the effect/vibe/experience of the game writing, how it's working as the big picture.

2. *Artist as questioner*: The artist/developer asks questions about the work. The questions could have been set ahead of time ('Could you particularly consider X character and how they contrast with Y?'), and they should be prepared in advance. After each question the responder(s) can answer, expressing opinions in direct response to the question, but it's best to not ask for change suggestions, yet. Example questions: Did you understand what to do? What did you enjoy? Were you frustrated at any point? How did you feel about X's voice?

3. *Neutral questions*: Responder(s) are invited to ask neutral questions of the artist about the work. The artist/developer responds, but try not to apologise, make excuses, or talk at length – it's the questions which are the useful things here. Questions are neutral when they don't disguise an opinion. For example, if you are discussing a particular plot beat, 'Why did you have that weird memory part of this scene?' isn't a neutral question. 'What guides your choices of memories referenced here?' is.

4. *Opinion time*: Responder(s) state opinions, subject to permission from the artist/developer. The permission is basically so you talk about things that are useful, rather than things you can't or haven't yet work on. You begin: 'I have an opinion about _____, would you like to hear it?" The artist can say yes or not right now, etc., and doesn't have to give a reason. It might be someone asks to give an opinion on the sound you've used, but it's all placeholder at the moment; in that case you might say 'not right now'.

It's important to note this is not a rigid framework but points from which conversations can be had. This is not a survey! It is a structure for a conversation. I think the most useful thing it does is very clearly set out that feedback is a process that should be supported by facilitation, that everyone should be in a useful and prepared mindset, and that there are different kinds of feedback which can be requested or offered which can be useful in different ways.

Exercise 13 (2 hours to plan and prep overall, 1 hour prep and 1 hour practice for each of the three sessions – 8 hours total)

This exercise can only be done in a group, and with existing written material, so I propose a series of small workshops where you produce, crit, and improve a piece of work together with one or more peers. If you group is more than five people, then break the crit and feedback sessions into groups of three so everyone has a go at facilitating feedback.

Prep: 2–3 hours. You will need to find a group of people, and if six or more people, break people into three-person groups within the main workshop. You might like to have a shared Google Drive with a resources folder, and a folder per person for drafts and final works, so you know where to go to read others' work in prep. You should photocopy/scan the relevant parts of the book on critical response and whatever creative writing prompt you use for session 1, so your pals can also come prepared. Make sure people have read the exercise before the first session so they're comfortable with the writing time. You may also want to put some seeds in the resources folder.

1 hour: In session 1, pick one of the exercises in 'Tools for Starting' that result in a piece of writing, and discuss the exercise so everyone understands it, then work on the piece together or async (whatever works best for you all.) Set a clear page limit of two-three pages.

1 hour: Before the next session, everyone should read their crit group's pieces and read this section of the book on the crit process and Critical Response Theory.

1 hour: In session 2 you will co-run a one-hour feedback session where you take turns to facilitate feedback on each other's work (make sure you don't facilitate your own). You don't have to do the strict version that I set out as a model in this chapter, but each person should decide the structure beforehand (or indeed how structured they want to be). Whoever is the feedback lead in each 20-minute feedback session should take care to be clear how the feedback session will work and keep it to time.

1 hour: Before the next session, redraft your work based on the feedback you received.

1 hour: Then spend the final session sharing your redraft of the work. Each person should read (or hold a reading of) their final piece, then talk about what they changed and why. Finish with a short reflection time where everyone talks through what they found useful and what they found challenging.

You could skip session one and bring an existing short story, poem, script, etc. to the group. But make sure it's still a short piece. No longer than five minutes to read aloud.

Leave time at the end of sessions to discuss and decompress, check in with your peers. For some people, opening themselves to crit can be a vulnerable-feeling process. Take time to acknowledge and discuss that, if you feel it might be helpful.

A Note on Playtesting

'Playtesting' is the accepted feedback term in videogames, but I'd like to argue that it's not as useful a term as is widely accepted. It is ill-defined across the industry, and mixed up with product and software-testing principles which don't adequately address the needs of seeking feedback on creative works. (I'm talking about playtesting specifically as a feedback mechanism here, rather than for quality assurance and bug-fixing purposes.)

Playtesting means different things to different parts of the industry. When some people use the word they only mean chatting casually while playing a build with game dev peers; when others use it, they mean a formally managed focus group of target audience members. My main problem here is that the word 'playtesting' is monolithic in people's minds but can take a number of forms in reality and on a studio-by-studio basis.

Playtesting with strangers and peers might be very useful – but it will be useful in different ways, and only if you ask a lot of questions to better define your playtesting framework. Questions like: Who are you playtesting with? Where and for how long? What kind of information are you collecting and how are you analysing it? What's their experience and perspective? How are you supporting and gathering feedback? How are you resourcing it, and how might your resources exclude certain perspectives?

For example, short, 30-minute invited feedback sessions where you watch someone play a demo for the first time will work well for, for example, gameplay-focused games where you want to test gamefeel, open-world games where you want to test wayfinding, or puzzles where you need to balance difficulty, etc. But they are very often insufficient models for getting feedback on story-driven games, where the effect you're interested in might be broader or not as obvious as 'it was fun' or 'they solved the puzzle'. What if you want feedback on how the structure shapes a whole ten-hour game? In that case you don't want to ask someone to waste time playing the game to discover a problem you've already identified. You want a trusted peer – a story professional with common vocabulary – to spitball structural ideas with, perhaps working together with Post-its and whiteboards.

That's why I think the Critical Response Process is so useful. It informs a better definition for playtesting by asking you what the project needs at whatever point in the process you're in and also to think about what you need, depending on the scope you have for change and the kind of feedback you're able to act on. Playtesting might mean internal or external, peers or the public, a single feature or the full game, early stages or nearly finished – but if you approach playtesting from a Critical Response mindset, you will be able to think these questions through with your colleagues and collaborators and arrive at a specific and useful definition.

Critical Response thinking (in asking you to prepare yourself for feedback) can also help you learn to set boundaries for feedback, supporting your being able to listen to feedback neutrally and learning to *listen between the lines*. People can be very solution-focused. When people offer solutions, you might need to listen to what's not satisfying them, instead of simply taking their suggestions on how to fix it. This is especially true with story. Someone could dislike a character, but what if you wrote them to be dislikeable? Instead of thinking 'that person needs to be nicer', ask yourself 'is the dislike serving the purpose I wanted, or is it perhaps being too distracting'.

Critical Response is a valuable lens which allows you to mould the ill-defined 'playtesting' into something that works for you and your project. When people use the word 'playtesting', ask them to define what they mean, what you're testing, and how the process will be designed to support that.

For a much more in-depth exploration of playtesting methodologies in an indie game dev setting, I recommend the GDC 2017 talk by Adriaan de Jongh 'Playtesting: Avoiding Evil Data' (Jongh, 2017),[1] and 'Part 12: Playtesting' in *A Playful Production Process* (Lemarchand, 2021).

---

[1] youtu.be/6EUeYu0aPn4.

Prototyping

Once you have an idea or a brief, you need to test it. It's perfectly possible that you'll start from a place where you need to develop story and writing but there aren't any tools in-engine to implement it yet, or that process is too laborious for testing things quickly and to present for sign-off.

That's where prototyping comes in. By far the cheapest means of testing it out is *paper prototyping*. Can you devise a tabletop role-playing game with the characters you're thinking of? Can you produce a quick script to see how it feels on the page? Can you draw a diagram of the experience? Many people turn to interactive fiction tools like Ink or Twine to test their writing, but it's important to realise that *tools shape your thinking*, particularly about how choice and pacing and branching can work. You should use a variety of tools to explore content, form, and execution. Here's an exercise to explore prototyping and how it can support writing in games.

Exercise 14 (5 hours: 1 hour prep and planning, 2-3 hours for mock-ups, 1 hour to reflect)

Take an existing story IP (film, TV, fiction – not a video game) and two characters from it. For example, the television comedy *Grace and Frankie*, using the eponymous characters.

Brief – You've been asked to develop a sequel as a mobile-only story-driven video game with simple puzzles, and you've been asked to produce a vertical slice as proof of concept. As a writer you need to get a sense of their voices and player choice. The vertical slice (VS) will be for a crucial plot beat where character A (Grace) tries to get some information from a reluctant character B (Frankie – who's probably been up to some hijinks, and doesn't want to admit it, then the puzzle can tackle solving the problem).

The scene will be a preamble to an amusingly themed match-three puzzle. Try to mock up and explore this scene in at least three ways:

- A one-page script using A4
- A one-page script using A5
- Ideating using a large surface, such as Post-its on a wall
- Drawing up a detailed brief or form for the work, and then answering it
- Sending text messages back and forth to yourself (focusing on line length on mobile)
- Pen-and-paper sketches
- A Twine or Ink prototype
- A storyboard
- Anything else you can think of

Reflection – What fitted you best, what took the most time, what offered the most useful insights? Does working on a whole wall full of Post-its feel different to working on a piece of paper or within an interactive fiction tool? Does writing on mobile or A5 help you get a better sense of readability? What else did you learn about how your prototyping tools affected your work? What story decisions did the process lead you to?

Developing Character: Dialogue

Writing better character-driven dialogue is not a mysterious process. It's a craft you can hone through a simple principle: listening. This is a proposal for a two-day workshop (run it over a weekend or a couple of weeks using four evenings) for two or more people (max, probably 12) to immediately improve your dialogue skills.

Writing Begins with Listening

This is a two-day workshop for any level, including entry-level. It's a two-day set of practical exercises for developing naturalistic, character-driven dialogue for games.

There will be additional stylistic and formal needs of games (is it a Tolkienesque fantasy setting with speech bubbles? or a noir detective game with full-screen width dialogue display? made for animation, where the animation needs space to be expressive? are you writing for 'sounds like speaking' or are you writing for 'sounds like you're reading a book'? etc.). But no matter what formal restrictions you're writing for, if you want your characters to sound roughly like 'real people', then this is a good foundational workshop. It's best done with at least two people, because like any good creative process, it's made immeasurably better through discussion and crit.

Exercise 15 (At least 2 days, with extra time to prepare and run comms. Could be run over several evenings. You may again want to produce a shared Google Drive folder for resources, worksheets, and a place to share your work.)

A TWO-DAY DIALOGUE WRITING WORKSHOP: PREPARATION
Aims

- To develop a common vocabulary for dialogue.
- To develop a sense of what it means to construct naturalistic dialogue.
- To practise and reflect in a supportive peer environment.

Resources

- Worksheets
- Listening materials/time
- Reading

Worksheet Template

Here are example worksheet headings for a voice sheet. Feel free to add headings relevant or interesting to you/your context.

Voice Sheet

Produce a Google Doc or print out with room for adding text with headings, such as shown in the following:

Character name
Origins
Age
Gender
Personality summary
Voice style and features
Code switching
Attitude to laughter, pauses, and other natural additions to speech
Line length
Rhythm
Imagery
Interruptions
Common phrases/idioms/pet names
Hesitation and surprise noises

Listening

This book is being written during a global pandemic, so I've produced a workshop that can be run in that context (from home, over remote communications, splitting work into feedback sessions and self-led sections). In a non-pandemic time, the first half of this workshop would be to send you out to cafes for a day just to *listen. To go to places and* record snippets and listen. To make sure you capture people of different ages, backgrounds, ethnicities, power differentials (i.e. friend to friend, adult to child, colleagues), gender IDs, etc. as possible, and to listen.

In a pandemic world, the next best thing is to try to find YouTube, TikTok, etc. footage of people talking 'naturally' (not podcasts because people are still performing). If you're struggling for 'live' sources, I can recommend the Listening Project, which is a British Library and BBC UK-wide project of one-to-one conversations between people who know each other (not totally natural, but close). What's especially good about this is the regional variation. It's obviously pinned to a UK 'voice', but there's a reach richness of class, regions, ages, gender/racial backgrounds, and more in there.

There are over a thousand dialogues in there, and they can be accessed for free at sounds.bl. uk/Oral-history/The-Listening-Project.

Reading

Read *Playwriting* by Stephen Jeffreys (2020), the 'Dialogue' chapter. Remember you can request books at your local library, or you could also buy one book and share it between you. I strongly recommend you don't leave this part out.

A TWO-DAY DIALOGUE WRITING WORKSHOP: STRUCTURE

Day 1: Listening

Day 1 will include a couple of group meetings, but much of it can be done solo. You may also want to split it into two half-day sessions. Start off by meeting for an hour with your peers and reflecting on how you currently feel about your dialogue skills – where you want to develop, the challenges you feel you face, influences, and the context for your learning. This will help you support one another in a more targeted way as you crit throughout the day, and help everyone realise where they're starting from. Work out how you're going to follow the workshop, and check in on how everyone is feeling.

30–45 Minutes: Listen (Solo)

Listen to excerpts of four or five of the Listening Project conversations. Or find a conversation online which is 'natural' and not too performative (TikTok, YouTube, etc., all good resources), and not actors performing or improvising. Or spend a little more time (a whole afternoon, perhaps) wandering around a town centre, café, bus stops, shops, listening to people and writing down what they say and how they talk. I think it's okay to record people so long as you delete the recordings when you're done, but if you're uncomfortable with this, the Listening Project or other online resources are the place to go.

30–45 Minutes: Transcribe (Solo)

Choose a short excerpt from one to two of the conversations to transcribe.

1 Hour: Describe (Solo)

Once you have written the conversation word-for-word, choose one of the speakers, and build a character and voice sheet for them. The aim is to build on what you have learned from the listening. This might include:

- Name
- Age
- Appearance
- Mannerisms
- Voice
- Vocal tics, habits
- Imagery
- Idioms
- Rhythms
- Pauses
- Interruptions
- Motivations in life
- History/education
- Character traits

- Moments of poetry
- More!

This is as if you were creating a character for a game, based on the person you have listened to.

1 Hour or More: Reflect (Group)

When you and your peers have at least one character/voice sheet each, come back together to talk about the exercises, share your character sheets, what you pulled out, what you noted, and why you made those decisions.

Self-Guided Homework (Solo)

1. Read the 'Dialogue' chapter from Stephen Jeffrey's *Playwriting*. (1 hour)
2. Find an example of a scene you really like from a piece of popular television with a strong presence voice/format, e.g. *Grey's Anatomy, Avatar: The Last Airbender, Star Trek: Deep Space Nine*. Transcribe the dialogue, including stage directions and write some notes on how the dialogue is effective at communicating/using
   - Character
   - Power dynamics
   - Interruptions
   - How does it feel natural?
   - How is it actually stylised?
   - Anything else you've learned from the reading (2 hours)
3. Take two characters drawn from the recordings/the sheets made by everyone (i.e. you can choose other people's characters), and write a one- to two-page scenario between them, where character 1 tries to convince character 2 to do something they are unsure about. This is not about the story/plot/setting, choose a silly thing like 'get them to lend them a book', or 'get them to allow them to borrow a dress', make it set in 'our' world; the crucial thing here is to focus on the construction of the character through voice. (1 hour)

Aim to produce naturalistic dialogue where if you cover the character names you can still tell who is talking. Aim for people who talk in natural rhythms, with natural hesitations and constructions, but with enough style to be readable. Aim to use stage directions to hint at body language where people would naturally do that rather than speak their subtext. The first two reading and transcription exercises should have provided you with a good foundation for this task.

Useful further reading is to find artists and writers annotating their own work, or seeing how they transfer it from one medium to another. *Fleabag* went from a one-woman stage show to a TV script. Or Stewart Lee (2010) annotating his stand-up.

Day 2: Writing

Today you're going to reflect on the 'homework', and you're also going to do writing from the world and characters of one of your own works, or if you're not currently working on something, using existing characters. You will use everything learned the day before to inform your dialogue style and structure.

If in day 1 you found you tended to overwrite lines (most people do not talk in paragraphs), today (if you write in Google Docs or Word or a script editor) I want you to switch to A5 page format. If you write in a text editor, resize the margins or the window. Reduce your page width, and use this to be mindful of line length.

2 Hours: Share and Reflect 1 (Group)

Come together and share and reflect on your work from the previous day.

Start off by discussing the reading. What did it help you articulate? Was there anything you took away which was valuable? Did you disagree anywhere?

Follow by sharing the transcriptions. What did you learn from these? How did they differ from the 'natural' speech of the listening exercise? How have they stylised characters, patterns of speech, and made their dialogue demonstrate the relationship between characters and exposition of the plot?

Then do a group crit on the writing exercise; perform the scripts together. You will already immediately get a sense of what feels natural and what feels stilted just from reading out loud. Discuss what feels effective and what might need more work; discuss character mannerisms, voices, line length, rhythm, identity; think together about what a redraft could focus on.

Then we'll do a final writing exercise. To prepare for this, read the following and help one another to prepare a scenario. You will all write for the same scenario.

1 Hour: Prepare (Group)

Take the world of one of the shows of which you transcribed the exchange, and choose two characters from the show. Together, collaboratively create a character and voice sheet for the characters, and decide among yourselves on a scenario where one of them wants to get something from the other. Make any rough planning notes you might need to write the scene. Refer to the previous day's work if you wish.

1 Hour: Write (Solo)

Individually, write a one- to three-page scene based on the scenario, including stage directions.

Strive for a dialogue style which is strong in characterisation, and fairly natural in terms of brevity and sentence structure, but reads much more neatly than dialogue for speaking.

(You might like to include interesting choices, of one to five words, that a player could make throughout or at the end. You could choose one choice to write for thereafter, have the choice pay off no matter what comes next, or write two alternate passages following the choice – do this only if you feel confident that you will benefit from it and not get lost in document formatting. The focus is still dialogue.)

1 Hour: Share and Reflect 2 (Group)

As a group, read and reflect on the scripts you have written. As you will have worked on the same characters and scenario, it will be interesting to see how someone else has approached the task, and hopefully you will be able to draw out the places where you have all made good choices.

2 Hours: Redraft, Edit (Group)

Some different options for this final work time; choose on the basis of what you feel will be most interesting/useful:

1. Spend at least a short time redrafting one or both of your written pieces.
2. Spend some time editing someone else's script.
3. Repeat any of the exercises using what you have learned.

1 Hour: Present and Reflect (Group)

Present your work; reflect and discuss:

- What did you find easy?
- What was difficult?
- What did you like?
- What did you learn?
- How might you develop either of the pieces/voices/characters?

Before you finish, make notes somewhere you can come back to when you pick up writing work in the future: a notebook where each week you note down what you learned that week, a text doc you add to with things you learn, or some Post-its you can stick on your wall. Make sure you reinforce your learning by trying to write more solo, together, or by preserving your reflections somehow.

Finally, congratulate yourself on a great solid piece of work!

Developing Story: Structure

As a writer you cannot only concentrate on character voice, dialogue, scenes, and plot beats, you often need to understand and refer to a wider/bigger picture of structure, plot, and character development. This structural view of storytelling might be something established by the creative director or narrative designer; or it might be a loose connection of plot and gameplay which you're expected to deepen, develop, and map character journeys to.

Post-its, whiteboards, large pieces of paper – big thinking is your friend here, and the best way to do big thinking is to have a big space.

Take as an example the following whiteboard which I developed as part of my work on *Mutazione*. When I came to the game there was a very well-developed world and plot (the creative director had an extremely strong sense of the events of the 100 years prior to the game's events, and a day-to-day sense of plot beats, subplots, and set pieces, for which they'd already commissioned animations). But the thing was a mess in storytelling terms. The characters were drawn, but not all of them had a journey where they changed. And there were too many subplots, which meant you lost the A plot. Doing this process with the creative director I was able to work with him to add the red materials – places where we added details so their characters developed – and it enabled me to point out that one or two of the days could be combined because not much character work happened, and we could cut one or two subplots to keep the pace moving. In this greyscale print of the whiteboard picture, the 'red' additions are a lighter grey than the 'black' text of already-existing beats.

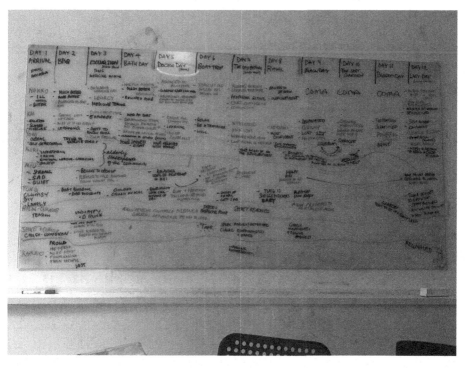

There are many theories of character arc/psychologies of change you could use for your underpinning as a storyteller, but in this context, it was an ensemble cast story and a naturalistic character development. One of the pillars was a community that had faced a crisis, and fallen out of balance – not meaningfully healed following it. Therefore, everyone needed a problem that should be 'healed' or reconciled by the end of the story. This big picture helped me then draw up a full-game redraft proposal; every conversation in every location at every time of day shook up to serve the A plot, drawing in a different character and subplot per day.

These big-picture views are vital, as a writer, to get a sense of how each smaller moment needs to contribute to the whole – depending on what your pillars, and genre, and storytelling format might be. It involves a level of instinct that you can develop through crit – either by asking people to look at your high-level versions of a story and reflect on it/what might be missing, by workshops, or by your examining successful works and figuring out how they were successful. Here are a few exercises which could help you towards a greater sensitivity to developing structure. If it's been a while since you read the chapters of Part I: Theory which touch on story structure, it's worth rereading those too.

Exercise 16 (1 hour prep and planning, 1 hour to produce the diagram)

Pick an episode midseason from a well-established ensemble cast TV show like *The West Wing*, *Star Trek: DS9*, or *Grey's Anatomy*. Produce an episode pitch document no longer than two pages.

- Name the main characters of the episode.
- Name and summarise the A plot of the episode.
- Name and summarise the B plot which contrasts/leavens the episode.
- If there's a little C plot, name and summarise that too.
- Describe the pillar for the episode.
- Describe the key character journeys and how they relate to the pillar.
- Draw a diagram which lists characters and plots on one axis, and scene numbers on the other. Mark a dot against each character and plot which is developed in each episode.
- Write a short summary on how the episode's structure is effective.

Example Diagram

I have made this up for a hypothetical episode of *The West Wing*, but I'm sure it bears some resemblance to one episode or another.

	1	2	3	4	5	6	7	8	9	10	11	12	13	14
The President	X			X						X		X		
CJ		X			x	X					X			X
Josh	X	X	X	X	X	X		X	X	X		X		
Donna		X				X					X			
Toby	X		X	X	X		X			X	X		X	X
The vice president				X				X				X		
A lobbyist					X		X							

A plot: How can they pass a vital healthcare bill without enough votes in their party?	X			X	X	X		X	X	X		X
B plot: CJ and Toby struggle over how to present a PR opportunity which Toby thinks is frivolous.		X			X	X			X			X
C plot: Josh's assistant Donna isn't talking to him (he forgot her birthday, but she won't tell him that).	X				X				X			

Exercise 17 (0.5 days prep, 2 hours exercise)

Pick a linear story-driven videogame you have played all the way through, or play a short story-driven game like *Life is Strange 2: Episode 1* and produce the same document as described earlier for at the scenes in that game. The shorter the game/episode, the more you can focus on the structure doc. An ensemble cast diagram will look very different to a single protagonist/hero's tale and you might want to draw out different details – character developments instead of subplots.

Exercise 18 (1 day to play game, 1 day to workshop design pillars and make notes, 0.5 days to produce design proposal)

The purpose of this exercise is to produce a design proposal for the structure of the beginning of a story-driven game. We're going to take an example game and

- Reverse-engineer some design pillars.
- Look at how the opening of the example game satisfies those pillars through its story structure.
- Turn those pillars and the approach the game takes to supporting them into a mock design proposal.

225

To begin, pick a non-linear, multiple pathway game like *80 Days*. Play enough of it to work out three to five design pillars for it. Define pillars which are specific, and about player experience. An example for *80 Days* might be

- Tempt the player into bad decisions and reward them with interesting story.
- Deconstruct the classism and racism of the original text.
- Tell the story through worldbuilding rather than plot.
- Discomfort and delight in equal measure.
- Every playthrough should tell a good story.

These example pillars are drawn from the interview 'Narrative and Design Insights from *80 Days*' Writing Lead' on gamedeveloper.com (Nutt, 2015) and a GDC talk 'Leading Players Astray' (Jayanth, 2015).

If you feel a little lost in defining design pillars, do what I did: reverse-engineer them from interviews or talks from the developers. Make sure you pick an example game that has a GDC or gamedeveloper.com design deep dive as a resource. For further reading on design pillars, you can also reference Chapter 7 'Project Goals' in *A Playful Production Process* (Lemarchand, 2021), which defines the pillars or principles for a game's design and development.

Next, play your example game's beginning a couple of times with those pillars in mind. Make notes about the first three beats in the story and how the initial structure and writing set up the pillars. In *80 Days*, you might focus on the first three possible stops from England. These notes will help you identify how the storytelling and writing is successful in order that you can imagine you are proposing them to a creative director, for which you will make a structural design proposal document.

To prepare for this, keep notes in whatever way suits you as you detail the possible places/ experiences in reach, pathways to them, characters you can meet, place information, items you can exchange, and key events that can occur in those first three beats. The headings you use or way you map this will depend on the game you pick and what works for you. The key thing here is to be able to summarise how these first steps in the game will set up the player's experience of the player character, the world, and gameplay, and how they set up to fulfil those pillars.

Finally, turn this research on the game into a one- to two-page story-driven design proposal. Summarise the proposal as if you're pitching the beginning of the story experience to a creative director. Headings you might like to consider are

- A summary of what this section of the writing/story should do.
- How does/can the player explore?
- Writing style, format, and approach.
- Genre and character voice notes.
- How does it set up the pillars, world, and future development?

- How does it introduce the player to the world and characters?
- How does the writing interact with tutorials and mechanics?
- What should the player feel/understand by the end?
- References/examples in other works.
- Design questions, process proposals (what next?)

Focus on it from the perspective of a writer – make sure you include notes on pacing, character development, line length, narration, and exposition.

This is an advanced exercise because much of it leaves the format up to you – use it as an opportunity to work out *how you think* and *how you can present your thinking to others*. Part of this exercise will be deciding what details to include. How are the characters developed? Who do you meet? What would you describe the game pillars as, and how does the part of the game you're considering contribute to them? Note real-world references, and if you have questions, note them down too. Describe how player choice operates in the location (restricted to begin with?) and how the place should make the player feel. Remember that your pillars are the brief you're trying to satisfy with the proposal.

And remember that this is advanced – it involves a lot of possible ways you could approach it, and a decent amount of narrative design and general game design thinking too. If it's something you feel like you need more experience or reading of games and game design theory before you tackle it – that's okay! Or perhaps, find a game design peer to double up on this exercise with; have them set the example game and the pillars, and discuss your proposal with you when you're done.

Exercise 18a (0.5–1 days to become familiar with tool and plan writing, 0.5 days to write and test, 0.5 days to redraft)

This exercise is written with Ink/Inky as an example tool, but you can use any tool, like Yarn or Twine. Just make sure you read the beginners guide for whatever you choose and are comfortable with beginning, branching, coming back to the same place, and ending a piece of writing in it. Spend time getting a feel for what you think will work for you.

You also need to have done the previous exercise or have another small and clear brief for a piece of writing.

Let's assume you're going to use Inky. If you haven't used Inky before, it's essentially a tool for producing interactive writing. An Ink file is a text file that you could open with any basic text editor, but the *language* Ink is a simple way to mark text with simple symbols and conventions so it can be interactive. Inky is a free tool (Mac and PC) which allows you to write in Ink in a way which you can test the work, have errors highlighted, and keep easy track of your writing.

For an example of what I mean by 'mark text with symbols and conventions', this is how you would write a choice in Ink:

```
Preface to the choice.
+ [Choice 1] -> outcome1
+ [Choice 2] -> outcome2

== outcome1 ==
Text that you see after choosing 1.
->reunite

== outcome2 ==
Text that you see after choosing 2.
->reunite

== reunite ==
Then the text carries on.
```

If you were to visualise this exchange as a branch it would look like this:

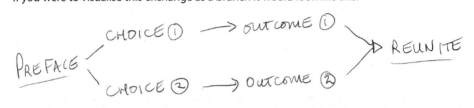

Reuniting branches is a good way to offer reward for choice, but not producing eight different outcome points you have to write for by the time you've offered only three choice points.

The 'player view' of the writing would be (on choosing choice 2):

> *Preface to the choice.*
> *Text that you see after choosing 2.*
> *Then the text carries on.*

You can download Inky, and take a look at both the Basics Tutorial and the Full Guide at inklestudios.com/ink. If you want to take longer than a day to explore the tool, feel free! But the focus of this exercise is just to get comfortable enough to add in simple choices amongst your writing and to be able to hit a 'play' function so you can test it.

Once you're ready to write, working in Ink (or your tool of choice) and without referencing the original writing (if drawing on the previous exercise), use the design proposal you produced or another small brief with a clear purpose to draft a piece/scene/encounter from your proposal/brief.

If you were modelling a piece of your proposal for *80 Days* that might be drafting the text for arriving at and exploring a single location. If you're working on something else, it might be a single conversation between the player character and another. Or a piece of more general interaction fiction. Make sure before you write you know precisely what genre you're in, who the characters are, what the place is, and the situation. Know where A is and where B is (what the scene/encounter should *do* – set up the world, characters, story). Then your job is just to write from A to B, with some simple pleasing choice in between.

There will be plenty mechanics you don't have time to reproduce or approximate; just ignore those. Focus on simple writing and choice, in the style of the game genre, game world, and using the proposal/brief as a basis for the scene/extract.

Try to make an experience which is no more than three to five minutes to play and keep branching minimal – start small and test often. How do you begin to feel about your process? Do you find it easier to write one single pathway through, and then add the choice in? Or do you like writing simultaneously? Once you have a first draft, stop for the day. Return to it at least one day later to reflect and redraft.

Is writing in a tool a bit too soon for you? Then replace it with the research and reading and experimenting you need to feel comfortable, before you return to concentrating on a short and very purposeful piece of writing.

No matter how many or which of these exercises you try, remember that you're trying to think structurally about a scene and how it contributes to the bigger picture of the storytelling. This won't be the work of writing a game, but this understanding of design proposals and structure will really help you think about how your writing should fit into them – that's why I've put these two exercises together.

Learning to Edit

If you are lucky, you will have the opportunity to edit your writing for a video game. If I were writing a guide for any other form of writing I would say that editing is an essential part of writing – and much more of the work than the first draft. But in a context where you might be brought on too late, with a poorly specified brief, what can be very large volumes of work, and with unfinished tools, you have to pay a lot of attention to honing and practising your craft. That first draft might be the only chance you get. You want to do your learning on exercises and self-set curricula, so that when you come to that of your work which will be for public consumption, if you put in some placeholder text and it comes that you never get a chance to redraft it before it goes to localisation, that it's the best you could do in that first sitting.

That doesn't mean you shouldn't advocate for time to redraft, or that your writing won't be improved by some distance and reading it amongst the whole, but this is a material reality of game writing that it's worth preparing for. All studios will be different: many might have tools ready for you to test the writing in situ already prepared, or be ready to work with you to develop them, or even have a narrative lead or editor who will do a pass on everything you write for this purpose. Story testing tools and editors are important, but you can't always rely on them being considered so.

In this context it's useful to develop the skill of producing second- or third-draft quality work at first draft – writing already edited, and going in to writing already prepared enough to know where the story is going and how you need to get it there. Unless you're working solo or collaborating in an amateur setting with no deadlines or resources on the line, you often won't have the luxury of using writing time to discover your characters and going back to fix their journeys later. So, that's why all of the tools we're practising here – a character sheet, a voice sheet, a clear brief about the purpose of the writing, the scene and the setting, and the practising of dialogue skills –allows you to write as well as you can the *first time*.

However, as we're thoroughly outside of the professional setting right now, when practising these skills, take the exact opposite approach: write easily, write lots, and don't overthink things. Get clumsy, overliteral, or uncharacterful lines on the page so you can look at them and make them better. It's better to have a line that reads 'I want the last biscuit' which you can punch up to read 'Don't want that last biscuit, d'you?'[2] than no line at all. You only get to the place I describe by starting from a place of messy, unworried abandon. You can't work with or learn from writing until it's on the page.

After just writing, the next and very simplest tool in your toolkit for writing well is simply this:

• Read it aloud.

Read your words out loud and you'll easily find the things which feel uncomfortable and unwieldy, unrealistic, or confusing about your writing.

Exercise 19 (0.5–1 days: 1 hour prep, 1 hour writing, 1.5 hours table read and discussion, 1 hour redraft, 1 hour reflection discussion)

Can be done alone, but it may be better in a group of two or three. Pick a TV IP which you and your group members know very well. If you can't agree on anything, pick a folk tale you all know (but archetypes aren't as useful as well-defined characters – TV is better).

Agree on a single scene set-up between two of the characters from that IP where they are in a known place, and one of them wants get a piece of information the other is unwilling to give. The idea is to remove all of the invention except the writing.

Write the scene. Set a limit of two to three pages for the scene. Do not get bogged down in stage directions. Everyone should take 30–45 minutes to write a version of that scene. Then do a table read (sit down and read a character each) of the script. If you are alone, just simply read it out loud several times. After the reading, discuss these questions:

• What worked well?
• What could be improved?

---

[2] This character is English.

- What didn't feel necessary?
- Did the characters have distinct voices?
- What felt untrue or difficult to say?

Then return to the script and redraft it primarily using cuts, resorting to new or rephrased lines only when necessary. Read again. Did it improve? Is there a principle or restriction you can draw from it for your next first draft?

- Distance

Another tool which other writing forms use is *distance*. The rule of 'put your book draft or play script in a drawer for six months', or if you don't have six months – 'the blank page draft two'. There are also shortcuts for distance to be found in other people: a dramaturg in theatre, a script editor in TV, an editor in fiction and poetry. These roles or this kind of wait allows you to become less involved in the minutiae or intent of the work, and be able to see it clearly, from several steps back. If you're lucky enough to be working with an editor on a project – accept their suggestions with joy and curiosity – ask for edit feedback sessions, ask about why they make certain changes, try to take general principles and lessons for both style and technique (edits may be towards a house style as well as technical improvements).

But to simulate distance you can use the 'blank page draft two' – a strategy I was taught as a playwriting student. It goes: write draft one of your script. Then, when it's finished, the next day, begin your second draft. Except you cannot reference draft one at all. Draft one was about finding your way, but now you know the story and the characters, so tell it from that perspective. Draft three allows you to review draft one (usually full of energy but a mess) and draft two (usually lacking in energy but structurally much cleaner) and decide what you want to take and edit, and what you want to rewrite for the balance.

Exercise 20 (1 hour for each draft, but at least 1 day between drafts; 1 hour for reflection)

Do a blank page redraft. Take the same provocation as exercise 19: two characters in a known place, from a known IP, where one is trying to get information from the reluctant other. Write draft one. Then, the next day, without referencing draft one, create a new blank page document, and write it again. The following day, compare the two drafts. What do you like about draft one, what do you notice about draft two? Can you see any habits in draft one you could use as a principle for avoiding in the future? Write your draft three. Then reflect on what you learned about self-editing.

- Do you have habits with how you begin sentences/speech?
- Do you slip into the same register for all characters?
- Do your characters speak too much?
- Do you characters speak their subtext too much?
- Does every line have a purpose? Does it move the action forwards?

- How much can you cut and have it still make sense?
- Try to cut one third of the total wordcount.

A final technique for developing your editing skills I'd like to offer is edit swaps. It's another way of getting someone else to leverage their distance to help you when you don't have time to wait for that closed-drawer six months (something most professional writers don't have the luxury for). As well as seeing how someone else edits your work, you'll get to try out the position of distance here too – in editing the work of your edit-swap partner.

Exercise 21 (1 hour prep, 2.5 hours workshop)

Edit swap – an exercise for two or more people.

In prep for a two-hour workshop, draw up a scenario with two characters. I advise choosing an existing IP and known characters for ease of working, but if you want to try out brief-setting you could add an hour or two on and build a world sheet, two character sheets, and two voice sheets. If you're running the workshop, make sure you write up the exercises and have shared the prep material beforehand.

At the beginning of the workshop the important thing is everyone should know what the situation going into the scene is and what it will be coming out of it. I usually suggest things like 'X wants something from Y' – information or an item – as it's a simple and easy-to-imagine set-up.

Take 45 minutes to write one to two pages of the script, ending in an interesting choice. Take 5 minutes' rest. Then swap your scene with another person, and spend 25 minutes editing; this is easiest done in shared Google Docs. Tips on editing can be taken from exercise 20.

Take 5 minutes to read the edits on your work. Then spend 25 minutes discussing everyone's edits together. You might like to use starting points such as:

- What surprised you about their edits
- What you think the biggest improvement was
- What you might have done differently
- What you thought worked best about their work
- Why you made the choices you did in editing theirs

Take the final 25 minutes to redraft your own piece a final time. Finish with a 15-minute reflection on what you learned about your writing.

Diagnosing What's Wrong

The more you learn the theory and practise via exercises such as these, the more you crit successful and unsuccessful works, the more you will develop instincts which allow you to diagnose quickly, and without trial or error, what's not working with a piece of writing or the premise for a piece of storytelling. Everything I've offered you as a tool to this point will lead you to this place, so I can't offer a specific and well-contained exercise. I invite you to listen to your disquiet, and as you develop your practice to learn to listen to your instincts.

If you have mocked up some writing in the game you're working on and it doesn't feel good to play, return to your mental checklists. Is it the style, a genre misfit, line length, form, pacing, too much plot, not enough character, structure, dissonance with other aspects? What should the story be doing in this moment, and what is preventing it from doing it? When you think about what the story/writing should be doing, consider that question from the perspective of:

- For the player
- For the character development
- For plot and exposition
- For gameplay and pacing

Crit is one of the strongest tools in your arsenal for identifying and developing your instincts on diagnosis. So, I offer you this idea:

Exercise 22 (several evenings; at least one to prep and one per crit club)

Form a small group of peers, and meet monthly over six months (you could do more regular intervals, but check people can do the prep comfortably).

Select five games that you will play in prep for the club. Games under 15 hours is ideal, and it's okay to use YouTube playthroughs instead of playing them. Make sure the games are useful examples for the interests of the group. And make sure the costs of participating are manageable. At the time of writing, there a number of subscription services which have good selections of games and which could make this affordable for everyone to participate.

Here's some selections I might choose if I were running a crit club using one of my current game console subscriptions. If I ran a crit club this way, it would cost everyone only the month's subscription to the service:

- *Call of the Sea*
- *Genesis Noir*
- *Knights and Bikes*
- *Raji*
- *What Remains of Edith Finch*

Take turns chairing the discussion – the act of preparing questions for a discussion will enable you to think in extra useful ways about crit. Spend around 90 minutes discussing, and then take a 5-minute break. Take 10 minutes to make some notes about what you might take from this game to your own practice – whether dos or don'ts. Then take the final 15 minutes to discuss.

Here are some discussion prompts for a crit club:

- How did the game make you feel?
- How did it achieve this?
- Was there a central character? How was the player supposed to relate to them?
- How did you feel about the character voices and journey?
- How did the writing and story interact with gameplay?
- What did you think about structure, pacing, and formal constraints?
- How did the game use choice and agency?
- How did it use genre conventions?
- What do you feel wasn't so successful?
- If you were to change one major aspect of the game/genre/story, how would it change?
- What might you have done differently?

Try to avoid discussing the plot or overall story (i.e. saying what happened) alone; the idea is to discuss how the story is put together and how the story is told. Also, take care to not only focus on the narrative design but on the design of the storytelling in the whole of the game. If you're writers, focus on writing. The narrative design is relevant, but discuss the writing angle specifically, and make sure you all understand that, and that your topics and chosen games support it.

Advocacy, Diversity, and Representation

One of your jobs as a writer is to advocate for the best version of the story possible, and sometimes that will be about advocating for different perspectives in the writing of the story. Remember that in building and developing any story you have an ethical duty (in my opinion at least) to not carelessly perpetuate harmful stereotypes and to reflect the breadth of your audience in the characters you develop. That might mean advocating internally for changes to the personnel, process, or story in order that you can fully reflect (among others):

- Disability
- Women
- BIPOC
- LGBTQ+ folks
- Older people
- Bodily diversity
- Working-class experiences
- Mental health struggles
- Neurodiversity
- Non-Western or non-White cultural and religious assumptions

Of course, you might not be writing a naturalistic or 'serious' story, but that still doesn't mean that you shouldn't challenge your approach to the characters or storytelling from these angles. I've talked in the Theory section (Part I) about how that should ideally include hiring diverse folks – and that might be out of your control – but one thing a writer can reasonably advocate for is *diversity consultation*. It's an imperfect solution in some ways, but there are people (not just in games; it's very common in literature where there's often just one author, so the multiple perspectives are even harder to come by) who do this job for a living.

Diversity consultants should be brought on board in time to make changes. They should be a professional (they'll often come with skills in recommending solutions as well as spotting specific problems – something you won't get from general playtesting feedback). When you invite someone in to do paid work as a diversity consultant, you should be clear about what's possible to change and what isn't. You should understand if they specialise in a certain area (i.e. LGBTQ+ history in South America). You should resource time to make changes they suggest. You'll want to make sure that if the art is stylised it's not perpetuating any harmful visual stereotypes. You need to be prepared to cut things.

For example, I was brought on to do some work on a horror game where one of the characters was a trans woman; the brief included a clear exposition of their being trans for a general audience. It seemed to me that there was no way for this person to disclose their transness without that disclosure being a 'twist' (which is often a clumsy stereotype), so I advocated for a paid trans consultant. We worked through the character and the setting and story, and there was no way to express their transness without outing them as a plot point, and there was no character-driven reason we could see that they would. In the end, the best thing to do was to cut that detail from exposition. It was okay for them to be canonically trans in our heads, but the writing shouldn't try to communicate it, and there was no reason the story should either.

You may also want to hire diversity consultants in different languages if localising a game so you can make sure the translation of the game uses up-to-date terminology (i.e. the most common gender-neutral pronouns for a non-binary character). Equally you may want to bring accessibility consultants on board to advise on line length, font size, and text effects, early enough to request font size, colour blindness, simplified language, or screen-reader features.

Getting used to defining briefs for yourself will also help you define a brief for a diversity consultant, and you could also work with them on a brief before delivering them materials to assess. Consider things like: How are you going to provide them with materials? How will they comment and feedback? How many iterations will there be? These practical questions should also be a part of it.

It's not easy to advocate for these things in a situation where resources run out quickly and time is critical, but it is ethical. If you go into every project asking these questions from the beginning, you will be more likely to succeed in moving towards and advocating for better diversity and representation in your games. Making games for more people.

Tools for Collaboration: Design Documentation

What if you want to propose creative or design changes from the perspective of the story? The most useful way you can do this is by using *design documentation*. Now, your collaborating studio might have a recognisable format they already prefer, in which case it's good to familiarise yourself with it. But if they don't, it's worth thinking in 'design document' format when trying to present changes you need to write the story well.

A good design document should

- Be short and succinct (one page)
- Describe the change proposed/describe the proposed feature (if new)
- Describe how the change/feature contributes to a pillar/solves a problem
- Describe whom the change will affect
- Provide work estimates/adjustments to scope that result

Here's an example for you to consider from my work on *Mutazione*.

Case Study: Gardens or Story?

There came a point in my narrative design for *Mutazione* where I had to push the creative director for an answer to a particular question: a key design decision that would – depending on what our CD's final decision was – make a radically different game to the one we ended up with. Neither would have been better or worse (although it may have found different playing audiences), just a point where a story proposal demanded we ask which of these creative directions most align with the CD's vision for the game. My question was

- Is the game about the gardens? Or is the game about the story? Which comes first?

The design challenge was that we had these wonderful generative musical gardens, and we had this idea for a world, and a story, and a bunch of characters, but we hadn't quite worked out how to make them work together. There were seven gardens which could be completed in any order, there was no clear 'puzzle' for them yet, and so we weren't sure how we would lay the clues for them. There was also a whole string of garden-related subplots around *medicine mixing* – where Kai could encounter members of the community with medicinal needs, and as part of caring for them and learning Nonno's practice, she could grow and gather plants, and with a medicine book, mix medicines to solve their problems. She was to do that in Nonno's house (you may still notice the mixing materials in the background of his kitchen).

This question 'What is the priority: gardens or characters?' was vital, because while the story could feature gardens or the gardens could allow a story to emerge, it was vital for the storytelling and design of the game to know *which came first*. Is the most important thing the ensemble cast of characters – their lives, troubles, secrets, and resolution? Or is it about the gardens, about the ecosystem? The community of humanoids were often articulated by creative director Nils Deneken's vision as being part of the organism which encompasses the gardens, and the question therefore was: are the gardens the way in, or is the community?

If the former, then the gardens should draw you back to the characters; they should solve interpersonal issues, and move the story forward, not offer medicinal puzzles. Kai's focus should be on the mystery behind the people and their history, not trying to dig up references in a book, find ingredients for mixing. Likewise, if it was the gardens which were the most important thing about the game, everything should come back to them. We should make the medicine mixing important – not just side quests, but the heart of the game. The gameplay in this case would have to involve satisfaction from solutions more than discovery. The characters would be pieces in the puzzle, more than the puzzle themselves.

Nils's decision was that it was the ensemble cast who were the priority. The community. The characters he had pulled out of his head almost a decade ago, fully formed, who had kept him company as he developed the world, the backstory, the *placeness* of *Mutazione*.

A solution: It was clear that we should shape the storytelling around the characters and their lives, and that gardens are a part of that. So, in design discussion with the rest of the team, we decided that each garden would be unlockable and completed on a certain 'day' in the game, and that each garden Mood would link to the theme of that day. That the unlocking would be done by a 'song' which would enable that day's Mood's plants to grow, and that the song would be learned from a member of the community enabled me to weave it back and forth between story and characters, and gardens. The storytelling would also be resonant: on the 'Harsh' garden day, it would feel like the community was having a 'harsh' day. And the main garden of the day should link to the main B plot of the day – should 'solve' a problem for a character, and the central character from that B plot would be connected to what you grow, and how you therefore move the community closer to balance.

The implications:

- Instead of plants growing slowly, developing each time game-time moved forward, they would now grow in large 'steps' each time you sang a mood song to them.
- Cut medicine mixing as a feature entirely (it would have taken a lot of work to implement, when we now knew we needed a revised time system and garden unlocking feature, and a whole new Garden UI).
- Cut the *Medicine of Mutazione* book (though I did take a big piece of that lore and fold it into hints in the encyclopaedia, and into little asides and stories members of the community might tell).
- Cut the medicine plot lines (which didn't move character/plot forward, just were mini puzzles to solve, rather than the development of the gardens as puzzles).
- We needed to associate each garden with a character/subplot.
- Through connecting the mood of the day with the storytelling/mood of the encounters you might have, I restructured the plots and subplots so they would mirror the mood. This meant cutting whole subplots, removing entire days when they strung out the

storytelling too much, and reordering plot events to better serve the symbiosis, in the hope of reconciling the theme of the game through the gardens helping the community.
- Recognising that the gardens did not have to be puzzles – they had to be activities, not things that could block progress, but considered as a place you would enjoy spending your time.

With all of that for context, now take a look at the design documentation I drew up following that meeting. Bear in mind this is a very major change with a lot of knock-on effects. The scope of a design doc can be much smaller.

Story First, Garden Second: A Design Proposal
August 30th 2018.
In order to better integrate the gardens and puzzle solving into the game we are removing free-flowing time from the garden functionality – instead of being moved forward by game-time they will be moved forward by one of seven 'songs' which Kai learns from other members of the Mutazione community.
Each complete garden will be a beat that you have to complete by the end of the relevant day.
You will only be able to make plants grow if you have learned the song for the specific mood of the plants. For example, if you plant a garden in both pacific and euphoria, but you only have the euphoria song, when you sing it, only the euphoria plants will grow.
The garden/character/mood relationship proposal:
Each mood will need to be completed on a discreet day in the game. We will provide hints towards one in particular so that the player can feel supported in moving the story forwards. Here is the proposal for that.

Character/hint/garden/mood connection proposal:

Character	Garden	Mood	Day
Nonno (*seeds*)	Rooftop	Pacific	2
Miu (*swim trip*)	East	Melancholia	3
Ailin (at the bathhouse, giving Kai treatment? Humming the melody because of Kai's 'harsh' mood)	Beach	Harsh	4
Dots (*visit the dots*) *Consider making this a Dennis day where you finally break the ice with him*	Tree Crown	Euphoria	6

Tung (*on boat trip*)	Tung's	Wanderlust	5
Jell-A (*hint to where to find otherworldly spores and evanescence, garden suggestions, OW song*)	Dark	Otherworldly	6
Mori (*praying for Nonno*)	Temple	Spooky	7

Required changes from narrative in order for this to work:
- In introducing the rooftop garden Nonno will hint that there are other songs you may find throughout the community.
- There is a specific order in which you unlock moods (proposed above).
- Garden per day require beats for:
  - Song discovery (early in the day)
  - Garden hint
  - General hints
  - Garden completion
  - A conversation with the character related to that mood which makes it meaningful
- Therefore, we need a full redraft around this critical path, weaving it back into the main events.
- Medicine and encyclopaedia combine (only a tiny bit of the medicine book should be moved over, but HN needs to look through it to work out what).
- Decide on who and where for each song and garden hint.
- Rewrite the encyclopaedia so there are more concrete hints for where plants are found.
- Do we need to alter Karoo's poem? (check, probably not)
- Characters know the songs, but it's what Nonno gives you (a drum?) that makes it work – something around resonance?
- Mori is a useful character for garden conversations – place her gardening more often.
- Characters should give you seeds to hint at 'moods'.
- Characters should talk about the gardens and how their moods are being shaped by them.
- You can undo a garden mood but that shouldn't affect the writing.
- When Nonno introduces the seeds, he won't be explicit about the whole mood system, he will instead present things in a mysterious way encouraging Kai to learn on her own. He will instead talk about his narrative perspective – the instrument you are given belonged to Manii, talk about how most things grow at a normal rate but you can encourage their growth through resonance, he teaches you the first song – Pacific Song – and encourages you to use it. He doesn't call it that, the now simplified mechanic needs to still preserve some mystery to be gently rewarding.

Mock-ups and workflow:
- CD will decide on the definitive placement of 15 plants (at least 2 from each mood, including the tonic ingredients) which will not be moved in later design revisions (as these will be the ones referenced in a concrete manner by narrative).
- HN needs a mock-up of learning and 'using' a song.
- Secrets for *delicate* and *toxic* plants mechanic should be sprinkled throughout.
  - Encyclopaedia (narrative)
  - UI (gameplay programmer/designers)
- We need a new variable management system for garden completion.
- Work out what all the new character activities are – make sure I list them for feeding back to Nils to revise the composition and placement.
- Relevant cuts (medicine mixing, medicine book).
- Character song sharing mock-up (is it a text style?).
- Garden completion mock-up (for the player only, we'll imply Kai 'feels' it through the follow-up conversations with Nonno, etc.).

Song possible names:
- Spooky Song
- Melancholy Melody
- Otherworldly Oratorio
- Pacific Prelude
- Wanderlust Waltz
- Harsh Hum
- Euphoric Prayer

Timescales for major redraft around this principle:
New timeline for all written work, including redraft.
September:
- Days 1 and 2
October:
- Days 3 and 4
- Encyclopaedia
November:
- Days 5 and 6, journal, environment clicks
- Independent proofreading can start
December:
- Days 7 and 8, opening and ending
January:
- Days 9, 10, 11, inventory/GUI pickups
February:
- Polish, copy for talking about the game, game description for stores, etc. PR beginning
- Independent proofreading finishes

Of course, that wasn't the final time the process was revised. We needed more funding at a certain point and found a new partner who also required localisation in 15 more languages than we were planning for. This meant introducing a last-minute localisation system and process, which revised our launch to September. We also later cut and combined a couple of days to improve pacing. But this is really the moment we pinned down the narrative design, in order for the writing to be effective.

This is a narrative design proposal with an impact on writing. But it's worth considering what a design proposal might look like from a writing perspective. So, take a look at one of the 'time of day' redraft proposals I signed off with the creative director following this proposal. Bear in mind I was working with a fixed palette of 'activities' (arrangements of characters in a place) and animations which had already been commissioned. When something is labelled as a 'BEAT' it means it's one of the mandatory conversations that need to happen – when you have all of the beats for the game-time-of-day, time moves forward. That's my MVP path as a writer.

In this proposal format I used several conventions we'd established in-house. They were that

- Each location with characters in it is named.
- Then the filename for the conversations is listed – and for the most part also tell me the one sentence description of what happens.
- Also listed is their plotline (a subset of conversations which had implications for my setting them up).
- The 'activity' is in italics (the group and animations of characters).
- Each is shaded depending on status: Blue = exists, and needs minimal redrafting. Yellow = exists but needs complete redraft. Green = needs creating and writing.
- If I needed more description for a conversation, it was noted below.

Location_Name
Filename_also_description (Plotline: X) activity
Possible expanded description

In lieu of colours, I'm going to use

- Dotted underline for 'done'.
- Single underline for 'same name but complete redraft'.
- Double underline for 'completely new'.

This one-line summary document helped me draw the picture of the time of day for the creative director to sign off, helped me understand the shape of the time of day, possible pathways through it, and to bear in mind what variables to consider when writing – and if I needed to gate conversations or branch them on variable or inventory checks. I already knew the story, characters, and places extremely well, so after a 'set-up' pass where I created and cut and wired everything, I just went into every file and listened to the characters talk, writing down what they said. This doc is still fairly narrative design interested – as I was doing both tasks on the game. But the writing info is also all there. It's both a proposal, and – once signed off – a working brief.

Just a note to say that this could feel a little overwhelming to look at! All of this combined shorthand was developed across the span of a whole project, so it's natural it might feel like a lot. If it feels like too much, you might want to just ignore most of the stuff connected to gating and implementation. I'm including these for completeness, but you can ignore variables, plotlines, and activities, and just look at how the doc summarises place, people and conversation contents for a specific time of day. If a narrative lead hands you this, you'll already be familiar with the tools and notations, and will be extrapolating

- Where?
- Who?
- What happens?
- What else is happening around them?
- What are the mandatory convos and what's optional?

Characters, voices, and places are all already known, and you have a one-line summary, so when you sit down to write each conversation from a doc like this, you just have to worry about the words.

Day 3 Afternoon. Game Time: 17
Redraft proposal

Indoor_archive
Ibn-Al Hatham (plotline: Archive chats) *YokeEat* **BEAT**
Yoke chats about a particular writer. Make sure there's a hint for the garden branched on a variable check for non-completion
Yoke_Claire_hints_EastGarden_again (plotline: Archive chats) *YokeEat*
Second hint

Indoor_bathhouse
Bathhouse_blocked (plotline: bathhouse block) *ailinsalon* **BEAT**
Ailin bathhouse issues can't do treatment right now
Everything_going_wrong (plotline: bathhouse block) *ailinsalon*
Ailin sadness chat 2 – chime with Mood for the day
AT17_fall_ailinsalon (AT17 fallbacks)

Indoor_Kai's home
Blackpool_lily_reminder (day 3 garden) *nonnobedsit*
Nonno_Gaia_memories_Day_3 (day 3 nonno) *nonnokitchen*
Nonno_East_garden_info (day 3 nonno) *nonnokitchen*
AT17_fall_nonnokitchen

Town_East_village

Garden_hint_miu_01 (plotline Day 3 Garden) **new activity** *eastgardenhang*
Miu hangs out in the east garden. Hint if garden not grown, nor Lily in inventory.
Garden_hint_miu_02 (plotline Day 3 Garden) *eastgardenhang*
Garden_miu_complete (plotline Day 3 Garden) *eastgardenhang* **BEAT**
Garden completion convo with Miu – you give her flower and she opens up a little.
Possible if **GardenMelancholia = true**. Needs several gates and variable checks internally
 too. 1. If gave lily already it moves time on. 2. If didn't give lily allows you to give it if in
 inventory, 3. If no lily and not given before, gives a hint. Variable created/check =
 GaveBlackpoolLily Can complete both Lily and Garden Beat.
Give_Blackpool_Lily_before_garden **BEAT**
Possible if **GardenMelancholia = false** but you have the Lily in an inventory check, she
 opens up a little and hints at how nice it would be if you finished the garden. Completes
 Lily Beat.
Give Blackpool lily after garden **BEAT**
A convo where you can give the lily, IF you have it in the inventory AND you haven't
 already given it. sets a variable **GaveBlackpoolLily** and moves time forwards. Completes
 Lily Beat.

Town_southside

Mori_gardening_day_3 (Day 3 Garden) *morigarden* **BEAT**
Mori gives you seeds, hints, delicate hint, make sure there's a BRANCH in case you already
 completed the garden
Mori_Garden_gossip (Day 3 Garden) *morigarden*
Mori gossip to point you towards other chars
AT17_fall_morigarden
Lolabye_rain_coming (plotline: Rain) *spikeplaysguitarboat*
Spike on boat singing – rain coming
AT17_fall_spikeplaysguitarboat
Fishing_alone (plotline: Rain) *bopekfish*
Bopek fishing alone but tomorrow the others might fish with him
AT17_fall_bopekfish

Town_treesqaure

Dots_Bully_Day_3 (plotline: Dots Day 3) *dotsausagebully*
Dots in tree square – down to trade, sausages bullying them/pretending to trade/maybe
 trying to come up with a new scheme featuring Dots.

Town_tung'sYard

Dennis_tung_talk (Plotline: Tung Dennis) *worktalk*
Tung_shows_dennis_his_boat (Plotline: Tung Dennis) *worktalk*

Tree_crown
Hostile_dot_guards_1 (plotline hostile dot guards Act 1) *dotguardstrunk*
Guards_recognise_you (plotline: hostile dot guards act 1) *dotguardstrunk*
Dots_run_and_hide (plotline: hostile dot guards act 1) *dotvillagelifeday*
Dots_still_hiding (plotline: hostile dot guards act 1) *dotvillagelifeday*
Dots_not_scared (plotline: hostile dot guards act 1) *dotvillagelifeday*
Talk_to_farmer_dot (plotline: hostile dot guards act 1) *dotfarmerwork*

Underground_jella's_lab
Jellasnoozing

Exercise 23 (1 hour for prep, choose the story and make up a problem; 2 hours to produce the proposal)

STORY SOLUTION EXERCISE

It's time to take another well-known story. This time take a religious tale, myth, or folk tale – as we need high level creativity, not specificity for this exercise. You're going imagine a problem and then make a high-level proposal for adding a character or changing the story that's not already explicit in the common telling of the story. Perhaps you're trying to make it adapt to some imaginary gameplay. Or trying to update it for modern sensibilities.

You need to decide what your problem is before proposing a solution, but don't take too much time about this – it's the proposal that's the exercise.
Using some of the following suggested headings, draw up a proposal of no more than two pages (aim for one) which clearly expresses the proposal, the problem it solves, and its impact on the project.

Proposal title and date
Problem proposal sets out to solve
Proposed solution
Short summary of proposal: who, what, where, when, why, how
How it solves the problem
Impact on full team (i.e. art, animation, set-up time, how much is your department, what cuts might be needed to make time for it)
Impact on writing
Risks and rewards
Other key details

In case you're not sure what I mean by 'create a problem', here're several examples of what a problem set-up could be and a solution you could create a design proposal for. My examples are all very Western European folk-tale influenced though; please do use examples close to your own cultural contexts.

Rapunzel (early project suggestion). Problem = gender. All of our hair swinging mechanics are very fun, but the source material feels pretty outdated in gender terms. Feel like it would be much fresher and more interesting if we do a gender swap, or make gender less binary, a princess as the player character, and Rapunzel as someone with an extraordinarily long beard, perhaps? Then the hair + player co-op is much freer of the older gendered expectations and can be lighter. (Bonus: Does hair have a different or richer significance for you? For example, if you're a Black writer, could you lean into the specific storied history of Black hair and take a different ownership of the source material and make the mechanics more interesting? What does it look like to use Black hair in a Rapunzel story? I couldn't tell this story well, but maybe you could.)

Red Riding Hood (mid-project suggestion). Problem = needs a character addition. A lot of the main action of the original story takes place in the cottage, but most of our gameplay is in the forest, taking the form of puzzles that the player solves as Red does tasks for Grandma before the Act 3 wolf gambit. It would be good to develop Red's character more during this time and to give the player more diegetic hints. Propose addition of a Farmer's Lad that Red meets around the forest. Propose that we extend the time period to years, not days, so the Farmer's Lad and Red can mature, develop, and in the end, the Lad can be revealed to be the Wood Cutter. We can also see Grandma needing more help and get more attached to her with a time extension in the story.

Cinderella (later project suggestion). Problem = character detail. Let's add into the backstory of Cinderella that her birth mother gave her a simple necklace on her deathbed. Have the memory be important so it can come up in X scene (necklace is all she has) and pay off in Y scene (evil sister breaks the necklace, Cinderella is at her lowest moment before the fairy godmother arrives). The memory will be a way of humanising Cinderella unique to our telling, and lead us to a clear emotional low, ready for the next act – where things get interesting.

Working with such broad examples isn't ideal, but the important thing is to understand that design proposals – whether writing them, communicating them, or receiving them – might be a part of your practice. It's valuable to think about how to communicate a proposal succinctly, in solution-focused terms, and understand that every proposal needs to understand its impact on the wider project.

What Happens When You Don't Get What You Need?

The last thing to say in terms of tools for developing is that almost every development process is deeply imperfect. You need to feel confident in advocating for better writing, tools, and storytelling, but also you need to be prepared for the fact that the answer will often be no, or some version of not now, which probably means never.

Part of being part of a team is picking your battles, understanding the politics of the team, and sometimes putting something down to experience – you did your best within the circumstances, and maybe this one won't be high up in your portfolio. Your practice will be much more about doing the best you can with the tools and processes you do have than it will be about inventing new ideas, characters, and worlds.

The final thing to remember is that, relatively speaking, writing is cheap.

Writing Is Cheap

Writing is absolutely the easiest thing to cut or change when compared to art, animation, or design features.[3] Acknowledging that is a big part of being a writer in a game dev process. A few examples:

- Did the art team not correctly interpret how a creature looks? Too bad, there's no time to redo the artwork, so change a couple of words in the description so it's now right.
- Don't have time to develop a rich trade mechanic as we don't have the 12 weeks of programmer resources it would take? Cut trade from the world; any plots that now involve exchange will use a simplified inventory variable system and/or cuts.
- Don't have time to implement and produce assets for a location midway through the player's journey? Cut it; now we're revisiting a location which is already built and has assets. Completely rewrite the story for that to happen.
- The creative director has decided they don't want to make a horror game anymore; they want to make a sci-fi game. Completely retheme the story in the new genre.
- We don't have time to make the rest of the game. This is now the game; refit the story so that works.

Here's a phrase to learn and use carefully:

That change isn't trivial.

Sometimes the writing taking the burden of the pressures of a game dev process is the right thing to do, and sometimes there are better solutions. Your job as a writer is to *clearly communicate* the impact of a change, to *take the time to understand the problem*, and to *scope the change or cut you're being asked to make*. If changes requested of the writing truly are easy and they don't damage the story – make them. If it's more complicated than that, communicate, if possible, by being solution-focused.

For example, perhaps someone else is assuming it will only take you a day to incorporate a character name change, but your understanding the story tools much more intimately means you know it will take you a week. Perhaps, though, if they resourced a tool for 'find

---

[3] Although remember that writing is only cheap before localisation and voice over processes have started. After that, anything except clear cuts is very expensive.

and replace' which takes half a day of a programmer's time, and you a day to implement and test, it would take the team a total of 1.5 days. Time to propose that alternative.

It's your job as the specialist to understand the impact on your work and to communicate the scope of incorporating it. If it's substantially more than the proposer has considered, that's when you use the nice, neutral phrase 'that change isn't trivial', followed by a clear scope outline and reasoning for the need for alternative solutions.

Developing Your Practice

Towards the end of this chapter the exercises have become a little more example-focused because in the end, some of your ability to develop your writing will be down to material and specific conditions. It will depend on the project, and the processes and freedoms you've been granted in your role, how well resourced you are, and the amount of agency you have in your tasks and role.

Remember to separate career from practice here. I'm trying to prepare you for the communication tools you'll use in a career setting, whilst encouraging you to develop your practice independently. Your dialogue skills, prototyping processes, editing skills, and critical learning are all things you can take care of in a small group of peers or in using some of these resources solo. The compromises and communication challenges of working on a game should be something you should be alive to when you join a team and as you learn to work with your collaborators.

CHAPTER 17

Tools for Finishing

This final chapter on tools for finishing is going to be much more practical and less focused on the act of writing itself. Tools for finishing will focus on the practical process of what writers do after the writing on a project is finished, offer productive ways to reflect on 'finishing' a project, and prepare you for moments of moving on – including from this book.

I will finish with some thoughts on putting together a portfolio (career) and developing a self-curriculum (practice).

In more author-led forms of writing, knowing when something is 'finished' is much harder. Finishing is less of a problem as a writer in games because you will often get little time and hard deadlines. 'Content lock' is a common term for a time after which no edits can be made – either to move into full quality assurance (QA), or localisation (loc) and/or voice over (VO) processes. Generally, finishing won't be your choice. Sometimes that might also be the end of your contract, and sometimes you will stay onboard to support a variety of other processes.

DOI: 10.1201/9781003182832-21

It will therefore be extremely rare that finishing – even making the decision at all – will be a process within your control. But on the rare occasion it is, here's a quote from Michael Atavar's *How to Be an Artist:*

> Knowing when to end a project, is a difficult art. Also completion itself is a complex process. It's easy to keep making, but arduous to come to an end. A finish requires application, stamina, determination.
>
> An ending requires –
>
> • Will power.
> • Clarity.
> • Overview.
> • Dedication.
>
> And 30% more work.
>
> The last 10% of any project will require 30% of your overall effort.

(Atavar, 2014, p. 229)

Or perhaps the pithier tweet from Ben Esposito I quoted in a footnote at the very beginning of this book:

> Nobody told me when you make a video game you have to make the whole thing.

(Esposito, 2018)

So, let us begin by tracing the practical role a writer might play after content lock, then move to means of reflecting on 'finished' work, and finishing by thinking through how you might move on from this book.

1. After content lock.
    • Loc and VO – Supporting these processes.
    • Quality assurance –Being a part of the QA process.
    • Marketing and PR – How you talk about the work/the game in public.
2. Reviews – Read reviews from critics you trust.
3. Reflecting on the project/work as a whole; your conditions as well as your work. Always be reflecting. How to deal with an art form which iterates in years rather than weeks.
4. Portfolio – How to make a portfolio.
5. Practice – How to set your own curriculum.

After Content Lock

'Content lock' can mean different things in different processes, and writing might have a different lock point than art, for example, and be specified differently: perhaps it's a complete lock – no more edits at all – or perhaps you're still allowed to attend to typos and are allowed to cut lines. The two important things to note:

- There will be a point in the process where you're no longer allowed to make changes.
- This point should be agreed and carefully specified between you and the rest of the team.

Understanding why lock dates apply will help you specify what kind of lock it is – don't be afraid to ask why they want to lock all changes by X date. If their answer is localisation, then you can ask for typos to be considered part of QA, not content lock.

Reasons you might specify a content lock:

- You don't want to introduce any further bugs into the game (including typos).
- You need to lock the content so it can be translated.
- You need to lock the content so it can be voiced.
- The game needs to be fully recorded and submitted to a ratings agency.
- It's just time to finish the game.

Content lock doesn't necessarily mean the end of a writer's involvement, however. When you spec out a piece of work asking if the team wants you on board to support loc, VO, and QA (whichever apply) is pretty wise (and a bit more money). You might also be useful in working out how to write about the game for the public.

Let's dig into what these processes could look like for a writer.

Quality Assurance

Games can produce very large volumes of text. As I touched on in Part I: Theory, proofreading large volumes of text requires tools – hopefully ones which you have anticipated the need for (and certainly will have if also preparing to extract the lines for localisation or VO scripts). I strongly recommend working with a professional proofreader – it's a genuine skill and important practice. It's also something not everyone is aware of so you might need to advocate for room in the budget for someone. If you end up doing it yourself, I strongly recommend extracting the text into a format different to how you wrote it – so you can try and look at it anew, and into a collaborative doc format where you can comment, flag, etc. in ways you can't in most game writing tools.

If you are lucky enough to work with a professional proofreader, then be ready to prepare an intro doc for them which explains new words from the universe of your game, and key spelling and grammar details: American or UK English, what style guide you're using (*The Guardian* style guide is the one I've most frequently used, but academic ones work too). And make clear any standardisations unique to the kind of writing in games, for example, have you decided to write laughter 'haha', do you allow the use of question marks for rising inflection rather than a genuine question. All of the extra things that come up in writing for reading like speaking. The most important thing is to be *consistent*. You will certainly make decisions with your proofreader too – when maybe you've not realised something needs standardising – but going in with a guide to new words, context, and already chosen standards will make this process much more effective.

Another part of QA – and by far the biggest for a writer – will be fixing bugs. Writing is often the cheapest way to fix things; if an asset is missing, then remove the text which references it, etc. You will also need to track down bugs in the logic of the writing, mark up which has been misapplied, and check that all branches of the story work together and make sense. If you've kept good documentation, you will know where to find things in the game to fix them, but ideally, you'll also have a 'find and replace' function in your writing tools. If you don't, then asking for one is worth it. Sometimes it might need to be done manually by a programmer, but that's better than nothing, and annoying them often enough might make them build you a tool instead. QA resources vary widely to just internal resources all the way to working with QA studios with dedicated people testing your game on all platforms several times a day for different things (performance, edge cases, specific bugs, logic, etc.).

Most QA processes will involve bug tracking software like Jira (or any task tracking software really, but Jira is the most well-known in my experience). If you find a bug, you will – to the spec agreed by your team – report it. At a basic level, a bug report describes a bug, marks how severe it is, assigns it to a person or department, and describes reproduction ('repro') steps, like the build you found it in, what you did to find the bug, and anything else that someone needs to reproduce it. You might also attach screenshots or video. If you receive bug reports for your writing, it's then your job to go through, find the bug, and fix it. This might be the first time that some of the team will have read your writing so it's also possible you'll get some feedback at this point, which honestly is typically inappropriate (content feedback should come earlier), but take the time to read it and consider if it's important.

It's also okay to explain that something isn't a bug. Example: A character uses an obscure and old-fashioned English idiom. A team member flags this as being nonsense. You could choose to update it, but if the character is meant to be obscure and old-fashioned, it's okay for them to not make sense because what the writing is doing is characterising them – the meaning *is* not making sense.

Loc and VO

Supporting VO might not be something a writer is involved in at all, but equally you might be called upon to assist in building the tools to express the text as a script, in supporting a voice director and during the VO process being on hand to answer questions about characters, tone, implication (and writing docs to hand this over – you will want to assist casting calls by describing characters and voices). If your VO process allows for 'rewrites' (i.e. the creative director wants to change a line that doesn't work well voiced during recording), then you may also need to be on hand to note changes and make them in the text. Make sure that if your game is going to be voiced you know if/how you might be called on to support the process.

The same preparations you make for a proofreader will also be helpful in supporting a localisation process. Expressed simply: localisation tools will extract strings of text from the game, give them a unique ID, and export them into a format that a localisation studio's software can read. Then, translators use their software to view strings and enter translations. The localisation software will then export finished translations so they in turn can be imported back into the game. This time the unique line ID will be also associated with a language, so when a game language is selected, the game will call the line ID in the relevant language for the relevant place. Ideally, a localisation tool should also allow you to see who's speaking, possible linked lines, and allow writer commentary. Writer commentary is vital for a good translation.

Every part of the game, from UI to dialogue, should be a part of this process. And you should also take a moment to think about if you need store copy (see the section 'Certification, Marketing, and PR') translated too.

Localisation can take a number of weeks or months, and you should both prepare for it and prepare to support it. During the localisation of *Mutazione* I spent the first hour of every day responding to questions in a group sheet where translators posted lines they had queries about – things like implications, idioms, or how I made up a word – so they could make sure their translation made sense. Imagine you're a translator looking at the word 'present' in a single word string of text. Does it mean 'here', 'gift', or 'to show something'? That might have three different words in French or German, and you might need to know the gender of who is 'here' or how formal the situation is for a good translation.

There also will typically be an LQA (localisation QA) process, where people fluent in the relevant languages play the game and flag strange translations in context (not in the localisation software). That will mean your team will also produce tools whereby players can identify a line's ID in play, and a shared feedback sheet where LQA can write up issues, and LQA and loc can discuss it.

You can also save a lot of time and make your localisation much better by preparing a doc in advance which sets out a context for the world, tone of the game, different kinds of text, and gives character descriptions and kinds of voice. If you put a lot of work into creating a strong naturalistic voice for each of your characters, then your translators need to know so they can find a local equivalent. Also, prepare your translators for the decisions you made to make your game more welcoming and approachable or inclusive – like using 'people who menstruate' rather than 'women' in a medical text which recommends a certain herb for period pains, or that you use they/them pronouns for a character. And make sure you find LQA team members with the LGBTQ+/relevant experience who will know how their specific language approaches these things.

Here's a little excerpt from the *Mutazione* localisation docs. First up a little extract (A–C) from the doc I produced for all the plant names I made up and how I came to that name from a combination of research and imagining. This allowed LQA to use the same reasoning. I've included a couple of the translation fields too so you can maybe see how the translators worked from my guidance. And then following that there's a page or two from the localisation context doc for tone and character.

Key	Description	French	German	Spanish
Aerorchid	Orchid is self-explanatory, the 'aero' was a word that felt like it fit nicely in front of it and it's quite slender and pointy (aerodynamic).	Aérorchidée	Luftorchidee	aerorquídea
Algifern	Half way between a fern and algae. It's a disturbing pale colour that made me think of plants that like the dark, such as algae.	Algifougère	Algenfarn	alguelecho
Améthriscus	The purple colour made me think of the precious stone amethyst; 'iscus' is a common end of plant name, like 'hibiscus'.	Améthriscus	Amethyskus	ametisco
Anarcadia	It's such a ridiculous-looking plant I decided to name it something outlandish. This is a combination of the words 'anarchy' and 'arcadia' (Arcadia is the ancient rural idyll from myth and legend).	Anacharis	Anarkadia	anarcadia
Anemone Tree	Looks a little bit like a sea anemone and a tree.	Arbre à anémones	Anemonenbaum	árbol anémona
Arrow Hat	Mushrooms very commonly have names that include words like 'fan', 'cap' or 'hat'. These are shaped like arrows.	Champiflèche	Pfeilhut	flechero
Astral Ragwort	Looked a bit like a night sky. Ragwort is a kind of plant in the real world.	Séneçon astral	Astralwurz	hierba cana astral
Atlas Leaf	It has big leaves. Atlas was big enough to hold the whole world up.	Feuille d'Atlas	Atlasblatt	hoja de Atlas
Bearweed	This name I think pre-existed my work on the game. It's kind of fluffy though, maybe that made someone think of teddy bears. Actually, that sounds like the kind of thing I would do. Probably I named this and forgot why.	Herbe des ours	Bärengarbe	hierba del oso

(Continued)

Key	Description	French	German	Spanish
Blackpool Lily	Dark glossy leaves made me think of 'black pool', and lily is obvious.	Nénuphar palustre	Schwar- zlachenlilie	lirio del pantano
Blue Claw	It's blue and the leaves sort of spider down like claws.	Griffe bleue	Blauklaue	garra azul
Blue Horsetail	Funny looking plant, don't know why I went with horsetail except that it's quite a well-known rural animal from our history, and a few things are named after them (horseradish, for example). I could sort of see people using these to play pin the tail on the donkey too. Looks like tails, is blue, blue horsetail.	Prêle bleue	Blauschweif	cola de caballo azul
Bluefern	It's a fern with a bluish colour.	Fougère bleue	Blaufarn	helecho azul
Bluenanas	It's a blue pineapple. 'Ananas' is 'pineapple' in basically every other language.	Ananableu	Blaunanas	piñazul
Boroboa	This is actually a play on words for a game I was playing at the time called Gorogoa.	Boroboa	Klecksie	boroboa
Butterweed	The ends looked like butterbeans so I called it butterweed. I also thought about the childhood game where you shine a buttercup under someone's chin in the sun and say 'you like butter' and could imagine the same for this. (Although, who doesn't like butter?)	Herbobeurre	Butterblüm- chen	hierba garrofón
Cacamba	It's a play on the word 'cucumber' although it's actually a salad leaf.	Cacombre	Kakamba	pepinoja
Cactus	Is a cactus.	Cactus	Kaktus	cactus

(Continued)

255

Key	Description	French	German	Spanish
Calamagrostis	It looked gross and a bit poisonous so I named it 'calam' for 'calamity' and 'agrostis' because it feels a bit like the word 'gross', the 'is' on the end is to make it feel more planty.	Calamistis	Bamgel	ascalamita
Cave Reed	It's a reed that grows in caves.	Roseau caverneux	Höhlenschilf	junco de caverna
Cerignola	It's a place in Italy. There are a few straight up Italian words in the game because the founders of the game were Nils (German) and Alessandro (Sardinian), and they enjoyed using Italian words as proper nouns. Or in this case an Italian proper noun as an English proper noun.	Cérignole	Cerignola	ceriñola
Cliff Shrub	It's a shrub that grows on cliffs.	Arbuste des falaises	Klippen-strauch	matojo de barranco
Coastal Orchid	It's an orchid that thrives by the sea.	Orchidée côtière	Küstenorchi-dee	orquídea costera
Cold Finger	Looks like fingers (yuck) and is blue.	Doigt glacé	Kalter Finger	manofría
Coral Weed	Looks a bit like coral, but grows above the ground. Added weed to make it sound like a plant that isn't coral.	Herbe coralienne	Korallenkraut	mata coralina
Coroca	I remember going through a bunch of existing plants before settling on this as a made-up word that sounded like my inspiration plants, but unfortunately, I can't remember what I went through. It's possibly also a word for a bird?	Coroca	Coroca	coroca

(Continued)

Key	Description	French	German	Spanish
Cotton Grass	It's grass that has cotton-like tops.	Herbe de coton	Baumwoll-gras	hierba algodón
Crab Tree	The harvest for this plant made me think of crab lures, so I called it a 'crab tree' and possibly wrote in the encyclopaedia that crabs like to hang around underneath it.	Arbre à crabes	Krabben-baum	árbol cangrejero
Cresset Reed	They're reddish and it made me think of the word 'russet'; 'cresset' is combined with 'crescent' and reed because it's reed-like.	Roseau torchère	Rostschilf	junco cobrizo
Crimson Lily	Beautiful lily-like leaves and a red flower.	Lys pourpre	Purpurlilie	lirio carmín
Cyanita	Mushrooms often end in 'nita', and the blue made me call it 'cyan' (the name of the blue used in printers).	Cyanite	Cyanling	cianita

[...]

Guidelines on tone.

On colonialism/racism: *Mutazione* is a story which at its heart is about intergenerational trauma, and the way that communities have to work together to live in harmony. Because of the themes of the game – the colonialism of science, isolated communities, mutants who are ostracised from the life of the mainland – we have taken great care to make sure that the game explores these issues, but *doesn't exploit them*. We've worked carefully with a diversity consultant to review the script, and we would appreciate it if you would take the same sensitivity into account when translating language. We're striking a balance between the colourful way our characters are represented, and making it clear that they're not caricatures. There are clear notes under the character section for each voice, but in general, if you're in any doubt, please check in with Hannah.

On sexuality and gender: We also have taken care to make sure that we don't dwell on other stereotypes, and wherever possible characters should not make gendered assumptions, including being alive to LGBTQ+ concerns. Kai herself is bi (thought it's not a focus of the story), and (for example) the now-not-used medicine book described a medicine for easing period pains as 'for people who menstruate' so as to be inclusive of transmen/non-binary folk who menstruate. It's a core value of Mutazione

(Continued)

Key	Description	French	German	Spanish
	that we not build assumptions into the game that could be alienating. This, I know, is a challenge for languages where gender modifies words that might be gender-neutral in English, but we'd like to encourage you wherever possible to not make assumptions about gender or sexuality in part of your language wherever possible, and to do research within your language to see what queer communities are currently doing with e.g. gender pronouns, etc. If in doubt, please reach out to Hannah.			

Character voices:

Link to illustrated Story Bible: (summary of overall story and gameplay) provided separately.

Kai (Player Character)

Key facts:

Age: 15

She/her (might be thinking about trying 'they' next school year)

Family: Gaia is her mother, her father died when she was 8 years old.

Granddaughter of Nonno and Dora (deceased) and has a baby brother (aged 3) whom she takes care of while her mother works.

Lives in an apartment in the city.

Goes to high school, captain of the swim team, serious crush on one of her teammates.

Notes on their voice:

Kai is hesitant and quiet to begin with, but only because she's among strangers. She's also quick-witted, outspoken, impatient, and has a fondness for slightly-bad jokes. She should sound like a contemporary teenager with an interest in sports, and other outdoorsy things, who's hands-on, and not very good at talking about feelings.

Nonno

Kai's Grandfather

Key facts:

Age: 63

He/him

Stubborn, intuitive, charismatic, highly intelligent.

Estranged widow of Dora, father to Gaia, grandfather to Kai and her brother.

Accomplished Shaman.

Currently dying.

(Continued)

Key	Description	French	German	Spanish
	Notes on their voice:			
	Nonno is one of the oldest people in the community, his language is often vague, because he's trying to get Kai to make her own connections and learn things for herself. He also likes to talk in metaphors, and sometimes rambles on in a way that's frustrating to Kai. I have styled him as a kind of older academic who used to be an explorer. Think 'Indiana Jones', but retired and kind of lonely'. Uses old-fashioned British English language.			
Tung				
Odd job man, Mechanic				
Key facts:				
Age: 18				
He/him				
	Son of Claire (mutant), and Gorm (human) who deserted his family when Tung outgrew him at age 5.			
	Maternal grandson of Mori.			
	Sensitive, insecure, hot-tempered, loyal.			
	Plays drums in the local band.			
	Notes on their voice:			
	Tung is defined by his inarticulacy. A lot of 'ums' and his words are clumsy, even when they're saying quite poignant or important things. He's young, only a bit older than Kai, but definitely less emotionally mature. He's bumbling and Kai enjoys riffing off him, but he lets her, because it's fairly close to the friendship he has with Miu. Vocabulary contemporary and young, except when he's talking about romance, where his soap opera obsession has made him very grandiose. Cadence: stumbling.			
Miu				
Hunter, Nonno's neighbour.				
Key facts:				
Age: 24				
She/her				
	Adopted daughter of Spike.			
	Lost husband RD and her kids to a disaster 4 years ago.			

(Continued)

259

Key	Description	French	German	Spanish
	Moved from the ruins of their old house to a small cabin next door to Nonno's.			
	Singer in the local band.			
	Notes on their voice:			
	Miu is very terse. She's in her mid-20s, but has gone through some serious trauma, and has dealt with it by repressing a lot of her feelings. Before the disaster she was naiver and was very funny in an open kind of way, but now she's incredibly deadpan, and speaks in the minimum number of words, always diminishing important sentiments a little after she speaks them. Her vocabulary is contemporary and young. Her tone is deadpan and terse.			
Mori				
Cook, Tung's Grandmother, Gossip.				
Key facts:				
Age: 69				
She/her	Suffers from gout and make sure everyone knows it.			
	She has been the main source of correspondence between Gaia and Nonno over the years.			
	Interferes because she cares.			
	Mother of Claire, grandmother of Tung.			
	Notes on their voice:			
	Mori is a larger-than-life character who is the community's main gossip and carer. She's always meddling and trying to winkle information out of people. She also cooks in the main eatery in the community, which she runs and grows vegetables for. She's an older lady, who will use old-fashioned sayings and idioms, but is also quite dirty in terms of sense of humour. Her words and tone are warm, she uses lots of endearments. She's of the same generation as Yoké and Nonno. I've given her a lot of old-fashioned English sayings and words, to the point where it doesn't matter that a lot of people won't have heard them before – they're about building character, meaning will be gleaned from context. Cadence: bubbling over with warmth, always interrupting, not always listening.			
[...]				

Certification, Marketing, and PR

Finally, as a professional writer, your skills could be extremely valuable in supporting certification, marketing, and public relations (PR) processes. This might include:

- Press kit copy[1]
- Press releases
- Store copy
- Ratings submission support
- Writing blog posts and guest articles about the game
- Being part of interviews with press
- Attending or doing your own streams
- Text in trailers
- Running social media campaigns

Text which describes and promotes the game will – alongside gifs and a good trailer – be the thing that convinces someone to give your game a try. It needs to be convincing, accessible, understandable, succinct, scannable, fit the room of the store/screen comfortably. It needs to get the player excited, but not overpromise and tempt poor reviews. You'll want a one-line description, and then a 50-, 100-, 300-, and 500-word copy version of any copy about the game.

Your team will also want a doc of common interview questions answered by key members of the team, so if someone sends in an email interview, people can copy and adapt an answer from the relevant team members. This is material a team should invest in; it's the first thing many people will see before any of the other writing you do, and it's something that should be done in time to get it localised if you're shipping the game in more than one language.

Then there're certification and ratings processes – ESRB and PEGI are the USA and European ratings agencies. To get an age rating for your game (necessary for all console platforms), your team will have to go through questionnaires and, in some cases, record every piece of possibly contravening piece of action or text, or even the whole game (with every possible choice) to prove the age rating you're selecting. That takes time! A writer can definitely be useful in quickly pulling up, e.g. uses of the word 'damn', or quickly confirming whether there are direct references to alcohol, and making changes if you're required to hit a certain rating.

Then 'cert' is the process that some consoles require your game to pass to be ready to launch – not just that the game runs, but that it runs to a certain spec, and that you have all of the relevant store copy, in the right languages, with the right store assets.

If you're a writer supporting this process, make sure you go through and discover all of the necessary fields for each of your platforms and processes, so you know that, e.g., you need to pick two genres, and need a translation of 'mutant-soap-opera' in every language.

---

[1] For an example of a press kit, check out mutazionegame.com/presskit. So many of my case study examples are *Mutazione,* but not much else of my game work is out of NDA, I'm afraid.

Ideally much of this will be supported by a marketing, publisher, or PR professional, but if you are a prominent writer on a story-driven project without a very large team, it might be very valuable for you to be a part of shaping how your team talks about the game as well as how it was written.

Reviews

Some people live by an ethos of 'never read the reviews'. They are probably the lucky kind of people who don't need to find good pull quotes or respond to poor reviews mentioning a game-breaking bug with a fix and an apology in hope they'll rescind it. As a writer, you may very well not be involved in that part of the 'finishing' process of post-launch support,[2] and thus be able to choose to not read them. The most important thing here is another 'who am I' moment.

I read the reviews. I read all of them! I'm pretty robust and able to identify the difference between someone the game wasn't for (a surprising amount of people who don't like reading will play a story-driven text-heavy game) or who just doesn't *get* it, from crit which I can consider and internalise and think about. All of the rules of crit from the Critical Response Process outlined in Chapter 16 apply here, so remember, with regards to reviews consider:

- Are you in a place to hear crit?
- What do you hope to discover from the crit?
- From what position, awareness, or perspective does the person offering the crit come?
- How does the format in which the crit is being offered affect the tone and content of the crit offered?
- Is the crit intended to be constructive?
- Who is the person offering the crit talking to?
- Does this crit point out a problem, or offer a solution from which you can articulate a problem?
- How can you carry this forward into your next work?

Just ask yourself if you want to read the reviews. If you don't want to that's okay. And allowing that to be your answer rather than reading a bunch of things and feeling like the past three years were a waste of time, or that you could never have fixed it because it was out of your control, or that everyone is a philistine – none of that is helpful to you and your practice.

---

[2] I'm not digging too deeply into post-launch support here because writers are rarely a part of it unless there's a long tail of extra content planned and funded. But it's worth considering that players might expect years of post-launch support and content from a game. It's about as exhausting as it sounds.

If you have to or want to read reviews, I recommend deciding how, why, and when. Don't read them obsessively every time you get a Google alert. Set aside time, absorb them, gather your pull quotes, note your bug reports, respond to anything you need to, and jot down any reflections for your practice in one of the practice/reflection note-taking systems you will have diligently built after this book's advice. If you might need to respond to reviews on storefronts, you might want to create 'form' responses in a sheet you and colleagues can copy and paste from if there's a known bug. Having such a sheet could also be useful if you need to take a breath before responding. Draft it in the sheet, and take five minutes to come back to it before posting.

You'll need to look at reviews more regularly at the beginning. You might also want a way of logging them and passing them to your PR or post-launch support team. But make sure that you are ready, you have room, you set aside time when you do it, so that you're not letting feedback disrupt or upset you. Take control of your feedback response, otherwise the feeling of having poured years into something that someone decided they didn't like in three minutes could fast become extremely draining and unproductive.

If you do end up drowning in crit, though, don't get angry at yourself; reach out to friends, colleagues, or professional mental health support resources depending on what you need.

Reflecting

That's the more procedural stuff out of the way. Aside from being on hand to fix bugs, support post-launch, and work on possible updates or new content, how do you deal with *actually being finished*.

Having come from performance has probably put me in the most useful position to be in when it comes to having developed a practice of finishing. In almost all of my early career as an artist my deadlines looked like me standing on a stage in front of an audience – really there's nothing about that kind of deadline which you can delay or shrink from. You're either doing your best or you're deeply embarrassed. I got good at deadlines.

The timescales of performance are also really helpful to the psychological process of finishing. The work I developed my practice in takes 12 weeks to make (pretty standard for a 90-minute piece of devised performance) and tours for a year – where with each performance you learn a little more about it. That's actually a pre-made finishing process – no choice on deadline, no option to defer, pre-made scope, no sense that a work defines you or holds a large chunk of your career or life in its stead, and a long process of reflection. You might also do lots of concurrent smaller works, interventions, pieces. I could come out of a year of my career having worked on or contributed to over 25 finished works.

In that context I consider my whole practice to be my *work*. Individual projects are sought out as ways to test or iterate, learn, and push myself; or to take a step towards a gnawing question at the heart of my practice (or because I need some money this month). It meant my work grew with me, and if I read a script for something I made five years ago, I can understand it as a stepping stone to where I am now. In performance you also learn more about a work each time you perform it. You're allowed to come to terms with your finishing out of those necessary material conditions; there's no delaying, there's no time to luxuriate, you're always moving on, you do many projects and are less invested in each one.

But what about in larger scale indie games where a project can take three to five years? Where there are so many things intersecting with your practice as to make it hard to unpick what you learned, or what you were stopped from doing out of necessity or someone else's vision? The moment of finishing might be out of your hands, but the process of finishing is much more than that – it's a process of reflection, of identifying what you learned, and that's a process you don't need permission to start.

In that way, it's good to break down 'finishing' into smaller time periods, or production phases. If you take time to reflect at the end of each month or production phase, use headings such as

- Challenges
- Wins
- Solutions
- Things out of my control
- What I might do differently next time
- What extra resources I need
- What I learned
- What I could have asked or said more clearly

You will give yourself room for much more iterative reflection, perhaps better equipping you for the next phase of work. Then at the end of each project go through the same reflection, but then add in cuttings from reviews and critical responses to the work that you found useful or to hold some truth. Paste them in a notebook or notes app and then reflect:

- Why is this useful?
- What does it articulate?
- Who is talking and why is their position relevant?
- How can I respond to this in my practice?
- What skills/experience/reading/tools might I work on to address this?

Make sure you're pulling out positive extracts too – learning from your successes is as useful as learning from your failures. 'It mattered to someone that I had a character address another character's language around mental health problems here' is something fortifying to hold close to your heart – and also to use to support your argument in your next project when you want your narrative lead to not allow the game UI voice to use the word 'crazy' pejoratively.

Your team or company might also have formal reflection and review processes, but make sure you have one of your own, even if there is a company debrief.

Portfolio

One of the most useful things you can do as a writer for games moving to a new project (or looking to) is have a clear, accessible, and easy-to-read portfolio website. Whether it's built in Tumblr, Squarespace, WordPress, or from hand, it doesn't matter. It does need to work well on mobile and in most common browsers. And you need a URL that you can still be proud of when you're ten years down the line.

You might still need to put together custom portfolios for certain applications or studios, but in general a public portfolio site linked to an active Twitter profile is one of the most effective means of reaching out for work.

What makes a good game writing portfolio? When I'm recruiting writers, at minimum I want to see

- **Landing page**
    A landing page with a picture, a short summary of you and your experience, and three clear representative writing samples. A clear 'contact' button with an actual email address.
- **About page**
    An about page which is a longer description of you and your practice, plus a CV-like list of crucial credits, qualifications, and experience.
- **Portfolio highlights**
    Writing samples: one short dialogue sample which shows you have a good ear for character, line length, naturalism etc.; one story-led design proposal; one interactive writing sample including well-written choices (a video if not playable in-browser). Each sample should have a clear statement explaining the brief, context from which it's excerpted, and any awards or review quotes or accolades associated with the work. If you've worked with/for someone on the sample, ask for an endorsement quote from your manager/collaborator you can include on the page.
- **Wider portfolio**
    A larger portfolio section with more examples of work – if you've worked in different mediums it might be useful to set up a subdomain which is games .yournamewebsite.com as the home for all of this, and link to your full website with poetry and fiction and TV writing from the root domain. Have a clear 'games writing portfolio' link from that root portfolio though.
- **Optional**
    Blog, link to social media.

These portfolio pieces are crucially *all things you don't need previous experience to work on*. You can, in fact, take a year to develop pieces for your portfolio (see the next section for a possible model for this).

And as I said – this is what *I* want to see – but it's also worth taking a look at people a couple of years ahead of you career-wise in areas you're interested in working in and seeing what they provide (don't use very established writers as an example, because by the point someone is operating on an established reputation, they will have outdated portfolios).

One very useful thing you can reach out to mentors for is a portfolio review. If the kinds of companies you want to work for aren't advertising entry-level positions, reaching out for a couple hour's portfolio review as a piece of mentoring from their story team could be a very valuable insight into what they'd want to see and a way to get them to be aware of you, maybe even recommend you to others.

Finally, don't be afraid of cold outreach. Some people hate receiving cold emails, which is fine; they probably won't remember you because they won't read it. But occasionally taking the time to do some cold applications is good practice and might result in making someone aware of you when they are recruiting.

The basic principles of a cold email:

- Research five to ten organisations you'd love to work with.
- Read their previous job adverts if possible, look through their work, familiarise yourself with them and their team size. Think about where they might be in a project cycle (did they just release something, ask them to bear you in mind for an internship on the next project).
- Be specific about what you want: paid work, shadowing, mentorship.
- Compose a careful and succinct email which explains.
  - Who you are.
  - What you have experience/interest in.
  - Why you're interested in them.
  - How you'd like to develop.
  - Your availability and what you'd like from them.
  - Add a link to your portfolio and attach a CV.
- Do not try and be 'original' or 'cute' or 'funny'. Be professional, clear, and above all *succinct*. Do not apologise for reaching out to them. Do not expect a response from them, and do not chase up the email.

Practice

I've spoken at length about how your practice belongs to you, and how that's an exciting and hopefully empowering concept. But what can that mean practically speaking?

A large part of this part of the book has been an invitation to build a mentor in your own mind. To take the time to learn about how you learn, work, and to give you a sense of ownership over your practice. I also shared a number of different exercises and practices, all of which I hope find a home in some of your practices, but none of which will work for everyone.

Exercise 24 (0.5 days of prep, thinking, rereading Part III; 0.5 days of planning)

As I leave you at the end of this guide to *Writing for Games*, the final exercise I would like to offer you is to *set your own curriculum*. To have a lifelong practice is to be a lifelong learner, except that your peers and critics and your tools for reflection are your teacher.

So, bearing in mind your resources (time, mental health, wealth, well-being, other skills), try this:

- Take a year.
- Split that year into 52 weeks.
- Mark the time that you need for rest and well-being very clearly.
- Identify some key things you want to develop – by picking exercises from this book, identifying resources you want to read/play/watch, and/or imagining other means of learning. Remember reflection time.
- Make sure you leave time to organise any group work.
- Don't be afraid to rework the plan as you learn what works and doesn't work.
- Plan it into the year.
- Put it into your calendar.
- Buy nice, new books/pens/notebooks if you can afford it – make a ritual out of things so it feels exciting.

That is, devise a year's curriculum for yourself. The following is an example of how that can work. I have made some basic decisions about the person completing it to show how to balance career, practice and person. This is a person without major caring responsibilities, who is a runner, working a day job in a country which takes Christian holidays, but who practises a different religion – and so needs to make room in their life which doesn't adhere with work holidays.

My Curriculum – 1 year

My availability/health/well-being: 2 half days per week. Some exceptions. I would also like to use 5 days of holiday this year to do an 'intensive' week on something. Make sure to pencil in holidays, and don't try and work when fasting, I need evenings for Iftar and am too wiped out on the weekends. Never sacrifice my running for the curriculum, running always makes me feel better, and should come first.

What I want to develop:
- Networks
- Dialogue skills
- Influences
- And revise my portfolio

Resources: Work will let me use the office after 6 pm for group work, but otherwise I want to use mostly free resources. Can afford one event though.

Things to bear in mind: My day job can be draining at unpredictable times, so before I check in on the next month's work, I should check in on how overwhelmed I'm feeling and not feel bad about deferring or cancelling a month.

Notes to self: Write at least a one-line reflection at the end of every week. Even if it's just 'went as planned' – but try and at least note down challenges, solutions, things I learned, and further leads. Also, is it worth blogging about this to keep myself accountable? Could also build my network a bit more …

Week	Summary	Detail
1	Prepare research weeks	Choose 3 each of games, texts, talks, and films/plays for reflection. Decide on the critical reflection framework – a common set of questions I'm going to think about.
2	Play & reflect	Play 1–2 games, and write critical reflections on them.
3	Play & reflect	Play 1–2 games, and write critical reflections on them.
4	Watch & reflect	Watch 2–3 films/plays and write up my reflections.
5	Read & reflect	Read excerpts and articles, write up my reflections.
6	Listen & reflect	Watch or listen to a number of talks, write up my reflections.
7	Week off – holiday time	No work on holiday!
8	Planning group work	Reach out to some people from my degree to see if anyone wants to do the dialogue workshop with me.
9	Prep dialogue workshop	Prepare to run the workshop – arrange space, send out materials, get work to set the space aside.
10	Week off – holiday time	No work on holiday!
11	Workshop	Dialogue workshop part 1: 2 evenings after work
12	Workshop	Dialogue workshop part 2: 1 evening and reflection. Ask if anyone wants to do a crit club starting later in the year – monthly? If not, can I do a solo one?
13	Reflection	Reflect on what I learned from dialogue workshop.
14	Portfolio piece	Rework one of my dialogue samples from the workshop so it's portfolio-ready.
15	Conference	Attend major game conference – go to talks, and also go to booths and talk to game makers. Try and meet other people with interests like me, and find new interesting people to follow on social media.

16	Research	Do some game jam research – something that fits in with my life/interest and where I'll feel useful, ideally in week 22? Look on globalgamejam.com.
17	Week off	Religious month – will be fasting, not a good time to do extra work.
18	Week off	Same as above.
19	Week off	Same as above.
20	Holiday week – actual holiday	Same as above – also taking time off work.
21	Admin	Confirm crit club first game, and find more talks and reading. Plan what I'm going to use the intensive week for – and plan out each day – make sure the plan means I have something finished by end of week.
22	Game jam?	Pencil in game jam here?
23	Reflection	Reflect on game jam experience. Is there anything I can include in my portfolio?
24	Influence building and networking	Crit club meeting 1 – hand over choice and running to next person in the club (we should share this).
25	Holiday week – intensive week – portfolio building	Make a piece of interactive fiction in Ink or Twine for release on Itch.io – brief: an interactive fiction adaptation of a short story from a collection by Izumi Suzuki I read recently. Day one: reread story and make notes about how to adapt. Day two: paper prototyping and planning: Day three: draft 1. Day four: draft 2. Day 5: polish and playtesting. Share on Twitter, see if I can get any responses/plays via Itch.io.
26	Holiday week – actual holiday	No work on holiday!
27	Reference building	Play crit club next game.
28	Rest	
29	Influence building and networking	Crit club meeting 2.
30	Rest	
31	Reference building	Play crit club next game and watch some GDC talks.
32	Week off	Religious new year – take a week to celebrate.

33	Reflection	Follow up new year with a reflection on what I've learned so far – both about learning and *from* the learning. Do I want to revise the plan?
34	Influence building and networking	Crit club meeting 3.
35	Portfolio building	Review my online portfolio and work out what's missing, and also revise how it looks/works – rebuild in a different CMS?
36	Portfolio building	Update all non-creative stuff including CMS for portfolio.
37	Reference building	Play crit club next game and read some gamedeveloper.com Deep Dives from writers and narrative designers.
38	Rest	
39	Influence building and networking	Crit club meeting 4.
40	Portfolio building	Decided I need to showcase my fantasy skills and team work. Will work on a 2-page design doc proposing a new area in a fantasy game from a story + world building perspective. What is the area? What kinds of items + characters + encounters are there? What purpose does it serve in the imaginary game's pacing/development?
41	Portfolio building	Redraft and then add the design doc to online portfolio.
42	Rest	
43	Reference building	Play crit club next game.
44	Rest	
45	Influence building and networking	Crit club meeting 5 – maybe agree if we want to continue next year/do something different.
46	Portfolio work	Add in and arrange the design doc, dialogue. sample, and short story Ink adaptation in portfolio
47	Career research	Look up some jobs I want to do and analyse the application processes and requirements. What am I missing? Is there anything I could apply to?

48	Career reflection	Redo my CV with the workshops I've organised and new things I've worked on this year. Reflect on what I want next steps in career to be (more game jams? offering myself for speculative work? finding a mentor? ask someone for a portfolio review?). And plan how to reach them – create tasks in calendar for next year's plan
49	Practice reflection	Reflect on what I developed this year and write a practice plan for next year.
50	Fun week	Do something fun to celebrate! Some kind of treat! Maybe could go to cinema or theatre with crit club pals.
51	Holiday week – actual holiday	No work on holiday!
52	Holiday week – actual holiday	No work on holiday!

I hope that's a useful example for an imagined year curriculum. You could also work on this with a couple of friends and make sure you're all planning in enough rest, and have a little Discord or Slack where you reflect and write up your process.

Conclusion

Throughout this book I've tried my best to give a useful overview of the theory, material conditions, and practice of writing for small- to mid-scale videogames. I've offered context for people new to games, and theory and vocabulary for people new to storytelling. I hope that I've also broken down some misconceptions about the craft of both storytelling and videogames as a medium, and equipped you to understand the structure and processes that might affect you as a game writer, as well as how to hold space for ethics and ethical labour processes. I'm also aware that what works for me might not work for you, and so strongly recommend you check out all of the other alternative resources I've offered.

But most of all, what I hoped to do was to give you the tools you need to build your own toolkit. To equip you to be your own mentor. And offer you the vocabulary, structures, and understanding you need to confidently advocate for and author better writing in videogames.

Don't be afraid to revisit parts of this book again and again, or to decide something isn't relevant, or to redesign or disagree with parts of it. It's drawn from my experiences, and there are many processes, genres, and game companies I've not worked with. This book isn't designed to be exhaustive – rather it's a starting point. The most important thing is that you use it to reflect and learn. To shape your own journey and practice in the way *you* need.

Writing this book was something I was surprised to find came quite easily. Having set out a structure and string of bullet points for each chapter, I found myself racing out 5,000 to 8,000 words per half-day sitting. It was quite thrilling and deeply rewarding.

Every month I find myself having to turn down several mentees and speaking opportunities – not because I think I am exceptionally good at these things, but because I think that perhaps there aren't so many people talking about this particular aspect of storytelling in games, in this craft-driven manner. Every time I added more to the book, I imagined the people I've mentored and the ones I wished I'd had time to. The talks I've given and the workshops I wish I'd been able to do. Every time I added to this book, I imagined being able to hand a free copy to a person who asked me how to get into or improve their games writing and say 'This is everything I would say if I taught you for a year'.

Writing for games is one of the most impenetrable kinds of storytelling and writing because it's so intertwined with a billion other disciplines, processes, and complex material/funding conditions – like any practice it takes *practise*, but with game projects running so long, and entry-level positions being hard to find, developing the craft can feel a little out of reach.

But it can also be thrilling in the scale of its challenges, hugely rewarding, and reach audiences across the world; seeing people and making people feel seen in a space made up of a beautifully collaborative material (between co-designers, and game and player).

Games can offer a distinct means of reimagining old stories, exploring eternal dilemmas, and producing entertaining experiences.

I hope that this book helps writing for games feel less distant and magical, and that it instead presents it as doable: offering you a means of pathfinding; setting waypoints for your practice and career, and a means of following and reflecting on them.

So much of storytelling is being actively human; learning to listen to people (whether speaking or not), learning about yourself in the world and in relation to others, and learning how we shape stories to reflect on the world: how we live together in it.

To have a lifelong practice is some kind of gift, I think. I owe so much to the people who have shaped mine: my mother, my dad, and brother; Rhian and Laura with whom I played epic hours-long adventures on school fields with. All the books, plays, poems, podcasts, TV shows, films, and art I've devoured. The teachers who saw something in me; the Theatre Writing Partnership which gave me my first theatre-writing opportunity; Carolyn Scott-Jeffs who nudged me towards a playwriting masters; The Royal Court young writers programme; and the many theatres who supported my performances, tours, and Edinburgh runs, especially Northern Stage and ARC. Dan Watts who tempted me back to Loughborough for a PhD, where I really learned to think deeply. My wonderful peers in all disciplines, like my dear friend Pat Ashe who somehow has time to read, watch, and play everything. My many mentors – but especially Alex Kelly. The gateways into games and interactive art: Hide & Seek, Duncan Speakman, The Pervasive Media Studio, Video Brains, Ed Key. And I also want to shout out Angus Dick, whose wonderful art is the cover of this book.

Thanks to all the people who helped me proofread this text, checked that my definitions made sense, and let me know when concepts needed clarifying and expanding: Char Putney, Jonathan Taylor, Martin Pichlmair, Douglas Wilson, Viv Schwarz, Maddalena Grattarola, and David King – thank you.

And finally, thank you to the co-owners of Die Gute Fabrik for the leap of confidence that they took not only in initially hiring me as a writer, but then in promoting me to narrative designer, then producer, then studio lead.

I often feel, when doing my job now – part creative director, part narrative design lead, part CEO – as if my life is a version of the movie *Slumdog Millionaire*. What a miracle it feels to have been equipped in my craft and life with the skills, tools for reflection, and lifelong practice that I have, and that I find using every inch of.

What a privilege to have learned from so many people, and finally, what a pleasure to now have an opportunity to share that with you, here, now.

I wrote this for you, for the love of learning, and for the love of the craft.

Pass it on.

Select Glossary of Games Industry Terms

AAA games (triple A games): The blockbuster, billion-dollar budget end of videogames.

Agile: A design philosophy which focuses on an iterative process where you build the simplest version of the design's features (minimum viable product, or MVP), and build on it again and again. It can be used to describe informal iterative design in general, or specific design philosophies and processes such as Scrum, which some people like to make slightly overwrought orthodoxies and training out of.

Barks: One-off lines which reinforce character and the drama of a moment; delivered not as part of conversation, but to liven up travel, battle, or the exploration of an open world area.

Game engine: Unity and Unreal are two popular game engines in the indie game dev world, but there are others, and studios can also build (or roll) their own. The game engine is an environment specifically geared towards the programming and making of games. It will have a bunch of basic systems, interfaces, and built-in tools, and allow you to build new tools, behaviours, and systems on top of these. A little like Word or Pages is a text editor which provides an environment for writing, and encodes things like italics, footnotes, and heading styles for you ahead of time.

Gamefeel: How the gameplay and mechanics feel to play. Might include how the game responds to a player's input; the visualisation of the interaction; and the reactions to the movement in haptics, sound, and other visual–tactile feedback.

Gameplay: How the player plays the game. It describes things like the 'core loop' of the game (the patterns of play the game teaches and expresses itself through), mechanics, and include gamefeel, the resistances, frictions, satisfactions, tactility of the gameplay systems.

Gate (verb): 'Gating' is a piece of common terminology for discussing how you pace access to story and other experiences throughout the player's exploration of space and time. In the metaphor you need the 'key' to the gate in order to open it and progress. The key you might need could be one or more of inventory checks for a certain item or number of items, having experienced a specific line or conversation, 'has met' variables (that you've met a character before), a certain time, proximity to a place, a threshold of something is met (clues, areas explored, level of character, tokens of another kind), etc.

III games (triple I games): Somewhere between indie and triple A, multimillion-dollar productions from smaller studios, perhaps in the range of 10 to 50 people.

Indie games: Independent videogames, smaller-scale productions with smaller budgets and teams. Typically, under $5 million and 20 people. Historically 'indie' has also referred to games made without publisher or platform support, but contemporarily this tends to refer to production and team size, and/or the aesthetics associated with smaller and more experimental productions.

IP: 'Intellectual property' is the extremely yucky game dev term for 'idea for a game/game world'. It's the stuff that you can trademark/copyright, protect via NDA, and license. Often when people say they're working on 'a new IP' it's a way of saying they're not working on a sequel or an 'existing IP' which has been licensed to them, like *Game of Thrones* or Lego.

JRPG: Japanese role-playing game.

Juice: The *je ne sais quoi* of game design. A simple jump can be made infinitely more satisfying by adding 'juice'. Think of the act of squeezing an orange. Imagine you simply command your hand to squeeze, and then you have a hand full of mush, not so interesting. So, imagine you add in resistance that is high at the beginning of the squeeze and then easier before a sudden stop, imagine that liquid squirts out, there is a squishing sound, and a drip afterwards. Congratulations, you added 'juice' to the experience and improved the gamefeel of the orange-squeezing gameplay experience. The mechanic is the fact you can squeeze. The gameplay includes orange squeezing. The gamefeel can be improved by adding 'juice'.

Loc (localisation): The translation of games writing into other languages. May include editing idioms, jokes, and cultural references so they are readable to a local audience.

LQA: Localisation-specific quality assurance.

Mechanics: The systems by which the player can affect the world of the game through their play. Can also have a more academic and precise definition, i.e. in the *mechanics, dynamics, aesthetics* framework of game design (Hunicke et al., 2004).

Middleware: Software which connects two things. FMOD and WWISE are two popular pieces of audio middleware which connect musicians with Unity through an audio-friendly interface.

Modders/modding: Someone who 'mods' is someone who 'modifies' an existing game to change it somehow. That might be adding new quests, it might be removing all the dragons because they annoy you, or improving the character generator's ability to model Black hair.

MVP (minimum viable product): Part of the Agile practice of design. The idea is to make the design idea, tool, or piece of gameplay in its most minimal functional way, and then to test or play it in order to know in which direction to improve and build on it.

QA (quality assurance): The people who will test the game to destruction. Their job is to seek out bugs, tell you their conditions (how to reproduce, or 'repro' them), so that they can be fixed by a member of the team.

Rigging: The act of articulating a character or game object so it can move and be manipulated – like applying skin to a skeleton.

SFX: Sound effects.

Shader: Something which produces visual effects in a game. More complex than animation, a shader manipulates pixels in the game to render dynamic effects like shadows, water, smoke, the wind through trees, and much more. A shader specialist will produce tools for their implementation and editing. Like the effect of smoke: they might create a particle system; define how it curves, moves, dissipates, and is coloured; and make an interface so these variables can be placed and set.

UI (user interface): The design of how the player interacts with the menus and on-screen materials.

Unity: A popular game engine.

Unreal: A popular game engine.

UX (user experience): The design of the flow of how the player moves through the game and its systems, including menus.

VO: Voice over.

Bibliography

Abbott, H. P., 2008. *The Cambridge Introduction to Narrative*. Second Edition. Cambridge: Cambridge University Press.

Aitken, N., 2017. *Writers of Color Discussing Craft: An Invisible Archive*. [Online] Available at: https://www.de-canon.com/blog/2017/5/5/writers-of-color-discussing-craft-an-invisible-archive [Accessed 4 October 2021].

Alder, A. & Ceremony, B. W., 2013. *The Quiet Year on boardgamegeek.com*. [Online] Available at: https://boardgamegeek.com/boardgame/161880/quiet-year [Accessed 22 October 2021].

Anon., uploaded 11 September 2014. *Mother Courage Documentary (Featuring Duke Special)*. [Online] Available at: https://youtu.be/x6obtAUsju8 [Accessed 18 October 2021].

Anthropy, A., 2021. *Rise of the Videogame Zinesters: How Freaks, Normals, Amateurs, Artists, Dreamers, Drop-outs, Queers, Housewives, and People Like You Are Taking Back an Art Form*. New York: Seven Stories Press.

Armitage, T., 2011. *Technology As A Material*. [Online] Available at: https://infovore.org/archives/2011/08/22/technology-as-a-material/ [Accessed 20 October 2021].

Atavar, M., 2014. *How to Be an Artist*. Third Edition. London: Kiosk Publishing.

Ayckbourn, A., 2002. *The Crafty Art of Playmaking*. Croydon: Faber & Faber.

"Badda-Bing Badda-Bang" Season 7 Episode 15 of Star Trek: Deep Space Nine, 1999. [Film] Directed by Mike Vejar. USA: Paramount Domestic Television.

Barry, L., 2009. *What It Is*. London: Jonathan Cape.

Bissell, T. & Burns, M. S., 2015. *The Writer Will Do Something*. [Online] Available at: https://matthewseiji.itch.io/twwds [Accessed 19 October 2021].

Boal, A., 1993. *Theatre of the Oppressed*. Tcg Edition. New York: Theatre Communications Group.

Boal, A. & Jackson, A. (Translator), 2002. *Games for Actors and Non-Actors*. Second Edition. Abingdon: Routledge.

Board Game Geek, n.d. The Quiet Year (2013). [Online] Available at: https://boardgamegeek.com/boardgame/161880/quiet-year [Accessed 22 October 2021].

Brecht, B., 1964a. Indirect Impact of the Epic Theatre. In: J. Willett, ed. *Brecht on Theatre*. New York: Hill & Wang.

Brecht, B., 1964b. The Street Scene. In: J. Willet, ed. *Brecht on Theatre*. New York: Hill and Wang.

Brecht, B., 1985. *The Messingkauf Dialogues*. London: Methuen London Ltd.

Brecht, B., Steffin, M. & Hare, D., 1995. *Mother Courage and Her Children*. Modern Plays Edition. New York & London: Bloomsbury Methuen Drama.

Burrow, C., 2021. It's not Jung's, it's mine. *The London Review of Books*, 43(2). https://www.lrb.co.uk/the-paper/v43/n02/colin-burrow/it-s-not-jung-s-it-s-mine.

Cameron, J., 2016. *The Artist's Way: A Spiritual Path to Higher Creativity*. London: Penguin Publishing Group.

Cardboard Computer, 2013–2020. *Kentucky Route Zero*. [Online] Available at: http://kentuckyroutezero.com/ [Accessed 19 October 2021].

Cardinale-Powell, B. & DiPaolo, M., 2013. *Devised and Directed by Mike Leigh*. London: Bloomsbury Publishing.

Cartwright, J., 1996. *Cartwright Plays 1: Road; Bed; Two; The Rise and Fall of Little Voice*. New York & London: Methuen Drama.

Dawes, K. Editor & Writers, V., 2016. *When the Rewards Can Be So Great: Essays on Writing and the Writing Life*. Forest Grove, Oregon: Pacific University Press.

Edgar, D., 1992. *How Plays Work*. s.l.: Nick Hern Books.

Edgar, D., 2009. *Open Learn – Start Writing Plays: Track 6*. [Online] Available at: https://www.open.edu/openlearn/history-the-arts/start-writing-plays?track=6 [Accessed 11th March 2021].

Egri, L., 1946. *The Art of Dramatic Writing: Its Basis in the Creative Interpretation of Human Motives*. New York: Simon and Schuster.

Elder, M., 2012. *The Guardian*. [Online] Available at: https://www.theguardian.com/world/2012/jan/26/doll-protesters-problem-russian-police [Accessed 10 Jul 2021].

Esposito, B., 2018. *Twitter.com*. [Online] Available at: https://twitter.com/torahhorse/status/993916034816950274 [Accessed 19 February 2021].

Fanon, F., 1952. *Black Skin, White Masks*. Penguin Classics 2019 Edition. London: Penguin Classics.

Fessler, E., 2020. *Kentucky Route Zero Act I Fulltext*. [Online] Available at: https://consolidatedpower.co/~eli/ActI.html#furniture-warehouse [Accessed 20 October 2021].

Flanagan, M., 2009. *Critical Play: Radical Game Design*. Cambridge: MIT Press.

Flock, I., 2012. *Someone Come Find Me*. [Online] Available at: https://invisibleflock.com/portfolio/someonecomefindme/ [Accessed 18 October 2021].

Goebel, W. & Schabio, S. eds., 2014. *Locating Postcolonial Narrative Genres*. London: Routledge.

Grip, T., 2009. *Puzzles in Horror Games Part 7: Penumbra Puzzles*. [Online] Available at: https://frictionalgames.com/2009-10-puzzles-in-horror-games-part-7-penumbra-puzzles/ [Accessed 5 September 2021].

Grip, T., 2013. *The Five Foundations Design Pillars of SOMA*. [Online] Available at: https://frictionalgames.com/2013-12-the-five-foundational-design-pillars-of-soma/ [Accessed 5 September 2021].

Grip, T., 2014. *4-Layers, A Narrative Design Approach*. [Online] Available at: https://www.gamedeveloper.com/design/4-layers-a-narrative-design-approach [Accessed 5 September 2021].

gypsy-traveller.org, 2021. *How to Open a Bank Account*. [Online] Available at: https://www.gypsy-traveller.org/advice-section/how-to-open-a-bank-account/ [Accessed 18 October 2021].

Hernandez, P., 2020. *My Mom Crossed the Border in Real Life. I Only Cross It in a Video Game*. [Online] Available at: https://www.polygon.com/2020/1/21/21070333/life-is-strange-2-episode-5-border-wall-interview-immigration-michel-koch-raoul-barbet [Accessed 4 October 2021].

hklive. n.d. Iconographia / Performance / 2006, 2007, 2008, 2009, 2010. [Online] Available at: https://hklive.tumblr.com/post/1132485081/iconographia-performance-2006-2007-2008 [Accessed 1 August 2021].

Huizinga, J., 1949. *Homo Ludens: A Study of the Play-Element in Culture*. 1998 reprint Edition. London: Routledge.

Hunicke, R., LeBlanc, M. & Zubek, R., 2004. *MDA: A Formal Approach to Game Design and Game Research*. [Online] Available at: https://www.aaai.org/Papers/Workshops/2004/WS-04-04/WS04-04-001.pdf [Accessed 4 September 2021].

Hustlers. 2019. [Film] Directed by Lorene Scafaria. United States of America: Gloria Sanchez Productions; Nuyorican Productions; Annapurna Pictures.

Ibsen, 1985. *A Doll's House*. Methuen Students Edition. London & New York: Bloomsbury Methuen Drama.

In Between Time, n.d. *In Between Time: About Us*. [Online] Available at: https://inbetweentime .co.uk/our-work/ [Accessed 1 August 2021].

Inkle Studios, 2014. *So What Is Eighty Days?* [Online] Available at: https://www.inklestudios .com/2014/04/15/so-what-is-eighty-days.html [Accessed 4 October 2021].

Jayanth, M., 2015. *Leading Players Astray: 80 Days & Unexpected Stories*. [Online] Available at: https://www.gdcvault.com/play/1022101/Leading-Players-Astray-80-Days [Accessed 2021 October 2021].

Jayanth, M., 2016a. *Forget Protagonists: Writing NPCs with Agency for 80 Days and Beyond*. [Online] Available at: https://medium.com/@betterthemask/forget-protagonists -writing-npcs-with-agency-for-80-days-and-beyond-703201a2309 [Accessed 4 October 2021].

Jayanth, M., 2016b. *GDC Vault: Forget Protagonists: Writing NPCs with Agency for '80 Days' and Beyond*. [Online video] Available at: https://gdcvault.com/play/1023393/Forget -Protagonists-Writing-NPCs-with [Accessed 4 October 2021].

Jeffreys, S., 2020. *Playwriting: Structure, Character, How and What to Write*. Reprint Edition. New York: Theatre Communications Group.

Jemisin, N. K., 2015. *The Fifth Season: The Broken Earth, Book 1*. Kindle Edition. New York: Little Brown Book Group.

Jongh, A. D., 2017. *Playtesting: Avoiding Evil Data*. [Online] Available at: https://www.youtube .com/watch?v=6EUeYu0aPn4&ab_channel=GDC [Accessed 20 October 2021].

Le Guin, U. K., 1998. *Steering the Craft : A Twenty-First-Century Guide to Sailing the Sea of Story*. Boston: Mariner Books.

Lee, S., 2010. *How I Escaped My Certain Fate*. London: Faber & Faber.

Lee, S. Q., 2017. Introduction. In: S. Q. Lee, ed. *How Dare We! Write: A Multicultural Creative Writing Discourse (Kindle Edition)*. Michigan: Modern History Press.

Lemarchand, R., 2021. *A Playful Production Process: For Game Designers (and Everyone)*. Cambridge: MIT Press.

Lerman, L. & Borstel, J., 2003. *Liz Lerman's Critical Response Process: A Method for Getting Useful Feedback on Anything You Make, from Dance to Dessert*. Washington DC: Dance Exchange, Inc.

life-is-strange.fandom.com, n.d. *Episode 1: Roads – Scene 5*. [Online] Available at: https://life -is-strange.fandom.com/wiki/Episode_1:_Roads_-_Script#Scene_5_-_Diaz_Garage [Accessed 4 October 2021].

Live, H. A. K., n.d. *Hancock and Kelly Live: Iconographia Performance*. [Online] Available at: https://hklive.tumblr.com/post/1132485081/iconographia-performance-2006-2007 -2008 [Accessed 1 August 2021].

Madden, M., 2005. *99 Ways to Tell a Story*. New York: Chamberlain Bros.

Martin, R., 2006. Staging the Political: Boal and the Horizons of Theatrical Commitment. In: J. Cohen-Cruz & M. Schutzman, eds. *A Boal Companion, Dialogues on Theatre and Cultural Politics*. Oxon: Routledge.

McCloud, S., 2006. *Making Comics*. New York: Harper Collins.

Melzer, A. H., 1994. *Dada and Surrealist Performance*. Baltimore, MD: Johns Hopkins University Press, Baltimore.

Molleindustria, 2011. *Phone Story*. [Online] Available at: http://www.phonestory.org/ [Accessed 19 October 2021].

Molleindustria, 2020. *Democratic Socialism Simulator*. [Online] Available at: https://www.molleindustria.org/demsocsim/ [Accessed 19 October 2021].

Montola, M., Stenros, J. & Waern, A., 2009. *Pervasive Games Theory and Design*. First Edition. Boca Raton, FL: CRC Press.

Moore, A. & Gibbons, D., 2012. *Watchmen*. International Edition. DC Comics, New York

Moore, S. M. A. H., 2014. *Women's Rights and Their Money: A Timeline from Cleopatra to Lilly Ledbetter*. [Online] Available at: https://www.theguardian.com/money/us-money-blog/2014/aug/11/women-rights-money-timeline-history [Accessed 18 October 2021].

Nicklin, H., 2019. *Hannah Nicklin: The Player is a Material Made Up of People (Freeplay '19 Keynote)*. [Online] Available at: https://www.youtube.com/watch?v=3gm97EKoypU&ab_channel=FreeplayIndependentGamesFestival [Accessed 4 October 2021].

Nicklin, H., 2020. *#Craft: Multiple Middles*. [Online] Available at: https://gutefabrik.com/craft-multiple-middles/ [Accessed 4 October 2021].

Norman, D., 2002. *The Design of Everyday Things*. New York: Basic Books.

NPR – Code Switch, 2019. *Transcript: Sometimes Explain, Always Complain*. [Online] Available at: https://www.npr.org/transcripts/782331005 [Accessed 4 October 2021].

Nutt, C., 2015. *Narrative and Design Insights from 80 Days' Writing Lead*. [Online] Available at: https://www.gamedeveloper.com/design/narrative-and-design-insights-from-i-80-days-i-writing-lead [Accessed 20 October 2021].

Osunwunmi, 2011. *Real Time Arts – RealTime issue #101 Feb–March 2011 pg. 24*. [Online] Available at: http://realtimearts.net/feature/Inbetween_Time_2010/10136 [Accessed 1 August 2021].

Passfield, S., 2018. *Playlist: Brecht National Theatre Files*. [Online] Available at: https://www.youtube.com/playlist?list=PLIWiVfxfZc0BeQzG1hk2dF4SgdBt2GK_z [Accessed 18 October 2021].

Pedercini, P., 2020. *Democratic Socialism Simulator: Release Notes*. [Online] Available at: https://www.molleindustria.org/blog/democratic-socialism-simulator-release-notes/ [Accessed 19 October 2021].

"Pink Champagne on Ice" Season 4, Episode 19 of The Mentalist. 2012. [Film] Directed by David Von Ancken. USA: Primrose Hill Productions, in association with Warner Bros. Television.

Queneau, R., 1981. *Exercises in Style*. New York: New Directions Paperback.

Schrank, B., 2014. *Avant-Garde Videogames: Playing with Technoculture*. Cambridge:MIT Press.

Shakespeare, W., 1606. *Macbeth*. s.l.: Act V, Scene VIII.

Shaw, J., Kelly, P. & Semler, L. E. eds., 2013. *Storytelling: Critical and Creative Approaches*. London: Palgrave Macmillan.

Shawl, N. & Ward, C., 2005. *Writing the Other: A Practical Approach*. Seattle: Aqueduct Press.

Short, E., 2016. *Beyond Branching: Quality-Based, Salience-Based, and Waypoint Narrative Structures*. [Online] Available at: https://emshort.blog/2016/04/12/beyond-branching-quality-based-and-salience-based-narrative-structures/ [Accessed 20 October 2021].

Short, E., 2018. *Not Exactly Mailbag: Worldbuilding from a Mechanic*. [Online] Available at: https://emshort.blog/2018/03/13/not-exactly-mailbag-worldbuilding-from-a-mechanic/#more-38045 [Accessed 19 October 2021].

Short, E., n.d. *Emily Short's Blog: Books Tag*. [Online] Available at: emshort.blog/category/books/ [Accessed 18 October 2021].

Short, T. X. & Adams, T., 2019. *Procedural Storytelling in Game Design*. First Edition. Boca Raton, Florida: A K Peters/CRC Press.

Solnit, R., 2019. *Rebecca Solnit: When the Hero is the Problem*. [Online] Available at: https://lithub.com/rebecca-solnit-when-the-hero-is-the-problem/ [Accessed 20 October 2021].

Star Trek: Deep Space Nine, Season 1, Episode 15: "Progress". 1993. [Film] Directed by Les Landau. United States: Paramount Television.

The Farewell. 2019. [Film] Directed by Lulu Wang. USA, China: Big Beach Films, Depth of Field, Kindred Spirit, Seesaw Productions.

The Killing. 1956. [Film] Directed by Stanley Kubrick. USA: Harris-Kubrick Productions.

Tufekci, Z., 2019. *The Scientific American – The Real Reason Fans Hate the Last Season of Game of Thrones*. [Online] Available at: https://blogs.scientificamerican.com/observations/the-real-reason-fans-hate-the-last-season-of-game-of-thrones/ [Accessed 25 February 2021].

Verne, J., 1873. *Around the World in Eighty Days*. 2020 Edition. London: Penguin Classics.

Vitale, A. S., 2017. *The End of Policing*. London: Verso Books.

When Harry Met Sally. 1989. [Film] Directed by Rob Reiner. Beverly Hills, CA: Castle Rock Entertainment; Nelson Entertainment.

Whitaker, J., 1991. *Jules Verne: Around the World in Eighty Days*. [Sound Recording] (BBC Radio Drama).

Index

Printed in the United States
by Baker & Taylor Publisher Services